—— 高等院校专业英语系列教材

旅游英语
（第4版）

李燕 徐静 编著

清华大学出版社
北京

内 容 简 介

本教材共分 17 个单元，主要包括：旅游咨询、预订客房、客房服务、餐饮服务、通信服务、会议服务、宴会服务、消遣服务、地陪服务、参观游览、景点介绍、旅游购物、解决投诉、应对难题、退房服务、传统节日和旅游广告。每单元由"单元目标""背景知识""实训材料""词汇扩展"等模块组成。每单元设定一个主题，同时涵盖听、说、读、写基本训练。

本教材构思独特、内容新颖、实用性强、使用面广，突出了"以典型工作任务为逻辑主线落实教学内容"的特点，可供高职高专及以上水平的旅游英语专业及旅游管理专业教学使用，也可作为旅游企业服务与管理从业人员的培训教材。

本书封面贴有清华大学出版社防伪标签，无标签者不得销售。
版权所有，侵权必究。举报：010-62782989，beiqinquan@tup.tsinghua.edu.cn。

图书在版编目 (CIP) 数据

旅游英语 / 李燕，徐静编著 . -- 4 版 . -- 北京：清华大学出版社，2025.3.
（高等院校专业英语系列教材）. -- ISBN 978-7-302-68423-7

Ⅰ . F59
中国国家版本馆 CIP 数据核字第 2025L35G05 号

责任编辑：张文青　陈立静
装帧设计：杨玉兰
责任校对：常　婷
责任印制：丛怀宇

出版发行：清华大学出版社
　　　网　　址：https://www.tup.com.cn, https://www.wqxuetang.com
　　　地　　址：北京清华大学学研大厦 A 座　　邮　　编：100084
　　　社 总 机：010-83470000　　　　　　　　邮　　购：010-62786544
　　　投稿与读者服务：010-62776969, c-service@tup.tsinghua.edu.cn
　　　质量反馈：010-62772015, zhiliang@tup.tsinghua.edu.cn
印 装 者：三河市天利华印刷装订有限公司
经　　销：全国新华书店
开　　本：185mm×260mm　　印　张：21.75　　字　数：522 千字
版　　次：2009 年 8 月第 1 版　2025 年 5 月第 4 版　印　次：2025 年 5 月第 1 次印刷
定　　价：59.80 元

产品编号：099137-01

PREFACE

随着我国旅游事业的飞速发展，旅游市场对旅游服务与管理人才的素质提出了更高要求，这对旅游英语专业教学是一个严峻的挑战。我们迫切需要培养出既通晓旅游管理专业知识，又具备英语交际能力的旅游服务及管理人才。本教材旨在为全国的旅游市场培养出更多更好的旅游专门人才，以满足不断扩大的市场需要。

作为湖北省省级精品课程及教育部高职高专英语类专业教学指导委员会精品课程"旅游英语"的配套教材、湖北省"十一五"规划课题"高职高专旅游英语教学模式研究"(课题编号：2008B145)的成果之一，本教材在编写过程中，结合了中国旅游市场的发展与相关职业的实际需要，体现了"教学内容职业化、课程结构模块化、实际操作标准化、顶岗实习规范化"的高职高专旅游英语教学模式。

根据旅游接待流程，我们将教材内容分为17个服务情景，以岗位工作环境为情境，以岗位职业语言为素材，内容包括：旅游咨询、预订客房、客房服务、餐饮服务、通信服务、会议服务、宴会服务、消遣服务、地陪服务、参观游览、景点介绍、旅游购物、解决投诉、应对难题、退房服务、传统节日和旅游广告。每个单元由"单元目标""背景知识""实训材料""词汇扩展"等模块组成，同时涵盖听、说、读、写的基本训练。

根据旅游服务的工作需要和教学反馈意见，本教材在第3版的基础上做了相应调整：增加了对话部分，使口语训练更加灵活；写作部分做了修改，为学生在应聘和实习中提供帮助；词汇扩展部分增加了最新的政策、法规及条例所涉及的词汇，为从业人员提供参考。

本教材可供高职高专及以上水平的旅游英语专业及旅游管理专业的教学使用，也可作为旅游企业服务与管理从业人员的培训教材。本教材配套资源丰富，主要包括电子课件、听力理解部分的录音、听力文本、导游须知电子手册。如有需要，可扫描本教材最后一页的二维码进行下载。

本教材由李燕、徐静编著，其他参与编写的老师有：伍光琴、黄玉珈、袁智英、刘晓菲、孙蓉、王晓真。我们在编写过程中得到了教学同行、业内人士及清华大学出版社的大力支持，在此一并致谢。因多方面原因，书中难免有疏漏之处，恳请广大读者提出宝贵意见。

李 燕

CONTENTS

- Unit 1　Giving Travel Information（旅游咨询）…………………1
- Unit 2　Hotel Reservation（预订客房）…………………23
- Unit 3　Housekeeping Services（客房服务）…………………44
- Unit 4　Food & Beverage Services（餐饮服务）…………………66
- Unit 5　Communication Services（通信服务）…………………84
- Unit 6　Meeting Services（会议服务）…………………104
- Unit 7　Banquet Services（宴会服务）…………………126
- Unit 8　Recreation and Entertainment Services（消遣服务）…………144
- Unit 9　Local Tour Guide Services（地陪服务）…………………160
- Unit 10　Visiting Places of Interest（参观游览）…………………183
- Unit 11　Scenic Spots Introduction（景点介绍）…………………200
- Unit 12　Shopping（旅游购物）…………………221
- Unit 13　Settling Complaints（解决投诉）…………………241
- Unit 14　Dealing with Special Problems（应对难题）…………………263
- Unit 15　Checkout Services（退房服务）…………………279
- Unit 16　Traditional Chinese Festivals（中国传统节日）…………304
- Unit 17　Traveling Advertisement（旅游广告）…………………321
- References　参考文献…………………342

Giving Travel Information
旅游咨询

Unit Objectives

After learning this unit, you should

- understand how to give travel information;
- master the basic words and expressions about travel information;
- get some cultural knowledge about travel information;
- find ways to improve your writing skills about A Letter on a Travel Reservation;
- be familiar with some typical domestic traveling routes.

Background Knowledge

When traveling, we may choose to travel by ourselves or attend package tours organized by the travel agencies that attend to the details of transportation, itinerary, and accommodations for travelers. We can also book train tickets, air tickets or passages there.

Types of Tours

1. inclusive tour(包价旅游)：A tour including transportation, hotels, transfers, sightseeing, and meals.

2. ecotourism(生态旅游)：The tour of organizing holidays to natural areas, especially areas that are far away such as the rain forest, where people can visit and learn about the area in a way that will not hurt the environment.

3. fly-drive package tour(自驾游)：An inclusive tour in which the traveler can have a self-drive rental car.

4. conducted tour (有导游陪同的旅游): A prearranged travel program for a group escorted by a guide.

5. foreign individual/independent tour (散客旅游): A prepaid tour including air, hotels, ground transfers, and prearranged sightseeing and guide service for individuals.

6. culture-oriented travel (文化旅游): A tour in which travelers can enjoy folkways and folk-custom.

7. escorted tour (全程陪同旅游): A prepaid travel program of sightseeing, meals and accommodations for a group accompanied by an escort from the beginning to the end of the trip.

8. cruise (豪华游艇旅游): A tour on a large ship or a boat for pleasure.

9. leisure travel (休闲旅游): A tour in which travelers can relax and do things they enjoy.

10. special interest tour (专门兴趣旅游): A tour designed for clients sharing curiosity or concern about a common subject.

11. agricultural tourism (农业观光旅游): A tour in which travelers can appreciate agricultural life, such as going to the orchard, etc.

12. sports tourism (体育旅游): A tour including exploring, climbing, car rally, etc.

Practice Materials

Listening

Dialogue 1

a. Listen to Dialogue 1 and decide whether each of the following sentences is true (T) or false (F).

1. _____ The man wants to make a reservation to New York next week.
2. _____ There are still tickets available for Flight 802.
3. _____ The next flight leaves at 9:30 on Tuesday morning September 13.
4. _____ The fare for one-way ticket is $196.
5. _____ The man reserves the Flight 807 finally.

b. Listen to the dialogue and answer the following questions.

1. What's the name of the airline company?

_____

2. When does the man want to fly?
_____

3. Is Flight 807 a direct flight?
_____

4. What's the man's name?
_____

5. What's the man's telephone number?
_____

c. Listen to the dialogue again and supply the missing words.
1. I'm sorry we are all _____ for Flight 802 on that day.
2. Shall I book you _____?
3. You want to go _____?
4. Can you also put me on _____ for the 12th?
5. I will notify you if _____.

Notes

1. the United Airlines	联合航空公司
2. reservation	(旅馆房间、饭店、飞机座位的)预订
3. available	可获得的，可用的，可看到的
4. book up	把……预订一空；已订满
5. alternative	选择余地；可供选择的事物(方式等)
6. direct flight	直航
7. first class or coach	头等舱票或经济舱票。普通机票包括头等舱票(First Class)、商务舱票(Business Class)及经济舱票(Economy Class or Coach)三种
8. fare	车费，票价
9. waiting list	等候批准的申请人名单
10. cancellation	取消

Dialogue 2

a. Listen to Dialogue 2 and decide whether each of the following sentences is true (T) or false (F).

1. The S.S. Newcastle is sailing for Hamburg from Northampton next Wednesday.

2. The man wants a ticket with a cabin for two.

3. The ticket will be 15 pounds.

4. The man wants 300 pounds of traveler's cheques.

5. If people want to cash the cheque, they need to sign their names at the top.

b. Listen to the dialogue and answer the following questions.

1. When do the passengers board?
_____

2. Is there a boat train?
_____

3. When and where does the boat train leave from?
_____

4. Where do passengers show their boat tickets?
_____

5. Where can the man get traveler's cheques?
_____

c. Listen to the dialogue again and supply the missing words.

1. Yes, that one will be all right. I'll _____.

2. Will you please _____ this card?

3. Will you sit down for a moment while I _____ the tickets?

4. If there should be any _____ in the sailing time, we'll contact you by telephone.

5. Will you please sign there, on _____?

Notes

1. book a passage	预订乘船旅行
2. sail for Hamburg	驶往汉堡
3. S.S. Newcastle	S.S. 纽卡斯尔号（船名）
4. from Southampton	从南安普顿出发
5. board	上船，登车
6. boat train	与船期衔接的港口联运列车
7. Where does it leave from?	它从哪里出发呢？
8. Victoria Station	维多利亚车站

9. pass 走过，经过
10. last-minute change 最后关头的变动
11. contact you by telephone 用电话与您联系
12. traveler's cheques 旅行支票
13. right over there 就在那边
14. sign 签字
15. Two hundred in ten-pound cheques and one hundred in five-pound cheques.
10 英镑一张的支票换 200 英镑，5 英镑一张的支票换 100 英镑。

Background Information

Book a Passage

Traveling by sea is a very convenient and economical way of traveling. It is more relaxing, comfortable and cheaper than traveling by airplane or by train. On some luxurious ships, there are various living and entertaining facilities, like restaurants, bars, theaters and even swimming pools, etc. The disadvantage of traveling by sea is that the speed is comparatively slow and some passengers are likely to be seasick with high wind. Booking a passage is just like booking an airplane ticket. The travelers can go to the agencies or just telephone them to book a passage. As traveling by sea is greatly influenced by the weather situations, there may be some changes of the sailing time. The agency clerks are responsible to inform the passengers of such changes. For the convenient contact with passengers, the clerks will ask passengers to write down the detailed personal information like name, address and telephone number, etc. Also, they will show the passengers a printed plan of all the cabins with different classes, direction, etc., so that passengers can choose the cabins they like. The boat trains can take the passengers to the port in time. Passengers only need to go to the appointed station on time and get on the train with the ship tickets.

Dialogue 1

Holiday Booking

Staff：Welcome Ma'am! What can I do for you?
Linda：Yes. I wanna go to Xinjiang to spend my holiday.

Staff: No problem. We can offer a tour along the Silk Road.

Linda: Very good. Is there a tour group that I can go with?

Staff: Yes, there is one this month.

Linda: Oh, great! So how long does it last?

Staff: Eleven days.

Linda: Fine. I have a 20-day holiday. So exciting! How many places will we visit?

Staff: We'll visit over 15 different places. Most of them are along the Silk Road.

Linda: Where will we stay for the night? Will we stay with the locals?

Staff: I'm afraid not. We can arrange hotels for you.

Linda: What's the price for this travel package?

Staff: Well, right now, it's RMB 2,200 yuan, including everything, such as airline tickets, tour guides, hotels and food.

Linda: Can I get a discount?

Staff: This is a special price. We cannot further lower the price.

Linda: I'd like a reservation for this tour. What do I do?

Staff: Please sign up here and pay a deposit.

Linda: Well. Okay. Thanks for your help.

Staff: I'm glad to be a help.

Notes

1. silk   丝绸
2. local   当地人
3. discount   折扣
4. lower   降低
5. sign   签字，签名
6. deposit   抵押金
7. FIT (foreign individual/independent traveler) (入境)散客
8. the Silk Road   丝绸之路
9. sign up   报名(或签约)参加

Dialogue 2

A Group Travel Reservation

(Brown telephones the Summer Travel Service, wishing to book a tour for his group. The

staff explains the details and reserves such a tour for the client on the phone.)

Staff: Good morning, Summer Travel Service. Can I help you?

Brown: Yes, please. I'm with an office supplies company in Beijing. We'd like to book a group tour.

Staff: We'd be glad to help you. May I have the name of the group, Sir?

Brown: Johnson Office Supplies Co., Ltd.

Staff: For how many people?

Brown: About 30.

Staff: What kind of tour do you have in your mind?

Brown: I think it should be something of incentive travel. In fact, we are planning a tour for our most hardworking staff.

Staff: Very good. Sir, have you read the proposal letter we sent to you?

Brown: Yes, I did. But we couldn't decide which place to go.

Staff: What about Yangzhou?

Brown: A good place. I've heard a lot about it.

Staff: It is a beautiful place, especially in April, the time of the year when you can see flowers everywhere.

Brown: That will be fine. Please reserve this trip to Yangzhou for us.

Staff: Okay, my pleasure. A flight to Yangzhou will depart from Beijing at 7:30 A.M., arriving at Shanghai Hongqiao Airport at 9:15 A.M., then a limousine will pick you up there and take you to Yangzhou directly. It is only two hours' ride.

Brown: Sounds good. Well, does the flight fare include breakfast?

Staff: Yes, you may have complimentary breakfast since it is an early departure.

Brown: Wonderful. Can you also reserve hotel rooms for the nights during our stay in Yangzhou?

Staff: Sure. For how many nights?

Brown: Arriving on Friday April 18 and leaving on Monday April 21.

Staff: That is three nights. Do you need a tour guide?

Brown: That would be better. But the guide must be able to speak English.

Staff: No problem, Sir. May I have your name and phone number?

Brown: I'm John Brown. Please call me at 010-2020-3548.

Staff: Yes, Mr. Brown, you have booked a 4-day-3-night group tour for 30 people to Yangzhou in the name of John Brown, arriving on Friday April 18 and leaving on Monday April 21. Will the company pay all the charges?

Brown: Yes, we'll send you a confirmation in writing. Thank you for your help.

Goodbye!

Staff: We're always at your service. Goodbye, Mr. Brown.

Notes

1. incentive	奖励
2. proposal	建议
3. reserve	预订
4. depart	出发
5. limousine	接送旅客的旅游车，豪华轿车
6. complimentary	(免费)赠送的
7. confirm	确认
8. incentive travel	奖励旅游
9. proposal letter	建议信
10. pick sb. up	接人
11. flight fare	机票费用
12. in the name of	以……的名义

Dialogue 3

Make Sure an Itinerary

(Tang Lin, a tour guide, comes to see Mr. Wilson, the tour leader of an American tour group. Tang knocks at the door and Mr. Wilson answers it.)

T: Tang Lin   W: Mr. Wilson

T: Good evening, Mr. Wilson.

W: Good evening, Mr. Tang. Come in, please.

T: Thank you. Well, I've come to talk about the itinerary for your trip. Can you spare me some time?

W: Sure. We received a copy of the itinerary from your Travel Service before we came. I hope there haven't been any changes.

T: No. Hardly any change at all. Since this is a big VIP group, everything must be well planned and made right.

W: That's right. Let's go over it again.

T: OK. First you will sightsee in Shanghai for three days. Then you will leave Shanghai for Wuhan by air. From Wuhan you will go to Chongqing by riverboat.

W: How long will the cruise trip take?

T: Three days. I'm sure you will enjoy the beautiful scenery along both banks of the Yangtze River.

W: You know what, my heart itches for the visit already.

T: And there are more. After spending two days in Chongqing, you will go to visit Beijing where a lot more excitements await you.

W: We'll stay in Beijing for four days, right?

T: Yes. And then you leave Beijing for home by air. The whole trip will last half a month. I hope everybody in your group will be physically fit for this long trip.

W: No problem. Everybody is as strong as a horse.

T: Good. If there should be any changes, please let me know in advance.

W: OK. Thank you very much for everything you've done for us.

T: My pleasure.

Notes

1. spare	抽出，腾出（时间、金钱或人手）
2. go over	查看，仔细审查
3. sightsee	观光，游览
4. riverboat	内河船
5. cruise	乘船游览
6. scenery	风景，景色
7. bank	河岸，堤岸
8. the Yangtze River	长江
9. itch for	渴望
10. in advance	提前，预先

Reading

Domestic Typical Traveling Routes

Beijing

Since AD 1000, Beijing, the city has served as a main or subsidiary residence for a series of dynasties. In Beijing you can see the Great Wall of China, the longest man-made wall in the world. Tour the Forbidden City where emperors have lived for more than 500 years. Walk through Tiananmen Square, and then see the Ming Tomb burial grounds for the 13 emperors of the Ming Dynasty...

Xi'an

Shaanxi Province and Henan Province are the cradle of ancient Chinese civilization. Here, in the fertile valleys of the loess-covered landscape, the ancestors of Chinese settled in the 3rd century BC. The fertile loess soil attracted the first human settlements, while irrigation difficulties forced people to work in close cooperation. As a result, the first and strongest states developed in this region. In Xi'an you can see more than 6,000 life-size terra-cotta warriors and horses recently excavated from the tomb of the first emperor of the Qin Dynasty. First discovered in 1974, each terra-cotta soldier and his horse have their own unique body and facial features, and more are being uncovered every year.

Guilin

Guilin, by the banks of the Li River in southern China, is justifiably considered to be one of the most beautiful places in China. Guilin literally means "Cassia Tree Forest". The landscape is characterized by terraced rice paddies, water buffalos, and bamboo groves, and peasants with turned up trousers and cone-shaped straw hats. Take a one-day cruise on the Li River to experience the magical beauty of the limestone rock formations and farmland commonly seen in Chinese landscape paintings. The Li River, limestone caves, Elephant Hill, and the pure beauty of this area are all attractions of Guilin.

Shanghai

Shanghai, the metropolis lies by the Huangpu River, the 80km long artery of Shanghai of which 30km of its upriver flows into the Yangtze River and thus guarantees access to the sea. The name Shanghai means "upriver to the sea". Shanghai Harbor is the third largest in the world. This beautiful city offers lots of sightseeing. For example, you may view the harbor from Huangpu Park and then visit the Jade Buddha Temple featuring two huge Buddha statues carved out of a single piece of white jade.

The Yangtze River

The Yangtze River is the largest river in China, known as the lifeline of China, which flows through nine provinces, with its 700 tributaries, covering an area of 1.8 million sq. km, which is 19 percent of the total area of China. Dynasty after dynasty people have marvelled at the majesty of China's Three Gorges. There are many wonderful cruises available on the Yangtze River with its majestic cliffs and soaring peaks. These cruises not only take you to the wonderful cities along the greatest and most historic river of Asia, but are commonly combined with excursions to many of the classic Golden Cities of China discussed above. Visiting the "Golden Cities" of China and possibly combining with a Yangtze River Cruise is highly recommended for those visiting China for their first time.

Extraordinary Tibetan Adventures

Tibet, used to be the mysterious, legendary and unknown Roof of the World, hidden and almost unreachable behind the highest mountains in the world, can be easily reached today from Chengdu, the capital of Sichuan province, to Lhasa. This is the safest way for visitors to travel to Tibet. The Himalayas are the youngest folded mountains in the world. Before the south Indian land mass began to shift northwards about 40 million years ago, the Tethys Ocean, one of the largest oceans in the history of the earth, occupied the area. Today, the Tibet-Qinghai Plateau is at an average altitude of 4,000 meters, the most elevated plateau on earth, covering 25 percent of the entire Chinese territory. The Tibetans have been nomads for centuries, crossing the highland pastures in the south with their herds of sheep, goats and yak. In contrast, the north is an uninhabited desert. Today, 3.66 million people live in the Tibet autonomous region, of whom about 3.14 millions are Tibetans. Tibetans also live in Qinghai, Sichuan and Yunnan provinces. Tibet Adventures allow you to experience the way of life, culture, history, and spectacular scenery unique to this part of China. It is said that visiting Tibet, the "Roof of the World", is as much a state of mind as a destination. Tours include visiting cities such as Lhasa known as "the City of the Sun" and Xigaze (Shigatse) where you will see beautiful palaces and cliff top monasteries, and attending colorful bazaars and relaxing in the beautiful Himalayan Mountains.

Travel along the Ancient Silk Road of China

This ancient trade route starts in the old capitals of Luoyang and Xi'an, and reaches the Yellow River at Lanzhou, follows along the "Gansu Corridor" and stretches along the edge of deserts and mountains. Before the discovery of the sea route to India, the Silk Road was the most important connection between the Orient and the West. The Silk Road experienced its last great era during the time of Mongols, when the entire route from China to the Mediterranean was part of one empire. At that time, Nicolo and Marco Polo travelled from Kashgar to the Far East along the southern route. The overland link quickly lost its importance as trade across the seas developed. Today it has been replaced in China with the railway line Lanzhou-Hami-Urumqi. The trade route was never known as the Silk Road historically. It was given the name by a German geographer Ferdinand Freiherr von Richthofen. Silk Road tours allow you to step back into the 13th century as you visit the cities of the legendary silk traders and monks. Travel through deserts where silk traders have travelled for thousands of years. You can discover the ancient mysteries of the Silk Road including bazaars where merchants haggle over camels and carpets, where you can meet the nomadic minorities of China, and attend music, dance and artistic performances. These tours are often combined with stops to Beijing, Xi'an, and Dunhuang to make your China travel adventure vacation complete.

a. Answer the following questions according to the passage.

1. Exemplify some famous scenic spots in Beijing.
   _____

2. What are the characteristics of the landscape in Guilin?
   _____

3. Give a brief introduction to the Yangtze River.
   _____

4. Which city is known as "the City of the Sun"?
   _____

5. What ancient mysteries of the Silk Road can people discover?
   _____

b. Translate the expressions into Chinese or English.

1. ancient Rome and Greece	_____
a course in ancient history	_____
_____	旧风俗
ancient ruins	_____
2. a two-year guarantee	_____
_____	在保用期内
give my guarantee to sb.	_____
be guaranteed to last for years	_____
3. stretch out one's arm	_____
stretch my patience to the limit	_____
_____	绵延数英里
stretch away into the distance	_____
4. turn the radio up	_____
turn up late for everything	_____
turn up a lot of new information	_____
_____	卷起衣袖

c. *Choose an appropriate word or phrase to fill in each blank to make each sentence meaningful, and change its form when necessary.*

cooperation	era	excursion	fold	literally
majestic	marvel	spectacular	territory	unique

1. Children are so excited about the _____ firework display on New Year's Eve.
2. Each person's fingerprints are _____.
3. I took what he said _____, but afterwards it became clear that he really meant something else.
4. Most of Britain's former _____ are now independent.
5. She _____ the handkerchief and put it in her pocket.
6. This cartoon was produced in _____ with the Walt Disney.
7. The Christian _____ is counted from the birth of Christ.
8. The great ship sailed slowly and _____ into.
9. The onlookers _____ that he was unharmed after a long fall.
10. The travel agency arranges _____ round the island.

d. *Translate the following sentences into English with words or phrases given in the brackets.*

1. 京都 (Kyoto) 是日本文化的发源地。(cradle)
_____

2. 旅游公司安排环岛旅行。(excursion)
_____

3. 这艘巨大的船缓慢而庄严地驶进了港口。(majestic)
_____

4. 我们在穿越英国湖泊区 (the Lake District) 的旅途中看到了不少美丽的景色。(scenery)
_____

5. 探险家们声称这块土地是英国领土。(territory)
_____

Vocabulary List

access	[ˈækses]	n./v. 进入；入口
adventure	[ədˈventʃə]	n./v. 冒险
ancestor	[ˈænsestə]	n. 祖先，祖宗
ancient	[eɪnʃənt]	adj. 古代的；古老的，旧的
artery	[ˈɑːtəri]	n. 动脉,（道路的）干道，干线；（河流的）干流
autonomous	[ɔːˈtɒnəməs]	adj. 自治的
bazaar	[bəˈzɑː]	n. 集市，市场，杂货店，百货店
burial	[berɪəl]	n. 埋葬
cassia	[ˈkasɪə]	n. [植] 桂皮，肉桂
cone	[kəʊn]	n. 锥形物，圆锥体
cone-shaped	[ˈkəʊnˈʃeɪptɪd]	adj. 锥形的
cooperation	[kəʊˌɒpəˈreɪʃn]	n. 合作，协作
corridor	[ˈkɒrɪdɔː]	n. 走廊
cradle	[ˈkreɪdl]	n. 摇篮，发源地
cruise	[kruːz]	n./vi. 巡游，巡航
destination	[ˌdestɪˈneɪʃn]	n. 目的地
dynasty	[ˈdɪnəsti]	n. 朝代，王朝
era	[ˈɪərə]	n. 时代，纪元，时期
excavate	[ˈekskəveɪt]	v. 挖掘，开凿，挖出，挖空
excursion	[ɪkˈskɜːʃn]	n. 远足，游览，短程旅行
extraordinary	[ɪkˈstrɔːdnri]	adj. 不平常的，特别的，非凡的
fertile	[ˈfɜːtaɪl]	adj. 肥沃的，富饶的，能繁殖的
fold	[fəʊld]	n./v. 折叠
gorge	[gɔːdʒ]	n. 山峡，峡谷
grove	[grəʊv]	n. 小树林
guarantee	[ˌgærənˈtiː]	n./vt. 保证，担保
haggle	[ˈhag(ə)l]	n./v. 讨价还价
herd	[hɜːd]	n. 兽群（尤指牛、羊群）
highland	[ˈhʌɪlənd]	n. 高地，丘陵地带
irrigation	[ˌɪrɪˈgeɪʃən]	n. 灌溉，冲洗
jade	[dʒeɪd]	n. 碧玉，翡翠
justifiably	[dʒʌstɪˈfaɪəblɪ]	adv. 可证明是正当地，有理由地
landscape	[ˈlændskeɪp]	n.（田野）风景，（陆上）景色
life-size	[ˈlʌɪfsʌɪz]	adj. 与实物大小一样的

limestone	[ˈlaɪmstəʊn]	n. 石灰石
literally	[ˈlɪtərəli]	adv. 照字面意义，逐字地
loess	[ˈləʊɪs]	n. 黄土
majestic	[məˈdʒestɪk]	adj. 宏伟的，庄严的
majesty	[ˈmædʒəsti]	n. 最高权威，王权，雄伟
marvel	[ˈmɑːvl]	v. 大为惊异，觉得惊奇
metropolis	[məˈtrɒpəlɪs]	n. (一个国家的)大都会，主要都市，大城市
minority	[maɪˈnɒrəti]	n. 少数，少数民族
monastery	[ˈmɒnəstri]	n. 修道院，僧侣
nomad	[ˈnəʊmad]	n. 游牧民中的一员
nomadic	[nəʊˈmædɪk]	adj. 游牧的
orient	[ˈɔːrient]	n./adj. 东方(的)
overland	[ˈəʊvələnd]	adj. 陆路的，经过陆地的，陆上的
paddy	[ˈpædi]	n. 稻，谷
pasture	[ˈpɑːstʃə]	n. 牧地，草原，牧场
plateau	[ˈplætəʊ]	n. 高地，高原
scenery	[ˈsiːnəri]	n. 风景，景色
spectacular	[spekˈtækjələ]	adj. 引人入胜的，壮观的
statue	[ˈstætʃuː]	n. 雕像
stretch	[stretʃ]	v. 伸展，伸长
subsidiary	[səbˈsɪdiəri]	adj. 辅助的，补充的
terraced	[ˈterəst]	adj. 成梯田(状)的
terra-cotta	[ˌterəˈkɒtə]	n. 陶瓦，赤陶；棕橙色
territory	[ˈterətri]	n. 领土，版图，地域
tributary	[ˈtrɪbjʊt(ə)ri]	n. 支流
unique	[juˈniːk]	adj. 唯一的，独特的
upriver	[ʌpˈrɪvə]	n. 上游
warrior	[ˈwɒriə]	n. 战士，勇士，武士
yak	[jæk]	n. 牦牛

Phrases

burial ground	坟场，公墓
limestone cave	石灰岩洞
rice paddy	稻田，水田
state of mind	心境，心情；思想(精神)状态

combine with	与……结合，联合
flow into	流入
marvel at	对……惊奇
turn up	调大，开大；到达，出现；发现；卷起，折起（衣服的下部）
in contrast	相反，大不相同

Terms

Buddha	佛
Himalayas	喜马拉雅山脉
Kashgar	喀什（中国新疆西部城市）
Lhasa	拉萨（中国西藏藏族自治区首府）
Mediterranean	地中海（的）
Mongol	蒙古人（语）（的）
Tethys	古地中海，特提斯海
Tibet	西藏
Tibetan	西藏的，藏族的，藏族人的西藏语，西藏人，藏族人
Xigaze	日喀则
Roof of the World	世界屋脊

Notes

1. the Great Wall 长城
2. the Forbidden City 故宫
3. Tiananmen Square 天安门广场
4. the Ming Tombs 明十三陵
5. terra-cotta warriors and horses 兵马俑
6. the Li River 漓江
7. Elephant Hill 象山
8. the Jade Buddha Temple 玉佛寺
9. the Yangtze River 长江
10. Three Gorges 长江三峡
11. the Tethys Ocean 古地中海
12. the Tibet-Qinghai Plateau 青藏高原
13. City of the Sun 太阳城
14. the Silk Road 丝绸之路

Writing

A Letter on a Travel Reservation

Task 1　Writing Skills

旅游服务机构可以为客户提供出展服务，海外订房、订票是其所提供的服务之一。

就海外订房、订票而言，除了电话直接预订外，个人和团体还可以通过书信、电子邮件、网络及传真等手段完成。运用现代通信手段进行预订既方便又快捷，现已成为常用的预订方式。

如果预订交通票据（如飞机票、车船票等），预订信应包括准确的人数、具体的日期、地点、航班号或车次等。如果预订客房，则应告知对方住宿的确切日期、住宿起止时间、对客房的要求等。此外，预订信的内容还可包括费用或抵押金的支付方式以及其他有关信息。

英文书信通常由下列五个部分组成。

1) 信头 (heading)

信头包括写信人地址和写信日期，通常写在信笺的右上角。比较熟识的朋友之间的通信，写信人的地址常可略去。

地址的写法通常是由小到大，如门牌号、街道名、市（县）名、省名、国名（邮政编码通常写在城市名之后）。这同中文书信的地址写法完全相反。

地址可以写 1~3 行，日期写在地址的下方（参见后文的信笺格式）。

日期通常有下列两种写法：

(1) 月、日、年：如 August 15, 2022

(2) 日、月、年：如 15th August 2022

2) 称呼 (salutation)

称呼指写信人对收信人的称呼，如"Dear Xiaojun"，写在信头的下方并位于信笺的左边。称呼一般以"Dear..."或"My dear..."开头，称呼后一般用逗号。

3) 正文 (body)

这是书信的主体部分，即写信人要表达的内容。正文要求文字通顺，层次分明，表意清楚。可以手写，也可以打字。

4) 结束语 (complimentary close)

它是书信结尾的恭维话，相当于文中书信最后的"祝好""致礼"之类的话语。最为常见的是以"Best wishes"（致以最好的祝愿）作为结束语。

5) 签名 (signature)

签名通常签在结束语下方的中间偏右的位置。签名应是亲笔书写，即使是打印出来的信件，最后仍需亲笔签名。在签名的上方可根据写信人和收信人的关系写上 Sincerely yours/Yours sincerely（用于长辈或朋友之间），或 Respectfully yours/Yours respectfully（用于对长辈或上级）。

Task 2 Sample Writing

1) Reservation of Tickets for Plane

Mr. Joe Johnson
Hubei Polytechnic Institute
No.17 Yuquan Road
Xiaogan, Hubei, 432000

July 15, 2024

The Reservations Manager,
China Eastern
258 Weihai Road, Jing'an District
Shanghai, 200034

Dear Sir/Madam,

  I wish to visit London on a business tour. Please kindly reserve for me a first-class seat on Flight MU551, departing from Pudong Airport, Shanghai, at 13:20 on 28th July and arriving at London Heathrow Airport at 18:05 local time on July 30. Please confirm the booking as soon as payment is made by cheque. If it has already been booked up, please let me know what is the next flight on which you can book for me and the departure time.

Yours faithfully,
(Signature)

【译文】
主题：预订机票

乔·约翰逊先生
湖北职业技术学院
玉泉路 17 号
湖北孝感，432000

2024 年 7 月 15 日

预订部经理

中国东方航空公司

静安区威海路 258 号

上海，200034

亲爱的先生/女士：

  我因公赴伦敦出差。请您为我预订 MU551 航班头等舱机票一张，时间为 7 月 28 日 13:20 从上海浦东机场起飞，在当地时间 7 月 30 日 18:05 到达伦敦希思罗机场。收到支票付款后请确定预订的机票。如果票已订完，请告知您能为我订的下一趟航班以及出发时间。

                  您忠实的

                  （签名）

2) Confirmation of Reservation

Dear Sir,

  We have acknowledged your letter dated July 15 requesting us to book one first-class seat for you on a flight from Shanghai to London.

  One seat has been reserved on Flight MU551 departing from Pudong Airport, Shanghai at 13:20 on 28th July and arriving in London at 18:05 on July 30 local time.

  The account will be sent to Bank of China, as requested.

                 Yours faithfully,

                  (Signature)

【译文】

主题：预订确认

亲爱的先生：

  我们已收到您 7 月 15 日的预订函，要求我们为您预订从上海到伦敦的头等舱座位。

  已预订东方航空公司 MU551 次航班的一张机票，该航班于 7 月 28 日 13:20 从上海浦东机场起飞，于当地时间 30 日 18:05 抵达伦敦希思罗机场。

  如您所要求的，账单将送到中国银行。

                 您忠实的

                 （签名）

Useful Sentences

(1) I would like to reserve a twin room at your hotel for four nights from June 8, 2024.
我想向你们旅馆预订一间双人房，2024年6月8日入住，总共四晚。

(2) Please reserve a single room under the name of Mr. Lin.
请以林先生的名义订一间单人房。

(3) If there is no room available for the above period, please inform me ASAP as I must look for another hotel.
如果在上述期间没有空房，请尽快告知，以便另寻旅馆。

(4) I would like to book a flight to Paris on January 8 on Air France, First Class and round trip.
我要订一张去巴黎的往返票，1月8日，法航，头等舱。

Task 3 Writing Practice

a. Filling the following reservation letter by translating the Chinese in the brackets.

Dear Sir/Madam,

　　Mr. Zhang Changjiang, our Sales Manager, _____.
(希望搭乘尽可能早的从北京飞往纽约的航班。)

　　We would be obliged if you could book one economy class seat for him on a flight leaving Guangzhou on or about May 17. _____ (我们已委托中国银行支付机票费和预约费), and we would ask you to submit your account directly to them.

　　We appreciate your early confirmation.

Sincerely yours,
Li Jing
Secretary to Mr. Zhang

b. Mr. Li Ming will fly to Wuhan on July 23 to attend a conference there. Please write to May Flower Hotel to reserve a single room for him for two nights from 23rd to 24th July.

Vocabulary Development

package tour	由旅行社全部代办的旅游
a long journey	长途旅行
air travel	航空旅行
conducted/guided tour	有导游的旅游

group inclusive tour	包价旅游
independent/do-it-yourself travel	自助游
international tourism	国际旅游业
normal/luxury tour/travel	标准/豪华游
outbound/inbound tourism	出境游/国内游
travel abroad	出国旅游
honeymoon trip/wedding vacation/wedding travel	蜜月旅行/婚假/旅行结婚
hot travel route/spot	黄金线路/景点
classic travel route	经典线路
domestic tourism	国内旅游业
excursion	游览
golden week for tourism	旅游黄金周
guide book	指南书，导游书
manuscript	手稿
on business	因公
sightseeing	观光
star grade hotel	星级宾馆
standard room	标准间
tourist guide	导游
business center	商业中心
castle	城堡
cultural heritage	文化遗产
hot spring	温泉
landscape	风景
monument	纪念碑
natural scenery	自然风光
pagoda	古塔
place of interest	名胜
place of historical interest	古迹
scenery	风景
summer resort	避暑胜地
tourist attraction	景点
view	景色

China Travel Service

The main travel agencies in China include the following:

China Tourism Group Co.,Ltd.	中国旅游集团有限公司
China International Travel Service Limited, Head Office	中国国际旅行社总社有限公司
China Youth Travel Service	中青旅控股股份有限公司
China Comfort Travel	中国康辉旅游集团有限公司
CITIC Tourism Group Co.,Ltd.	中信旅游集团有限公司
China Women Travel Service Co.,Ltd.	中国妇女旅行社有限公司
Hong Thai Travel Limited	康泰旅行社有限公司
Merchants International Travel Service Co., Ltd.	招商局国际旅行社有限责任公司
Uzai Group Co., Ltd.	众信旅游集团股份有限公司
Overseas Tour China, Shenzhen Co., Ltd.	深圳市海外国际旅行社有限公司
GZL International Travel Service Co., Ltd.	广州广之旅国际旅行社股份有限公司
Shanghai Jinjiang International Travel Co., Ltd.	上海锦江国际旅游股份有限公司
Shanghai Spring International Travel Co., Ltd.	上海春秋国际旅行社（集团）有限公司

（排名不分先后）

Hotel Reservation

预订客房

Unit Objectives

After learning this unit, you should
- understand how to reserve a hotel;
- master the basic words and expressions about hotel reservation;
- get some cultural knowledge about hotel reservation information;
- find ways to improve your writing skills about Reservation Application Form;
- be familiar with some famous hotels abroad.

Background Knowledge

Reservation is now widely adopted as a promotion method, and reservation makes it possible for hotels to be well prepared for guests' requirements when it comes to human resources, finance and carried goods.

Methods for Reservation

1. Telephone Reservation(电话预订): Telephone reservation is quick, personal and convenient, as customers could adjust their requirements timely according to the information provided by the front office on phone. Yet language may prove to be the main obstacle, such as foreign languages, dialects or even weak voice on the phone. To avoid mistakes, clerks answering the call must write down the reservation information carefully and repeat the information for guests to confirm.

2. Fax Reservation(传真预订): Fax reservation is more formal and accurate, and

decreases mistakes and future dispute.

3. Reservation on the Internet (网络预订): Reservation on the Internet is the latest method that is used by increasingly more people, as it is more convenient and cheaper.

4. Mail Reservation (邮件预订): Travel agent mainly adopts mail reservation.

5. Oral Reservation (口头预订): Oral reservation offers the chance for hotel to meet the guest's requirements as the guest will go personally or ask the agent to reserve in the hotel.

6. Contract Reservation (合约预订): Contract reservation is usually in place for long-term renting with commercial partners or travel agents.

Practice Materials

Listening

Dialogue 1

a. Listen to Dialogue 1 and decide whether each of the following sentences is true (T) or false (F).

1. _____ The two people have had a reservation in Xi'an before they telephone the hotel.

2. _____ They want to book a two-room suite.

3. _____ The Zhengyin Hotel has some suites when they book.

4. _____ The rate for one double room is 850 yuan.

5. _____ They will arrive at the hotel next week.

b. Listen to the dialogue and answer the following questions.

1. What's the name of the hotel?

2. How about the condition of the double rooms?

3. Does the rate include the breakfast?

4. How many nights do they want to stay in the hotel?

5. What's the date when they arrive?

c. Listen to the dialogue again and supply the missing words.

1. There are several hotels _____.

2. Can we make a _____ now?

3. Just a moment, please. I will _____ for you.

4. We don't have any _____ free at the moment.

5. Every room is _____ with radio, television, telephone and _____.

Notes

1. suite	套间
2. check	查看，核对
3. double room	双人房间
4. single room	单人房间
5. private bathroom	独立浴室
6. minibar	迷你酒吧（迷你冰箱）
7. rate	费用
8. arrive	到达

Dialogue 2

a. Listen to Dialogue 2 and decide whether each of the following sentences is true (T) or false (F).

1. The man books the room for himself.

2. The man wants a double room with a bath.

3. A queen-size bed is larger than a king-size bed.

4. A king-size bed costs a few dollars more than a queen-size bed.

5. The rate doesn't include the breakfast.

b. Listen to the dialogue and answer the following questions.

1. How many persons are there in his party?

_____

2. Do all the rooms in this hotel have a private bathroom?

_____

3. What's the difference between a king-size bed and a queen-size bed?

_____

4. What's the rate for a room with a queen-size bed for one night?

_____

5. Is there a discount for this room?
_____

c. Listen to the dialogue again and supply the missing words.

1. How many persons are there in your _____ ?
2. We can have one with _____ a queen-size _____ a king-size bed.
3. A queen-size bed is larger than the _____ double bed.
4. It _____ which you prefer or is most comfortable in.
5. _____ , what services come with that price?

Notes

1. party	在文中指同行者，同伴
2. either...or...	或者……或者……
3. a queen-size a king-size	两者均指特大号码
4. ordinary	普通的，一般的
5. double bed	双人床
6. put together	放到一起
7. depend on	依据，取决于
8. by the way	顺便问一下
9. fill out	填满
10. registration card	注册登记卡

Background Information

a. Types of Reservation

1. Temporary reservation happens when guests choose to reserve just the same day or a couple of days before they come to stay here. The hotel is supposed to give firm oral answer to such reservation through phone call or fax, and no confirmation mail is required. When guests fail to appear by the reservation's due time, the reservation is cancelled, which shall be made clear and noticed to guests when they make reservation by clerks.

2. Confirmative reservation calls confirmation from hotel, either oral or written when the hotel receives reservation from guests. Deposit money from guests is not demanded. When guests fail to arrive at the hotel duly, the reservation is cancelled automatically. This kind of reservation bears two advantages: one is that requirements from guests could be repeated and

guests could know whether the hotel has fully understood their requirements. And the other is that the hotel's responsibility and related issues are clearly stated.

3. Guaranteed reservation means guests promise to stay in the hotel or they will undertake economic loss. The guarantee can be advance payment, or credit card and sometimes contract. When guests break their promise, the hotel will keep a day's payment.

b. Failure of Reservation

There are usually three cases in which the hotel may fail to meet the reservation.

1. The hotel finds it impossible to provide rooms for confirmative or guaranteed reservation. When the situation occurs, the hall manager must come to handle it personally. After apologizing and explanation, the manager shall arrange for other hotels for the guests and send guests there free of charge, and the hotel shall take care of the part overcharged over the reservation with them.

2. When guests arrive at the hotel later and the reserved room has been sold, the hotel shall make efforts to help guests find other hotels in the vicinity and arrange vehicles for guests.

3. The hotel cannot find reservation record that guests claim they have done. Clerks are expected to help guests with accommodation while looking through the files.

 Speaking

Dialogue 1

Booking a Room

(Scene: A guest makes a call to the hotel to book a room for his wife and himself.)

R: Reservationist   G: Guest

R: Abby Park Hotel. Can I help you?

G: Yes, I would like to book a room for my wife and myself.

R: Certainly, Sir. Could I have your arrival and departure dates?

G: We will be arriving on Tuesday next week and staying for two days.

R: We have a double room for you with a nice view of the park. Would that be OK?

G: Yes, that would be great. How much is the room?

R: It is ninety-five pounds per night. It is a double room with a bathroom. There is a fridge, coffee maker and a television in the room.

G: Does the bathroom have a bath or a shower?

R: All our bathrooms have full size baths with a shower attachment.

G: Does the room have an Internet connection?

R: Yes, all our rooms have complimentary wireless Internet.

G: Excellent. Do you serve breakfast in the hotel?

R: Yes, breakfast is included in the price. Our guests have the choice of a full English breakfast or a continental breakfast.

G: That's great. Can I book the room?

R: Certainly, Sir.

Notes

1. arrival date	抵店日期，入住日期	
2. departure date	离店日期	
3. fridge	冰箱	
4. coffee maker	咖啡机	
5. shower	淋浴间，浴室	
6. attachment	（机器的）附件，附加装置	
7. complimentary	免费的，赠送的	
8. wireless Internet	无线网络	
9. full	丰富的，丰盛的	
10. English breakfast	英式早餐（熏肉、鸡蛋、香肠、烤面包、饮料等）	
11. continental breakfast	欧陆式早餐，简易早餐	

Dialogue 2

A Group Reservation

(Scene: A guest calls the hotel to reserve rooms for an American group.)

R: Reservationist   G: Guest

R: Shanghai Hotel. Reservation Desk. May I help you?

G: Yes, I'd like to make a group reservation in your hotel.

R: What kind of room would you like, Sir? We have single rooms, TWBs (twin beds with private bathroom), and deluxe suites in Chinese, Japanese, Roman, French and Presidential styles.

G: We'd like to have 12 TWBs and a Japanese suite.

R: Oh, I see. May I know the name of the group?

G: The American Education Delegation.

R: For which dates?

G: From May 23rd to May 27th.

R: May I have your name, Sir?

G: George Smith.

R: Oh, I see. The American Education Delegation would like to have 12 TWBs and a Japanese suite from May 23rd to May 27th. One moment, Sir. Let me have a check... Sorry to have kept you waiting, Mr. Smith. Yes, we can confirm you 12 TWBs and a Japanese suite from May 23rd to May 27th.

G: Thank you. Can you tell me how much you'll charge for a double room? And do you have a special rate for group reservations?

R: For one night, a double room in our hotel is 800 yuan and a Japanese suite is 1,200 yuan. And we offer a special rate for group reservation, a 20 percent discount. So, it's only 640 yuan for a TWB and 960 yuan for the suite.

G: That's great. Could you meet us at the airport?

R: Yes, of course. Our shuttle bus will be waiting for you at the airport. But could you give me the flight number, in case the plane is late?

G: MU435. Oh, yes. Have you got a big conference hall? We will have a meeting in your hotel during our stay in Shanghai.

R: Yes, Sir. We have a very nice multi-function hall on the second floor. But I'm afraid you'll have to speak to the sales manager about that. Would you please hold on, and I'll check whether I can put you through.

G: That's fine. Thank you.

R: I'm always at your service.

Notes

1. deluxe — 精装的，豪华的
2. delegation — 代表团
3. confirm — 确定，证实
4. special — 特别的，特殊的，专门的
5. meet sb. at the airport — 去机场接某人
6. shuttle bus — 往返汽车
7. multi-function — 多功能
8. put through — 穿过；使从事，使经受；完成；接通电话

Dialogue 3

Registering a Tour Group

A: Tour group coordinator   B: Tour group guide   C: Mr. Smith

A: Good evening. Who is the tour guide, please?

B: That's me.

A: How do you do? My name is Wang Nan, the tour group coordinator. Welcome to our hotel. I'd like to reconfirm your reservation.

B: How do you do? My name is Liu Ming, the tour guide. This is the leader of the tour group, Mr. Smith.

A: How do you do, Mr. Smith?

C: How do you do, Mr. Wang?

A: Is there any change in the number of your group members?

B: No.

A: Very good, Sir. You have made a reservation for 12 double rooms and 4 single rooms. Here is the rooming list. Do you have a group visa?

C: Yes. Here you are.

A: All right. I'll make a copy of your group visa. Please wait a minute.

……

A: Here are the room cards and breakfast vouchers, Mr. Liu. Are you going to divide them yourself?

B: No, I will give them to Mr. Smith. He will divide them.

A: May I confirm your check-out time? According to the schedule you will check out at 8:00 A.M. on the 18th, is it right?

B: Yes, we would like to change our check-out time to 8:30 A.M.

A: No problem, Sir. What time will you have a morning call?

B: The morning call will be 7:00 A.M.

A: I see. 7:00 A.M. on the 18th. Could you please place your luggage in front of your room door by 8:00 A.M.? The bellman will pick them up. Anything else?

B: No. Thank you.

A: If there is any change, please inform the Front Desk.

B: OK. Thank you.

A: You're welcome. Enjoy your stay.

> **Notes**
>
> 1. visa　　　　　　　　签证
> 2. make a copy of　　　复制，复印
> 3. voucher　　　　　　凭证，收据；代金券，票券
> 4. divide　　　　　　　分发
> 5. schedule　　　　　　时间表
> 6. check out　　　　　　结账后离开
> 7. luggage　　　　　　行李
> 8. in front of　　　　　在……的前面
> 9. bellman　　　　　　行李员；传达员
> 10. pick up　　　　　　捡起

Reading

Passage 1

Hotels

When you are traveling, whether on business or for pleasure, you often need to stay in a hotel. The kind of hotel you choose is probably decided, above all, according to how much money you want to spend. There are small hotels with very few services, where the prices are low; or there are large hotels with all the very latest comforts, where you could spend all the money you have in the bank for one very comfortable night.

There are several different kinds of people who go to hotels. Some want to live rather than just stay in a hotel; the hotels which are designed to meet their needs are called residential hotels. However, most people who stay in hotels are either business people or tourists on vacation. Some hotels are designed particularly for one of these two groups: commercial hotels are usually located in the business section of a town, while vacation hotels (which are also called tourist hotels) may be by the sea, in the mountains, or near other beauty spots. In large cities, many of the hotels are designed for both kinds of guests.

In most hotels, there are two kinds of rooms: single rooms, for the use of one person, and double rooms, for the use of two people. In addition, in larger hotels, there are also suites, which include two or more rooms connected together—perhaps a bedroom and a living room. These are usually for people who are very rich or very important.

What is it like staying in a large modern hotel? In your room, you will probably find a radio, a color television set, an ice-box filled with cold drinks, a machine for making coffee, and many other kinds of equipment to make your stay comfortable. At the head of your bed there might be a panel of buttons. You could lie in bed and press these buttons to turn on the air conditioner, lock the door, turn off the radio and television, and turn out the light.

If you are hungry, the easiest thing to do is to telephone the Room Service and order food to be brought up to your room. However, it may be more interesting to try the different places to eat in the hotel. You might decide to have just a snack in a small coffee shop, or to eat a complete meal in one of the smart restaurants. After your meal, there are probably several places to go for a drink.

There are many other services as well. If your clothes are dirty, you can send them to be washed or dry-cleaned. If you are on business, you can have your letters typed for you. If you feel ill, you can call for the hotel doctor.

If you are staying in a tourist hotel, you can probably go to the swimming pool or the tennis court to get some physical exercises. Some hotels even have ponds filled with fish for guests who enjoy fishing. In the evening there may be concerts given by famous singers, or movies may be shown, or magic tricks may be performed, or you may prefer to go dancing.

Hotels have changed greatly over the years, but the basic idea of hotels has remained the same: to provide shelter for travelers. Today, they have become one of the biggest industries in the world, and have kept up with modern developments in science and technology. However, no matter how modern and comfortable a hotel building is, the most important feature is the people who work there: a small old hotel where you are given a warm welcome is a much nicer place to stay than a large modern hotel where nobody smiles or does anything to help you.

a. Choose the best answer for each of the following questions.

1. In Paragraph 1, the writer states that one's choice of a particular hotel is made mainly according to _____.

   A. how much one is willing to pay for a night
   B. whether one is traveling on business or for pleasure
   C. whether the hotel is in the central part of a city
   D. how good the services of the hotel are

2. All the following kinds of people usually stay in hotels except _____.

   A. people who travel on business   B. tourists who are on vacation
   C. people who want to live in a hotel   D. students who study in universities

3. Which kind of hotels is usually located in the business section of a town?

A. Residential hotels   B. Vacation hotels

C. Commercial hotels   D. Tourist hotels

4. Which room in a hotel is the most expensive?

A. A single room   B. A double room

C. A living room   D. A suite

5. The main idea of Paragraph 4 is _____.

A. the way to turn on the equipment in a hotel

B. the equipment of a modern hotel room

C. the use of a panel of buttons in a hotel

D. the food in an ice-box in a hotel

6. Paragraph 5 is mainly about _____.

A. how one can get something to eat in a hotel when hungry

B. where one can go for a drink in a hotel

C. what one can get in a coffee shop

D. when one should order food from the Room Service in a hotel

7. What kind of hotel may provide a swimming pool or a tennis court?

A. A residential hotel   B. A commercial hotel

C. A tourist hotel   D. A country hotel

8. What feature of a hotel is the most important in the writer's eyes?

A. Modern equipment in the rooms

B. Smart restaurants and coffee shops

C. Activities organized at night for pleasure

D. A warm welcome given to travelers

9. This passage is about _____.

A. the history of hotels   B. the modern equipment in hotels

C. hotels in general   D. the most important feature of a hotel

b. *Choose an appropriate word or phrase to fill in each blank to make each sentence meaningful, and change its form when necessary.*

commercial	double	dry-clean	panel	section
snack	spot	residential	tourist	vacation

1. Fontbonne is a liberal arts college, located in a _____ suburb of St. Louis.

2. Cambridge is always full of _____ in the summer.

3. Employees are entitled to four weeks' paid _____.

4. The film was highly praised, but was not a _____ success.

5. Signals control each _____ of the railway track.

6. On this map X marks the _____ where the treasure is buried.

7. Do you need a _____ room or two singles?

8. Premier Gardens is one of a half-dozen subdivisions in California where every home cuts power consumption by 50%, mostly by using low-power appliances and solar _____.

9. Drinks and light _____ are served at the bar.

10. Natural-filled duvets must be _____ by a professional.

c. Translate the following sentences into English with words or phrases given in the brackets.

1. 她是那种人们非爱即恨的人。(either... or...)
_____

2. 该课程除了介绍一般的电脑知识，还提供实际操作的机会。(in addition)
_____

3. 该宾馆为客人提供擦鞋服务。(provide for)
_____

4. 员工需要跟上最新的技术发展。(keep up with)
_____

5. 不管要花多少时间，我也要做完这项工作。(no matter how)
_____

Vocabulary List

button	[ˈbʌtn]	n. 按钮
comfort	[ˈkʌmfət]	n. 使人舒服的事物
commercial	[kəˈmɜːʃl]	adj. 商业的
double	[ˈdʌbl]	adj. 双的，双人用的
dry-clean	[ˌdraɪˈkliːn]	v. 干洗
equipment	[ɪˈkwɪpmənt]	n. 设备，装备
feature	[ˈfiːtʃə]	n. 特征，特点，特色
ice-box	[ˌaɪsˈbɒks]	n. 冰箱，电冰箱

latest	[ˈleɪtɪst]	adj. 最近的，最新的，最现代的
locate	[ləʊˈkeɪt]	v. 位于，坐落于
panel	[ˈpænl]	n.（机器、设备等的）仪表板，面板
particularly	[pəˈtɪkjələli]	adv. 特别，尤其
perform	[pəˈfɔːm]	v. 演出，表演
remain	[rɪˈmeɪn]	v. 保持，仍然存在，继续存在
residential	[ˌrezɪˈdenʃl]	adj. 住宅的，与居住有关的
section	[ˈsekʃn]	n. 部分，区域
shelter	[ˈʃeltə]	n. 居住地，居所
snack	[snæk]	n. 小吃，快餐，点心
spot	[spɒt]	n. 地点，场所
suite	[swiːt]	n. 一套房间，套间
tourist	[ˈtʊərɪst]	n. 旅行者，旅游者
vacation	[veɪˈkeɪʃn]	n. 假期，休假

Phrases

on business	出差
above all	首先，最重要的是，尤其是
according to	根据，按照
rather than	而不是
either...or...	不是……就是……，要么……要么……
on vacation	在度假中
in addition	另外，除此之外
fill with	使充满，装满
at the head of	在……的最前面
turn on	打开
turn off	关上，关掉
turn out	关掉，熄灭
as well	同样，也，还有
swimming pool	游泳池
tennis court	网球场
physical exercise	体育锻炼
magic trick	魔术表演，魔术戏法
prefer to	宁愿，更喜欢

provide...for	为……提供
keep up with	跟上，赶上；不落人之后
no matter how	无论如何，不管怎样

Passage 2

The Profile of Hilton

Ever since Conrad Hilton opened his first hotel in 1919, the Hilton organization has built a reputation for quality, value, integrity and strength. For more than 100 years, "Hilton" has been standing for excellence in the industry. Hilton Hotels Corporation offers five-star luxury hotels in many places like London, Tokyo, Hong Kong, Singapore and Bali. In addition to that, Hilton International has a global network, which provides its customers with nearly 6,800 hotels in about 122 countries worldwide.

As one of the best brands in this field, it is not only well-known and well-respected, but also referred to as a market leader. Holding the belief that "Travel is more than just from A to B. Travel should inspire new ideas", it tries to deliver outstanding products, services and experiences to each customer.

In today's increasingly competitive hotel industry, the winners are those with the best brands that offer the most attractive marketing program.

Hilton Hotels Corporation has been a leader in creating diversity program. It is now able to offer guests the widest possible range of hotel experiences, including four-star city center hotels, convention properties, all-suite hotels, extended stay, mid-priced focused service, destination resorts, vacation ownership, airport hotels and conference centers.

In 1999 the corporation established a new family of brands: Doubletree, Embassy Suites Hotel, Hampton Inn and Hampton Inn & Suites and Homewood Suites by Hilton. In November 2000, Hilton Group and Hilton Hotels Corporation formed a joint venture company to expand their business on a worldwide basis. Owned equally by Hilton Group and Hilton Hotels Corporation, this joint venture has been headquartered in Brussels, Belgium since then.

a. Answer the following questions according to the passage.

1. When did Hilton open his first hotel?

_____

2. How many hotels does Hilton Hotels Corporation include in the world?

_____

3. In today's hotel industry, who are the winners?
_____

4. What kinds of new brands did the corporation establish in 1999?
_____

5. Where is the headquarter of the joint venture?
_____

b. Choose an appropriate word or phrase to fill in each blank to make each sentence meaningful, and change its form when necessary.

| in addition to | belief | joint venture | be able to | ownership |
| refer to | stand for | diversity | establish | headquarter |

1. She also learned a kind of alphabet for the blind, in which different finger positions _____ different letters of the alphabet.

2. _____ giving a general introduction to computer, the course also provides practical experience.

3. We should get a thorough understanding about the cultural _____ of the United States.

4. Will you _____ glance over my report before I send it to the committee?

5. It can also _____ a conflict or disagreement, often involving violence.

6. The source of our outside financing is _____, compensation trade and bank loan, etc.

7. His second novel _____ his fame as a writer.

8. There was a happy chime of _____ and practice in everything she said.

9. The company is to relocate its _____ in the Midlands.

10. The family possessed documents that proved their right to _____.

c. Translate the following sentences into English with words or phrases given in the brackets.

1. 我觉得旅游这个主意很吸引人。(attractive)
_____

2. 北京饭店在质量和服务方面赢得了很好的声誉。(reputation)
_____

3. 在竞争激烈的酒店行业中，北京饭店一直处于领先地位。(competitive, industry)
_____

4. 华为是一个享誉全球的知名品牌。(brand)

_____

5. 她到此准备长住一段时间。(extend)

_____

Vocabulary List

attractive	[ə'træktɪv]	adj. 有吸引力的，漂亮的，诱人的
belief	[bɪ'li:f]	n. 相信，信念，信仰
brand	[brænd]	n. 商标
competitive	[kəm'petətɪv]	adj. 竞争的
convention	[kən'venʃn]	n. 习俗，会议，集会
destination	[ˌdestɪ'neɪʃn]	n. 目的地，意图
diversity	[daɪ'vɜ:səti]	n. 不同，变化多端，不同点
establish	[ɪ'stæblɪʃ]	v. 建立，确立
extend	[ɪk'stend]	v. 延伸，伸展，扩大
headquarter	[hed'kwɔ:tə]	n. 总部，总公司
industry	['ɪndəstri]	n. 工业，产业
integrity	[ɪn'tegrəti]	n. 正直，诚实；完整
luxury	['lʌkʃəri]	adj. 奢华的
offer	['ɒfə]	v. 提供
ownership	['əʊnəʃɪp]	n. 所有权，所有制
property	['prɒpəti]	n. 财产，资产，所有权
reputation	[ˌrepju'teɪʃn]	n. 名誉，声望
vacation	[veɪ'keɪʃn]	n. 假期
well-known	[ˌwel'nəʊn]	adj. 著名的，众所周知的
worldwide	[ˌwɜ:ld'waɪd]	adj. 世界范围的

Phrases

marketing program	营销计划
joint venture	合资企业
be able to	有能力做……
refer to	涉及，提及
stand for	……的立场，代表
in addition to	除……之外
not only...but also	不仅……而且

Terms

Conrad Hilton	[ˈkɒnræd-ˈhiltən]	康拉德·希尔顿
North America	[nɔːθ-əˈmerɪkə]	北美
London	[ˈlʌndən]	伦敦
Tokyo	[ˈtəʊkiəʊ]	东京
Bali	[ˈbɑːli]	巴厘岛
Brussels	[ˈbrʌslz]	布鲁塞尔
Belgium	[ˈbeldʒəm]	比利时

Notes

Hilton Hotels Corporation（希尔顿酒店集团）：希尔顿是国际知名的酒店管理公司，旗下拥有十八个酒店品牌。希尔顿一直致力于实现"让世界充满阳光和温暖，让宾客感受到希尔顿的'热情好客'"的创始愿景。在其百年发展历程中，希尔顿为超过30亿名宾客提供过服务。2020年，希尔顿推出 Hilton Clean Stay（希尔顿清洁无忧住）服务，实施行业领先的清洁标准和消毒标准。在2020年"道琼斯可持续发展指数"评比中，荣膺"全球产业领导者"殊荣。

Doubletree（逸林酒店）：希尔顿逸林酒店作为希尔顿旗下的一家快速扩张的高档酒店品牌，在全球拥有超过510家高档酒店、逾210,000间客房。希尔顿逸林酒店及度假村可提供全方位的服务设施，其中包括餐厅和休息室、客房服务、健身俱乐部、商务中心、会议及宴会空间。"This summer is packed with the fun of kids at doubletree!"（今年夏天，逸林酒店充满了孩子们的快乐）是其著名的广告语。

Embassy Suites Hotel（大使馆套房酒店）：大使馆套房酒店是希尔顿旗下的品牌之一。第一所大使馆套房酒店创建于1983年，它在套房系列的酒店中是档次最高、规模最大的。在其旗下的每一家酒店，客人们都可以享受到拥有露天庭院和两个房间的套房。

Hampton Inn & Suites（汉普顿旅馆）：汉普顿旅馆酒店是希尔顿旗下的品牌之一，遍布美国、加拿大和拉丁美洲，客人能够非常轻松方便地找到。不管是商务还是休闲，不论是单间还是套房，客人们都能享受到特有的服务。

Homewood Suites by Hilton（家木套房酒店）：家木套房酒店是希尔顿旗下的品牌之一，其服务旨在使入住的客人有家的感觉。

"Travel is more than just from A to B."（"旅游不仅仅是从A地到达B地。"）

——Hilton 著名的广告语

 Writing

Reservation Application Form

Task 1　Writing Skills

为了确保顺利入住酒店，根据国际惯例，客人须提前预订房间，一般情况下都是通过电话或网络来预订。对酒店工作人员来说，一方面要学会制定简洁明确的预订单，另一方面要确保准确无误、快捷清楚地填写订单。

制定和填写酒店预订单应注意的事项：

(1) 涵盖个人资料。个人资料包括客人的姓名、单位、国籍、城市、地址、电话、传真、电子信箱和证件等内容，由于客人来自不同的国家和地区，同名同姓的人较多，为了避免可能出现的误解，填写预订单时，一定要做到准确无误。

(2) 清楚登记客人的要求。为了客人的方便，同时也为了酒店的有效管理，制定预订单时，务必明确客人进店和离店的时间、房间类型、是否有特殊要求等。填写预订单时，尽可能逐项填入。

Task 2　Sample Writing

Sample 1

DATE APPLIED May 10, 2024	A RESERVATION APPLICATION	NEW BOOKING CANCELLATION AMENDMENT ON WAITING LIST	
GUEST NAME John Pany	ARRIVAL 5/10/2024 MONTH/DATE/YEAR	DEPARTURE 5/18/2024 MONTH/DATE/YEAR	
COMPANY General Motors	TRANSPORTATION ARRANGEMENT SINGLE TRIP	ROUND TRIP	
TITLE Manager	FLIGHT ETA 8:00 A.M. May 10	ETD 11:30 June 4	
TYPE OF ACCOMMODATION REQUIRED Single room with mini bar		RATE SPECIAL DISCOUNT CORPORATE DISCOUNT TRAVEL DISCOUNT AIRLINE DISCOUNT	
PERSON One			
FIRM/TRAVEL AGENT Pacific Travel Agent	PAYMENT INSTRUCTIONS ROOM　　　　ALL EXPENSES GUEST　ACCOUNT		

NAME OF APPLICANT John Pany	A/C NO. 2123994000323	
PHONE NUMBER 001-445-237-6567	FAX NUMBER 001-446-238-7865	REMARKS SPECIAL RM RT APPROVED BY
RECEIVED BY Tom Lee	RECONFIRMED BY Kate Jude	
VIP APPROVED BY	CIP APPROVED BY	
Pleae note that reservations are held until 6:00 P.M. unless arrival details are notified.		

Sample 2

HOTEL BOOKING FORM

Please fill out the reservation request form below, we will send the Confirmation Invoice detailing the bookings, terms & payment via e-mail within 24~28 hours.

Surname: <u>Miller</u>

Other name: <u>Dillon</u>

Company (if any): <u>Universe Computers</u>

Address: No. 280 <u>Deland Avenue London</u>

City: <u>London</u>

Country: <u>Great Britain</u>

Tel: <u>002-885-813-3598</u>

Fax: <u>002-885-814-8320</u>

E-mail: <u>miller@hotmail.com</u>

(Please check again if your e-mail address is correct)

Check-in date: <u>December 21, 2024</u>

Check-out date: <u>December 28, 2024</u>

Name of Hotel: <u>Sunny Hotel</u>

Second Choice: <u>Seaside Paradise</u>

In which City: <u>Honolulu</u>

No. of Room Required: <u>Five</u>

No. of Adult: <u>Eight</u>

No. of Children: <u>Two</u>   Age: <u>Five</u>

Occupancy: Single, <u>None</u>; Double bed, <u>Four</u>; Twin bed, <u>One</u>

Price Per Room Per Night in This Hotel: <u>$150/room</u>

Any additional information or requirement:

Task 3 Writing Practice

a. Match the following groups of words and phrases.

1. reservation　　　　　　　a. 登记入店
2. ETA　　　　　　　　　　b. 交通
3. ETD　　　　　　　　　　c. 预订
4. cancellation　　　　　　　d. 估计的离开时间
5. transportation　　　　　　e. 成年人
6. check-in　　　　　　　　f. 双人床
7. check-out　　　　　　　　g. 占用，使用
8. occupancy　　　　　　　　h. 结账离店
9. adult　　　　　　　　　　i. 估计的到达时间
10. twin bed　　　　　　　　j. 取消预订

b. Write a Reservation Form according to the given information. Add some more information if necessary.

澳大利亚人 Tom Stiffens 想通过网络预订一家泰国酒店，他到达的时间是 2024 年 5 月 2 日上午 9:30，从曼谷入境。5 月 8 日下午 2:00 离开。他需要一标准间，他家住悉尼市马克大街 204 号，电子邮箱是 sn@sust.com，护照号是 0332404165。

Vocabulary Development

bellboy	负责行李的男服务员
cashier	收银员，出纳员
lobby	大厅
front desk	前台
information desk	信息台，资讯台，问询处
switch board	电话总机，服务台
receive a reservation	收到预约
periodic report	定期报告
check-in	入住饭店
check-out	离开饭店
wake-up service	唤醒服务
luggage deposit	行李寄存
large-scale hotel	大型酒店
information tracing system	信息追踪系统

advance payment	预付款
deposit money	定金，保证金
leaving notice	离店通知单
lodge claim or complaint	提出索赔，提出意见
guest room	客房
occupied room	有人入住的房间
customer resource	客户资源
walk-in guest	没有预约的客人
guest with reservation	预约的客人
currency exchange	货币兑换

Housekeeping Services
客房服务

 Unit Objectives

After learning this unit, you should

- read, comprehend and translate the passages and dialogues about housekeeping into Chinese;
- know how to give information about housekeeping;
- master the basic words and expressions about housekeeping information and use them to make sentences;
- get some cultural knowledge about housekeeping information;
- comprehend the dialogues, practice listening skills and talk a little about housekeeping;
- find ways to improve your writing skills on Help Wanted Ads.

 Background Knowledge

Types of Housekeeping

1) single room　　　　单人房（一张单人床）
　　double room　　　　双人房（一张双人床）
　　twin room　　　　　双人房（两张单人床）
　　double double　　　双人房（两张双人床）
　　big single room　　 大床房（一张双人大床）
　　triple room　　　　 三人房（三张单人床）

2) economy room (ER) 经济间
standard room (SR) 标准间
superior room (UR) 高级套房
standard suite (SS) 标准套房
deluxe room (DR) 豪华间
presidential suite (PS) 总统套房
3) studio room 工作室型客房（设沙发床或躺椅）
multi-functional room 多功能客房
combined type room 组合客房

Types of Hotels

inn 旅馆，饭店
lodge 小旅馆
tavern 酒店
caravansary 马车店，大旅馆
hostel 招待所
hotel 饭店，酒店
motel (motor hotel) 汽车饭店（旅店）
budget hotel 廉价旅馆
economy hotel (one-star hotel) 一星级饭店
some comfort hotel (two-star hotel) 二星级饭店
average hotel (three-star hotel) 三星级饭店
high comfort hotel (four-star hotel) 四星级饭店
deluxe hotel (five-star hotel) 五星级饭店

Types of American Credit Cards

(1) American Express（美国运通卡），是由美国运通公司 (American Express Company) 发行的信用卡，它可以在全世界大多数国家第一流的旅馆、餐厅及商店等处使用。

(2) Carte Blanche（全权卡），这是两个法语词，意思是"空白的卡片"(blank card)。原意是一个空白的文件，由一方事先在协议上签好字，然后送另一方填写其所同意的条件。

(3) Diners Club（大来卡）。第一张塑料付款卡。1981 年美国最大的零售银行——花旗银行 (Citibank) 的控股公司——花旗公司接受了 Diners Club Intenational 卡，并且巩固该公司在信用卡市场中所保持的强有力的位置。

(4) Master Card (万事达卡)，是美国三千家银行通过国际信用卡协会 (Interbank Card Association) 签发的信用卡。它是美国使用最广泛的信用卡中的一种，原名为 Master Charge。

(5) Visa ("维萨"卡)，是美洲银行发行的信用卡。该行是最先签发信用卡的银行。在各种信用卡中，美洲银行所签发的信用卡数目最多。美国加利福尼亚州以外的约 40 个州的银行，都可以代表美洲银行签发它的信用卡。该行的信用卡原名为"美洲银行卡"(Bank Americard)，于 1977 年改名为"维萨"。

(6) Discover Card (发现卡)，一般来讲免年费，有高信用额度以及提供较高的现金回扣。在北美持卡用户已超过六千万，已成为继 VISA、MasterCard、AE 之后的第四大信用卡。1985 年到 2007 年，由摩根士丹利等金融机构控股，零售商公司 Sears 推广发行。2007 年时，Discover Financial Services 成为一个独立的金融公司。

Practice Materials

Listening

Dialogue 1

a. Listen to Dialogue 1 and decide whether each of the following sentences is true (T) or false (F).

1. _____ The man is a waiter of a dining room.
2. _____ The guest was just about to go down for his supper.
3. _____ The guest would like a flask of hot water.
4. _____ There is no water in the flask.
5. _____ The guest himself will go and get some hot water.

b. Listen to the dialogue and answer the following questions.

1. What's the man's occupation?

2. What does the guest ask the man to do for him?

3. What does the guest need some water to do?

4. Is there any hot water in the flask?

5. What will the man do then?
_____

c. *Listen to the dialogue again and supply the missing words.*
1. When would you like me to _____ your room, Sir?
2. But before you _____, would you do this for me?
3. I need some hot water to _____ medicine.
4. I'm sorry that your flask is_____.
5. I will go and get _____ flask that's _____ at once.

Dialogue 2

a. *Listen to Dialogue 2 and choose the best answer to complete the statements.*
1. The guests are going to have _____ in the room.
   A. a meeting   B. a discussion
   C. a small party   D. a game
2. The guests want the girl to tidy up a bit _____.
   A. in the living room   B. in the dining room
   C. in the reading room   D. in the bathroom
3. The guests would treat their friends to _____.
   A. Chinese tea   B. coffee
   C. orange juice   D. beer
4. The girl will bring in some _____ together with the drinking water.
   A. fresh flowers   B. new cups
   C. fresh towels   D. clean bottles
5. What would the guests like to do while waiting for their friends?
   A. do some sewing   B. do some reading
   C. listen to music   D. do some washing

b. *Listen to the dialogue and answer the following questions.*
1. What does the girl want to do for the guests?
_____

2. What are the guests going to have in the room?
_____

3. Why is the bathroom in disorder now?
_____

4. Who will turn on the lights for the guests?
_____

5. Do you think the guests will have a good time that evening?
_____

c. Listen to the dialogue again and supply the missing words.

1. May I do the _____ service for you now?

2. I'll let the overnight _____ know.

3. Our friends seem to be _____ late.

4. Would you like me to draw the _____ for you?

5. Goodbye, Sir and Madam, and do have a very _____ evening.

> **Notes**
>
> 1. flask   长颈瓶，热水瓶
> 2. overnight   终夜的，一夜间的
> 3. cozy   舒适的，温暖的
> 4. typical   典型的
> 5. boiled water   开水
> 6. quite a mess   乱糟糟的
> 7. tidy up   整理

Speaking

Dialogue 1

Happy Birthday

H: May I come in, Mr. Paul?

G: Come in, please.

H: I'm here to say Happy Birthday to you.

G: Thank you. How do you know it is my birthday today?

H: We learned from the registration record. Please accept this birthday card and these flowers from us attendants.

G: I really appreciate your congratulations. It is very considerate of you.

H: It's our pleasure to do so. We wish you many happy returns of the day.

> **Notes**
>
> 1. registration — 登记
> 2. attendant — 服务人员
> 3. appreciate one's congratulations — 感激某人的祝贺
> 4. considerate — 体贴的，周到的
> 5. wish sb. many happy returns of the day — 祝某人健康长寿

Dialogue 2

Using a Safety Deposit Box

H: Good evening, ma'am. May I help you?

G: Yes. I'd like to use a safety deposit box.

H: Will the object fit into this size of box?

G: Let me see. I think it's OK.

H: Could you fill out this form, please, ma'am?

G: Here you are.

H: Thank you, ma'am. Would you like to use it until May 20th?

G: Yes.

H: This way, please. Your box number is 522.

G: Thank you.

H: If you would like to use the contents during the period of use, please come here in person. After confirming your signature, we will open the box.

G: I see. Thank you.

> **Notes**
>
> 1. safety deposit box — 保险箱，保险柜
> 2. fit into — （使）适合，刚好放入
> 3. fill out — 填写（表格等）
> 4. contents — （复数）所容纳之物，所有物
> 5. period of use — 使用期间
> 6. in person — 亲自

Dialogue 3

Seeing off Guests

G: Excuse me, have you made out my bill? I'm leaving in an hour. I'm going to pay my account right now.

H: Yes, madam. Here you are. That's the total amount payable at the bottom there.

G: Thank you. I don't want to come back to the room after I settle my bill at the Cashier's Counter. May I take my baggage downstairs now?

H: Yes, you may. Have you got your baggage ready?

G: Yes, I have packed everything up.

H: Shall I have the bellman help you with your things downstairs?

G: No, I can manage them by myself. I have only two bags. They're not too heavy.

H: Fine. Would you mind my checking the room?

G: Of course not. Let's go, shall we?

H: Yes, let's go. Is everything to your satisfaction during your stay here?

G: Yes, I'm quite satisfied. I have had a good time at your hotel.

H: After you, madam.

G: Now please do your duty.

H: Thank you for your cooperation. The desk lamp is there. The vacuum flask is not broken. Here are the teacups and saucers. The TV set is all right. Very good. You may go now. May I have the key back?

G: Yes, here it is.

H: Thank you. Let me carry one of the bags to the lift for you.

G: Many thanks. Let's be off now.

H: Here comes the lift. I wish you a pleasant journey. Goodbye.

G: Goodbye.

Notes

1. repairman	修理工
2. bellman	应接员，行李员
3. make out one's bill	结算账单
4. settle one's bill	结账
5. pack up	打包，收拾
6. would you mind doing sth.	您介意做某事吗
7. do one's duty	履行责任
8. cooperation	合作
9. desk lamp	台灯
10. vacuum flask	保温瓶
11. saucer	茶托

Reading

Passage 1

Tips on Service

Hotel workers depend on tips to augment their usually small salaries. Rather than being annoyed at having to tip the doorman who greets you, consider it part of the cost of travel and be prepared with the dollar bills you will need to hand out before you even getting to your room.

Doorman

Depending on the amount of luggage, tip $1 to $2 to the doorman who takes your bags and turns them over to a bellman. If you are visiting and have no luggage, you naturally do not need to tip him for simply opening the door for you. Tip him again when you leave with your luggage as he takes it from the bellman and assists you in loading it in your car or into your taxi. When the doorman obtains a taxi for you, tip him $1 to $3 (the higher amount if he must stand in the rain for a period of time to get it).

Bellman

Tip $1 a bag but not less than $2 to the bellman who carries or delivers your luggage to your room. When the bellman does something special for you, such as make a purchase or bring something you have requested to your room, but not room service deliveries, he or she should be tipped $2 to $3 for every service, at the time it is provided.

Maid

For stays of one night or more, the maid should be tipped $2 per night per person in a large hotel; $1 per night per person in a less expensive hotel. Give the maid her tip in person, if she can be found. If not, put it in a sealed envelope marked "chambermaid".

Valet

Valet services are added to your bill, so there is no need to tip for pressing or cleaning when items are left in your room. If you are in when your cleaning and pressing is delivered, however, tip $1 for the delivery for one or two items, more when several items are being delivered.

Dining Room Staff

Tips for dining room staff are exactly the same as they are in any other restaurant—15% to 18% except in the most elegant dining rooms where tips are 18% to 20%. If you are staying in an American plan hotel where your meals are included in your total bill, tips are as usual, and an additional tip should be given to the maitre d'hotel who has taken care of you during your stay. This tip ranges anywhere from $10 to $15 for a weekend for a family or a group of four people to $20 to $30 for a longer stay or a larger group.

a. Answer the following questions according to the passage.

1. In what situation can the doorman get higher amount of tips?
_____

2. How much should you tip the bellman when he buys something for you?
_____

3. What should you do if the maid you want to tip for cannot be found?
_____

4. Is it necessary for you to tip for valet services as usual? Why?
_____

5. Are tips for dining room staff much more than they are in any other restaurant?
_____

b. Translate the expressions into Chinese or English.

1. deliver an important report   _____
   delivery truck   _____
   _____   送信
   take delivery of the new car _____
2. press one's trousers   _____
   _____   按门铃
   press home one's advantage   _____
   press the trigger of a gun   _____
3. set one's seal to the proposals _____
   seal the parcel with sticky tape _____
   _____   密封的瓶子
   seal the document   _____
4. an elegant piece of furniture _____
   elegant manners   _____
   an elegant lady dressed in
   the latest fashion
   _____   最豪华、最有档次的酒店

c. Read the descriptions of three hotels in Bangkok and put the Chinese into English.

Each hotel room has _____ (空调), 24 hour _____ (客房服务), TV, radio and most have IDD phones. Other facilities include photocopying, typing, _____ (传真) and translation.

1. The Sheraton

This large hotel offers business people excellent facilities including translation and computer hire. It has a large pool and a wide range of sporting and leisure events.

2. The Ambassador

Tower complex with a big _____ (购物中心); business and sports center, a wide choice of _____ (酒吧) and restaurants; ideal for sales conferences.

3. The Regent

In a quiet location, close to the central business district. The business center is open daily, including shops, large pool, sauna, _____ (健身中心), tennis, _____ (会议室).

d. Translate the following sentences into English with words or phrases given in the brackets.

1. 这位年轻的女士有着非常优雅的举止。(elegant)
_____
2. 你的行李已经被搬上火车了。(luggage)
_____
3. 在这个价格范围内，有好几条旅游线路可供选择。(range)
_____
4. 不要为预订机票费神——导游已经帮你办理了。(take care of)
_____
5. 房租费包不包括早餐？(include)
_____

Vocabulary List

annoy	[ə'nɔɪ]	v. 使……恼火
assist	[ə'sɪst]	v. 协助，帮助
chambermaid	['tʃeɪmbəmeɪd]	n. 清理房间的女服务员
deliver	[dɪ'lɪvə]	v. 投递，送
doorman	['dɔ:mən]	n. 门卫
elegant	['elɪgənt]	adj. 优雅的
include	[ɪn'klu:d]	v. 包括

luggage	['lʌgɪdʒ]	n. 行李
purchase	['pɜːtʃəs]	v. 购买
press	[pres]	v. 熨烫
range	[reɪndʒ]	v. （在一定范围内）变化，排列
valet	['væleɪ]	n. 清洗、熨烫衣服的服务员

Phrases

additional tip	额外的小费
dining room staff	餐厅服务员
depend on	依赖，取决于
take care of	照看，照顾

Passage 2

Credit Cards

Today, more and more people in the United States are using credit cards instead of money to buy the things they need. Almost anyone who has a steady income and a continuous work record can apply for a credit card. There are many credit cards available: American Express, VISA, and Master Charge are some of the most popular.

If you have a credit card, you can buy a car, eat a dinner, take a trip, and even get a haircut by charging the cost to your account. In this way, you can pay for purchases a month later, without any extra charge. Or you may choose to make your payments over several months and pay only part of the total amount each month. If you do this, the credit company, or the bank that sponsors the credit card, will add a small service charge to your total bill. This is very convenient for the customer.

With the credit card in your wallet or purse, you don't have to carry much cash or worry about losing money due to carelessness or theft. The card user only has to worry about paying the final bill. This, of course, can be a problem, if you are charged more than you can pay for.

Many of us believe that it will only be a matter of time before credit cards replace cash and checks for both individuals and businesses.

People spend a lot of money in their daily lives. Working people spend their money on transportation to and from work, and on various expenses throughout the day. Most people enjoy shopping and buy many things that they need and want. They buy sports equipment, go to sporting events, and do many things that cost money.

However, many Americans don't pay cash or write checks for these things. More often they pay for things with credit cards. Credit cards are small rectangular plastic cards. Banks give these cards to their customers. When a customer buys something at a store, he shows his card at the store. This authorizes the store to charge the bank for the customer's purchase. The bank collects all the charges for each customer. Then once a month the bank requires the customer to pay all the charges for that month. The bank doesn't force the customer to pay the full amount. It allows the customer to pay for charges in several payments over a period of time. However, the bank requires the customer to pay interest on the unpaid part of the charges. In this way the bank allows customers to buy things that they can not afford at one time. People can use the cards to buy what they want and pay for it over a period of time. They also do not need to carry a lot of money.

So, a credit card is a card issued by a bank, allowing the holder to obtain goods and services on credit.

Choose the best answer for each of the following questions.

1. What are the most popular credit cards in the USA now?

A. American Express.　　　　　　　　B. VISA.

C. Master Charge.　　　　　　　　　　D. All the above.

2. Why do we use credit cards instead of wallets?

A. With the credit card in your wallet or purse, you can buy a car, eat a dinner, take a trip, and even get a haircut.

B. With the credit card in your wallet or purse, you don't have to carry much cash or worry about losing money due to carelessness or theft.

C. Because people spend a lot of money in their daily lives.

D. Because a credit card is a card issued by a bank, allowing the holder to obtain goods and services on credit.

3. What are the advantages of credit card?

A. A credit card is a card issued by a bank, allowing the holder to obtain goods and services on credit.

B. With the credit card in your wallet or purse, you don't have to carry much cash or worry about losing money due to carelessness or theft.

C. You can buy a car, eat a dinner, take a trip, and even get a haircut by charging the cost to your account.

D. Both B and C.

4. How long can you choose to make your payments by a credit card and pay only part of the total amount each month?

A. One week.   B. One month.
C. Several months.   D. Over several months.

5. Where is a credit card issued?

A. The credit card company.   B. The bank.
C. The holder.   D. Individual company.

Vocabulary List

steady	['stedi]	*adj.* 稳定的
income	['ɪnkʌm]	*n.* 收入
continuous	[ən'tɪnjuəs]	*adj.* 持续的
extra	['ekstrə]	*adj.* 额外的
popular	['pɒpjələ]	*adj.* 流行的
haircut	['heəkʌt]	*n.* 理发
sponsor	['spɒnsə]	*v.* 赞助
bill	[bɪl]	*n.* 账单
theft	[θeft]	*n.* 偷窃
amount	[ə'maʊnt]	*n.* 金额
add	[æd]	*v.* 增加
wallet	['wɒlɪt]	*n.* 钱包
purse	[pɜːs]	*n.* 钱包
carelessness	['keələsnəs]	*n.* 粗心
charge	[tʃɑːdʒ]	*v.* 收费
pioneer	[ˌpaɪə'nɪə]	*adj.* 早期的
respectively	[rɪ'spektɪvli]	*adv.* 分别地
individual	[ˌɪndɪ'vɪdʒuəl]	*adj.* 个人的
business	['bɪznəs]	*n.* 企业
equipment	[ɪ'kwɪpmənt]	*n.* 设备
rectangular	[rek'tæŋgjələ]	*adj.* 方形的
authorize	['ɔːθəraɪz]	*v.* 授权
force	[fɔːs]	*v.* 强迫
plastic	['plæstɪk]	*adj.* 塑料的
issue	['ɪʃuː]	*v.* 发行
obtain	[əb'teɪn]	*v.* 获得

Writing

Help Wanted Ads

Task 1　Writing Skills

与其他种类广告一样，招聘广告也是具有媒体倾向的。报纸上的招聘广告，为求经济，往往有不少缩写，而网上的招聘广告缩写相对要少些。无论是报纸招聘广告还是网上招聘广告，一般都应包括以下信息。

联系信息 (Contact Information)
主要包括：
(1) 公司名称 (Business Name)
(2) 公司地址 (Business Address)
(3) 公司电话 (Business Phone)
(4) 公司邮址 (Business E-mail Address)
或者：
(5) 联系人姓名 (Contact Person's Name)
(6) 联系人电话 (Contact Person's Phone)
(7) 联系人邮址 (Contact Person's E-mail Address)
(8) 联系人通信地址 (Contact Person's Mailing Address)

招聘工作信息 (Job Information)
主要包括：
(1) 就聘职位 (Position Title)
(2) 工作地点 (Location)
(3) 就聘公司名称 (Business Name)
(4) 工作描述 (Job Description)
(5) 就聘资格 (Qualifications)
(6) 福利 (Benefits)
(7) 聘用时间 (Days & Hours of Employment)
(8) 薪资额度 (Salary Range)

当然，出于种种原因，并非每个招聘广告都须载有上述所有信息。广告中的信息量多少，招聘单位或个人会有自己的考虑。但是有一条经验之谈：具体陈述了工作时间、报酬、福利的招聘广告，肯定能得到最好的反应。

另外，写作时还应注意招聘广告的写作特点和语言风格等。英文招聘广告的语言特点如下。

1) 创作新颖标题 (Creating Some Novel Headings)

为了吸引读者注意，获得最佳的广告效果，广告撰稿人经常会别出心裁地遣词造句，创造出新颖的标题。如：

Hero Meets Hero（英雄识英雄）

It Is You Who Make Everything Possible（创造一切全靠你自己）

Are You Ready to Accept Challenges from a Transnational Enterprise?（您愿意接受跨国企业的挑战吗？）

2) 多用省略句 (Employing Many Elliptic Sentences)

为了在有限的空间、时间、地点、费用范围内传播足够的信息以达到最佳的广告效果，英文招聘广告大量使用省略句。如：

Hard work and honesty a must. 工作勤奋和为人诚实是必备的条件。（主语之后省略了 are）

Read and Write English. 会读写英语。（省略了情态动词 can）

Qualifications needed：所需资格：（省略了从句 which are）

3) 利用各种短句 (Utilizing Various Kinds of Phrases)

一般用于说明工作职责和应聘资格（要求）两项内容中。如：

Good communication skills（良好的交际能力）

Ability to work in a team under pressure（能够在集体中承受压力进行工作）

4) 常用祈使句 (Using Imperative Sentences Frequently)

一般用来说明应聘方法。表示礼貌，使读者感到亲切，开头都用个"请"字。如：

Please apply in your own handwriting with full English resume and send photo to...

请亲自誊写详细的英文简历并附上近照寄至……

Please highlight the position you apply for at the bottom of the envelope.

请在信封下方注明你所应聘的职位。

Please call 0810-5808123-3629 for interview.

请致电 0810-5808123-3629 商定面试事宜。

5) 采用缩略词 (Making Use of Abbreviations)

为了节省广告撰稿人的撰稿时间与读者的阅读时间，以及节省广告的篇幅和费用，英语广告中能用缩略词语时都尽可能缩略。如：

Dept = Department 部门　　　　　CV = Curriculum Vitae 个人简历

JV = joint venture 合资　　　　　G.M.= General Manager 总经理

ad = advertisement 广告　　　　　add = address 地址

attn = attention 收信人　　　　　Corp. Ltd.= corporation limited 有限公司

ID = identification 身份证

Task 2 Sample Writing

One Native English Speaking Teacher Required

School：XXX Teachers College

Position：Oral English teacher

Expected Dates：Currently available

About the School：A teacher training college located in Cangzhou, Hebei Province, south of Beijing. Two hours and half by train.

Requirements:

1. Native English speaker

2. Teaching experience and BA degree

3. Female teacher preferred

Job Description:

1. Oral English courses

2. 16 hours a week

3. About 30 college students from 18 to 24 years old in each class

4. At least one year contract or longer

Remuneration Package:

1. Monthly salary：negotiable

2. One-way airfare for one year's duration

3. One furnished private apartment and utilities provided

4. Public holidays and one-month annual vacation with pay

Contact：

Add：

Zhang Hua

English Department XXX, Teachers College 061001

Tel：

E-mail：

Posting Dates:

招聘广告其他有用词汇

1) 个人素质 (Personal Qualities)

Mature, dynamic, honest 思想成熟，精明能干，为人诚实

Personal confidence and aggressiveness a must 必须有信心和进取心

Proficient in English and Mandarin 能熟练运用英语和普通话

A person with ability plus flexibility should apply 要有能力及适应力强的人

A stable personality and high sense of responsibility are desirable 须个性稳重，具有高度责任感

Enthusiasm, organized working habits are more important than experience 有工作热情和有条不紊的办事习惯，比有经验重要

Being active, creative and innovative is a plus 思想活跃，有首创和革新精神尤佳

The main qualities required are preparedness to work hard, ability to learn, ambition and good health 主要必备素质是有吃苦耐劳精神、爱学习、事业心强和身体棒

2) 语言能力 (Language Proficiency)

Ability to communicate in English is desirable 会用英语进行沟通

An excellent understanding of English would be mandatory 须具备出色的英文理解能力

Working command of spoken & written English is preferable 有英文说、写应用能力者优先考虑

Able to speak Mandarin and Cantonese 会说普通话和粤语

3) 电脑知识 (Computer Literacy)

Computer operating skill is advantageous 有电脑操作技术者尤佳

Good at computer operation of Windows 须精通使用 Windows 进行电脑操作

Be familiar with CAD/CAM preferable 熟悉 CAD/CAM 者优先考虑

4) 工作经验 (Occupational Experience)

Working experience in foreign company is preferable 有在外资公司工作经验者优先

At least 2 years in hotel management 至少有 2 年酒店管理的经验

Familiarity with international trade issues will be an added advantage 熟悉国际贸易事项者尤佳

5) 其他要求 (Miscellaneous Requirements)

Not more than 30 years 年龄不超过 30 岁

Male/Female 性别不限（男女均可）

Experience working with foreign companies 有在外资企业工作的经历

Good at developing new business relationships 善于发展新的业务关系

Traveling within China a must 必须在国内出差

Task 3　Writing Practice

a. Write a job vacancy advertisement according to the following information.

Great Wall Hotel 是一家著名的大酒店，现在招聘餐饮部经理一人，条件如下：

1. 中国公民，年龄 30~45 岁；

2. 酒店管理专业或相关领域的专科文凭；

3. 至少 5 年的酒店管理经验；

4. 具有良好的交际能力、英语会话和写作能力。

有意者请拨打电话 010-34567890 与王立先生联系。

b. Organize the following information into a help wanted ad.

Business Address：5026 N Broadway or 2815 W Montrose

Fax No.：773-463-7435

Contact Person E-mail Address：contact@neonexpressl.com

Position Title：Secretary/Administrative Assistant

Application Dates and Hours：Monday to Friday, 9:00 A.M.~4:00 P.M.

Qualifications：Good communication, bilingual, basic computer skills (Microsoft Word and Excel)

Salary Range：competitive, $8~$10/hour

Vocabulary Development

Words and Expressions

ventilator	换气扇
register	旅馆登记簿
valuables	贵重品
trolley	手推车
lobby	大厅
briefcase	公文包
trunk	大衣箱
suitcase	小提箱
front office	前台工作人员
assistant manager	大堂副理
duty manager	值班经理
guest relations officer	宾客关系主任
information supervisor	信息主管
information clerk	问讯员
reception supervisor	接待部主管
manager of room division	客房部经理

executive housekeeper	客房部主管
front office cashier	前台收银员
foreign exchange clerk	外汇兑换员
security guard	保安员
elevator operator	电梯工
automatic sliding door	自动滑动门
shower head	淋浴喷头
hair dryer	吹风机
wall lamp	壁灯
television remote control	电视遥控器
letter rack	信件存放架
key rack	钥匙存放架
hotel bill	旅馆账单
registration form	登记表
cigarette tray	香烟托盘
advance deposit	定金
rate sheets	房价表
imperial suite	皇室套房
presidential suite	总统套房
deluxe suite	豪华套房
junior suite	简单套房
mini suite	小型套房
unmade room	未清扫房
on change	待清扫房
baggage receipt	行李收据
storage room	储藏室
suit bag	衣服袋
traveling bag	旅行袋
shoulder bag	背包
name tag	标有姓名的标签

Useful Sentences

中译英

1. 我非常高兴为您服务。
I'm glad to serve you.

2. 我是楼层服务员，有什么能为您效劳的吗？

I'm an attendant on this floor. What can I do for you?

3. 对不起，让您久等了。

Sorry to have kept you waiting so long.

4. 如果您有衣服要洗，请放在洗衣袋里，每天上午 9:00 收取。

If you have laundry, leave it in the laundry bag. It'll be collected at 9:00 every morning.

5. 对不起，打扰您了，我现在可以打扫房间吗？

I'm sorry to disturb you. May I clean your room now?

6. 您需要热开水和冷水吗？

Do you need hot water and cold water now?

7. 先生，这是电灯开关，那是温度调节器。

This is the light switch and that is the temperature adjuster, sir.

8. 每天晚上 8 点钟至次日凌晨 2 点，饭店播放闭路电视。

There are closed-circuit television (in-house TV) programs from 8:00 P.M. to 2:00 A.M. every day.

9. 请您把您的名字和房间号码签在账单上。

Please sign your name and room number on the bill.

10. 您有事情唤服务员，请按电铃。

If you need help, please push the bell-button.

11. 当您离开房间时，请把房间钥匙放在服务台。

Please leave your key at the service desk when you leave your room.

12. 请告诉我您的姓名和房号。

May I have your name and room number, please?

13. 我是服务员，请让我看一下您的住房卡好吗？

I'm the attendant. Would you please show me your room card?

14. 您的房号是 731，我领您去。

Your room number is 731. Let me show you up there.

15. 您要新开水吗？

Would you like fresh hot water in the thermos now?

16. 您看房间是现在清扫还是等会儿？

Shall I clean the room now or later?

17. 这是您的房间钥匙。

Here is your room key.

18. 我可以来收长途电话费吗？

May I collect the bill for the long distance call?

19. 如果您希望我们帮您擦皮鞋，请将鞋放在门外。

If you want to have your shoes polished, please put them outside the door.

20. 您有衣服要洗吗？

Do you have any clothes to be cleaned?

21. 对不起，这件衬衫袖口熨坏了，我们赔您20元钱可以吗？

I'm very sorry. The cuff of your shirt was damaged when we pressed it. We have arranged to pay 20 yuan for compensation. Is it OK?

22. 您的衣服织补好了，您看是否满意？

Your coat has been mended. Is it all right?

23. 我可以补充您的小冰箱吗？

May I refill your mini bar?

24. 您需要叫早服务吗？

Do you want a morning call?

25. 请您与楼层服务台联系。

Please contact the floor service counter.

26. 马桶不能冲水了，我去找人来修理。

Sir, the flush is not working. I'll send someone to fix it.

英译中

1. Can I have my breakfast brought to the room?

我可以在房间用早餐吗？

2. I'm looking for the room 1208.

请问1208号房间在哪儿？

3. How about getting me an extra blanket and two pillows?

我想多要一条毛毯和两个枕头，可以吗？

4. I can't fall asleep because the tap is dripping.

水龙头漏水，吵得我无法入睡。

5. There is a hole in this coat. Please mend it for me.

衣服上有一个洞，请代为织补一下。

6. There is a button missing on my coat. Can you sew on a button for me?

我衣服上掉了一个扣子，你能帮我配一个吗？

7. Is there a dance hall here?

这里有舞厅吗？

8. Please clean it when I'm out.

请等我出去之后再打扫房间。

9. Some of my friends will come and see me this afternoon. Would you please bring me some more teacups and chairs?

今天下午有一些朋友将来看我，你能给我一些茶杯和椅子吗？

10. Can this room be kept for me?

这间房间可以为我保留吗？

11. I'll leave a note for him. Please give it to him.

我留下一张纸条，请转交给他。

12. If someone calls me, please tell him that I'll be back after ten o'clock.

如果有人打电话找我，请告诉他我在10点钟以后回来。

13. I'll be checking out around noon. Where can I pay my bill?

我要在中午结账，请问在哪儿付款？

14. Can you tell me something about the climate here?

您能给我介绍一下此地的气候吗？

15. Excuse me, but something is wrong with this socket.

对不起，这个插座坏了。

16. It's my wife's birthday today. I would like to order a cake.

今天是我夫人的生日，我想订个蛋糕。

17. The light of this room is dim. Please get me a brighter one.

房间灯光太暗，请帮我换一个亮点的灯泡。

18. What will the weather be like tomorrow?

明天天气如何？

Unit 4

Food & Beverage Services
餐饮服务

 Unit Objectives

After learning this unit, you should

- read, comprehend and translate the passages and the dialogues about food and beverage into Chinese;
- know how to give information about food and beverage;
- master the basic words and expressions about food and beverage information and use them to make sentences;
- get some cultural knowledge about food and beverage;
- comprehend the dialogues, practice listening skills and talk something about food and beverage;
- find ways to improve your writing skills about Invitation.

 Background Knowledge

Drinking

Drinking habits vary widely among Americans as they do among people from other lands. Some families never serve any alcoholic drinks, others have them before dinner, wine with the meal, and perhaps drinks after dinner. You are more likely to be offered a cocktail before dinner than wine with the meal. If you are not accustomed to American cocktails, be careful, because they are often quite strong. Women as well as men drink them, but you should feel free to ask for something less strong or a non-alcoholic drink if you wish. In some homes, cocktails may be served for an hour or longer before dinner. If you do not wish to have another cocktail, simply say "No, thanks".

Wine is becoming increasingly popular with Americans but is still not as common as in some other countries and not drunk as much as beer. Do not be surprised if you are offered milk, coffee, tea (iced or hot, depending on the season) or even Coca-Cola with a meal. Water is usually served in the restaurants without being ordered, although you may certainly order something else that you prefer to drink.

Eating out —— Who Pays?

If you've made an agreement to go out to eat with someone, you should be clear who's going to pay. If the other person suggests you have lunch with him or her, you might simply say something like this: "I'm afraid it'll have to be some inexpensive places as I have very little money." The other person may say: "OK, I'll meet you at McDonald." This means that you've agreed that each person pays for his or her own meal, i.e., you "go Dutch". If the person says, "Oh, no, I want to take you to lunch in a little restaurant I like very much", that means the person intends to pay the bill for both of you. If a person invites you to his or her home for a meal, it's understood that that person is paying; if you invite someone to your home, it's understood that you are buying the food. If you want to invite someone out for lunch, you must also make yourself clear by saying, perhaps, "I'd like to take you to lunch tomorrow at the Hostess Inn Coffee Shop." (meaning you plan to buy the food), or "Let's have lunch together tomorrow at Burger King. It's on me." American women used to expect men to pay all the meals, but today most women pay for themselves. However, you should always make your position clear. Being clear is the polite thing to do; it is lack of clarity that causes loss of face in this situation.

Practice Materials

Listening

Dialogue 1

a. Listen to Dialogue 1 and decide whether each of the following sentences is true (T) or false (F).

1. _____ Li Hua is a secretary of the Department of Foreign Languages.
2. _____ John is a professor from America.
3. _____ John would like to use chopsticks.

4. _____ John wants to have a little wine.

5. _____ The sea cucumber is very delicious.

b. Listen to the dialogue and answer the following questions.

1. Who is Li Hua?
   _____

2. Who is John?
   _____

3. What would John like to use, chopsticks or a knife and fork?
   _____

4. What would John like to drink?
   _____

5. What does John think of the roast duck?
   _____

c. Listen to the dialogue again and supply the missing words.

1. John is a professor from _____.
2. Would you like wine or _____?
3. Here's to your _____. Cheers!
4. Let's _____ the food. This is sea cucumber.
5. _____ yourself to the duck.

Dialogue 2

a. Listen to Dialogue 2 and decide whether each of the following sentences is true (T) or false (F).

1. _____ America has great cooking from all over the world.
2. _____ Americans can only eat Italian, French, German and Japanese food.
3. _____ Li Qian would like to have some American food.
4. _____ Li Qian would like to go to an expensive restaurant.
5. _____ Carl Cooper will take Li Qian to an elaborate American restaurant.

b. Listen to the dialogue and answer the following questions.

1. Which country is Li Qian in now?
   _____

2. What is Li Qian doing there?

_____

3. Is there a Chinatown in the city where Carl Cooper lives?

_____

4. What would Li Qian like to have, American food or Chinese food?

_____

5. What time will Li Qian pick Cooper up?

_____

c. Listen to the dialogue again and supply the missing words.

1. What do you _____ by "any kind of food"?
2. Our country's _____ up of people from all over the world.
3. _____ about some American food?
4. An expensive place would make me _____.
5. Great. I will pick you up at your _____ about 5. OK?

Notes

1. dean	主任
2. professor	教授
3. chopsticks	筷子
4. Here's to your health.	祝您身体健康。
5. Cheers!	干杯！
6. sea cucumber	海参
7. delicious	美味的
8. help oneself to sth.	请随便吃点……
9. tender	嫩的
10. crispy	香酥的
11. be made up of	由……构成
12. all over	遍及
13. old-fashioned	传统的
14. pick sb. up	（开车）接某人

Speaking

Dialogue 1

At the Chinese Restaurant

(The waiter is explaining something to Johnson.)

A: Excuse me, I'd like to try some Chinese food. Can you tell me where I should go?

B: We serve Chinese food here. But I'm not sure which style you prefer.

A: I have no idea about Chinese food.

B: It's divided into four big cuisines, or say four styles. They are Shandong cuisine, Sichuan cuisine, Cantonese cuisine, and Jiangzhe cuisine.

A: Is there any difference between Cantonese food and Beijing food?

B: Yes, Cantonese food is lighter while Beijing food is heavy and salty. The famous specialities of these two are Roast Suckling Pig and Beijing Roast Duck.

A: How about Sichuan food?

B: Most Sichuan dishes are spicy and hot. And they taste different.

A: Oh really? I like hot food. So what's your recommendation for me?

B: I think Mapo Tofu and shredded meat in chilli sauce are quite special. We have a Sichuan food dining room. May I suggest you go there? It's on the second floor.

A: Thank you.

B: My pleasure.

Notes

1. cuisine	烹饪，烹饪法
2. light	清淡的，易消化的
3. heavy	难消化的
4. salty	咸的
5. Cantonese	广州的
6. speciality	特制品，特产
7. Roast Suckling Pig	烤乳猪
8. Beijing Roast Duck	北京烤鸭
9. hot	刺激的，辣的
10. chilli	（干）辣椒

Dialogue 2

Having Chinese Food

A: Waiter   B: Mr. Frank

A: Mr. Frank, what would you like to have tonight, Western food or Chinese food?

B: When I was in America, my friend, Mr. Dull recommended me to have Chinese food, and I appreciated it very much indeed. What kind of cuisine do you have in your dining room?

A: We have Cantonese food, Sichuan food and Shanghai food. Which one do you like best?

B: I don't like anything greasy. I think I'd like to have Cantonese food.

A: OK. How about saute prawn section, saute lobster slices with mushroom?

B: All right. I'll take them both.

A: Mr. Frank, do you like to use chopsticks? If you don't, I'll get you the fork and knife.

B: If I can have them, that's so much better.

A: Do you like some soup?

B: Yes, but I don't know what soup you have.

A: We have sliced chicken soup, dried mushroom clear soup and so on.

B: Good. I prefer dried mushroom clear soup.

A: According to the specifications of Chinese food, we serve dishes first and then soup. We'll bring you some soup first if you like.

B: Yes, please. I'm used to having soup first.

A: All right, I'll get it for you.

Notes

1. oily	浸透油的，油腻的
2. greasy	油腻的
3. saute	嫩煎的，用少量油快炸的
4. lobster	大螯虾；龙虾
5. mushroom	蘑菇
6. specification	规格，说明书

Dialogue 3

At the Western Restaurant

(Wang Hong, the tour guide recommends a western restaurant to Mr. and Mrs. Brown. The couple are having their dinner in the restaurant.)

G: Miss Wang, a tour guide   T1: Mr. Brown, a tourist
T2: Mrs. Brown, a tourist   W: Waiter

T2: Darling, these days we have tasted different Chinese dishes of different styles. I want to have western food for a change today.

T1: Oh, Miss Wang, do you know any good western food restaurants around here?

G: Yes, very near the hotel, there is Red Rose Restaurant which serves western food. I'd like to make a reservation for you if you want.

T1: Thank you. Please make a reservation for 7:00 p.m. tonight.

G: All right.

(At the Restaurant)

W: Good evening!

T1: Good evening! I'm Mr. Brown. We have a reservation.

W: This way, please. Your table is near the window.

T2: Thank you.

W: Here is the menu.

T1: Thank you.

W: May I take your order?

T1: We haven't decided yet. Could you give us a little more time?

W: Yes, take your time, please.

T1: Can we get something to drink? I want a bottle of beer. My wife wants a cup of coffee.

W: Fine.

T1: Could you tell us your specials today?

W: The special for today is steak.

T1: I'll take this steak dinner. My wife will have the same.

W: How would you like your steak?

T1: I'd like it medium-rare.

T2: I'd like it well-done.

W: What would you like to go with your steak?

T2: Peas and carrots.

T1: The same for me, please.

W: What would you like for dessert?

T1: Ice cream, please.

T2: No, thanks.

T1: Could I have the check, please?

W: Here's the check.

T1: Can I pay for the bill by credit card?

W: Yes, of course. Here's your receipt.

Notes

1. Chinese dishes	中国菜
2. western food	西餐
3. for a change	变换一下（口味）
4. around here	附近
5. Red Rose Restaurant	红玫瑰餐厅
6. menu	菜单
7. order	点菜
8. a bottle of beer	一瓶啤酒
9. a cup of coffee	一杯咖啡
10. steak dinner	牛排晚餐
11. medium-rare	嫩的，半生半熟的
12. well-done	全熟的
13. peas and carrots	豌豆和胡萝卜
14. dessert	甜点
15. check	账单
16. receipt	收据

Dialogue 4

At the French Restaurant

(Hulot, a tourist who is visiting France, is having dinner at a French restaurant. He has no idea what to eat and is asking Michalle for advice, a local guide and also a regular customer to this place.)

H: This looks wonderful, Madame Michalle.

M: Yes, it's very nice. All our foreign visitors enjoy it. The food is wonderfully well-prepared. Let me know if you need any help with the menu.

H: Thank you. Mmm, can you tell me about the terrine?

M: Yes. A terrine is a kind of meat Pâté. It's meat turned into a paste. It sounds horrible but it's actually really good.

H: Mmm. Maybe another time.

M: You could try the ravioli. They are rather like your Chinese dumplings, and the sauce is delicious.

H: Sounds good. I think I'll have the lamb for the main course. What does it come with?

M: Well, you can have fries—French fries—or simple boiled potatoes.

H: I'll have the potatoes. What are you having?

M: I'm having my usual. I like the fish here. Would you like some wine?

H: Oh, yes. That would be lovely.

Notes

1. wonderfully		绝妙地，极好地
2. well-prepared		精心准备的，准备充分的
3. terrine		肉冻
4. meat Pâté		肉馅饼
5. turn into		（使）变成
6. paste		肉酱
7. ravioli		小方饺
8. sauce		调味汁，酱汁
9. lamb		羊肉
10. main course		主菜
11. come with		伴随……发生，与……一起供给
12. fries		炸薯条
13. French fries		炸薯条
14. boiled potatoes		水煮马铃薯
15. lovely		可爱的，令人愉快的，好看的

 Reading

Passage 1

American Food Habits

Generally speaking, salads are popular and are served all the year round. Many American people are trying to keep down their weight and so they are "calorie" conscious. This is evident in menus offering "low calorie" or "weight watchers" meals. In markets one can find "No cal" drinks (meaning drinks without calories) such as ginger ale or cola. "Diet" foods without sugar or salt are also available in food stores.

Waiters in American restaurants tend to assume that everyone drinks coffee. If a waiter suddenly asks "Now or later?", what he means is "Do you want coffee with your meal now or later?". Many Americans drink coffee with their meal. When dining out in the US we can ask for tea, milk, coke, beer, and so on, if we prefer these to coffee. American restaurants cannot serve beer, wine, or liquor unless they are licensed to do so.

The main course in American meals is usually meat, fowl or fish, but rarely is more than one of these served in the same meal (except that seafood can be used as an appetizer).

a. Answer the following questions according to the passage.

1. Why are many American people "calorie" conscious?
   _____

2. Are "diet" foods without sugar or salt available in food stores?
   _____

3. If a waiter suddenly asks "Now or later?", what does he mean?
   _____

4. Can all American restaurants serve beer, wine or liquor?
   _____

b. Fill the blanks with words given below, and charge the form when necessary.

assume	evident	conscious	available	course
license	rarely	prefer	serve	unless

1. His attention was not _____ to me.
2. I became _____ of a man staring at me.

3. The dress is _____ in all sizes.

4. Brown's formal title is "professor", but he _____ to be called "Mr.".

5. He _____ went anywhere except to his office.

6. What time is breakfast _____ in this restaurant?

7. The country _____ the landowners to fish in these waters.

8. The directors have a meeting every Friday, _____ there is nothing to discuss.

9. I _____ him to be able to read.

10. We had three _____; the first was soup, and then meat and fruit.

c. Translate the following sentences into English with words or phrases given in the brackets.

1. 越来越多的人对天然的健康食品感兴趣。(natural health foods)
_____

2. 他们的任务是一年到头地供应蔬菜。(all the year round)
_____

3. 有些人喜欢清淡的食物，有些人的口味却很重。(bland)
_____

4. 一薄片面包有九十卡路里。(calorie)
_____

5. 你可以住在饭店里或私人家里。(either...or)
_____

Vocabulary List

assume	以为
bland	清淡的
calorie	卡路里
conscious	意识到的
fowl	家禽
ginger ale	姜汁酒
unspiced	未加香料的

Phrases

keep down	控制

Passage 2

British Eating Habits

The British are traditionally conservative about their food and eating habits. But much of the food eaten in Britain now is not, in fact, traditional. The traditional cooked breakfast, for example, has been disappearing from the homes and hotels of Britain. More and more people are interested in buying "convenience food". Traditional foods are manufactured and processed and ready to cook or eat. Fresh fruit is a natural convenience food, available all the year round. With the changes in society, meals are becoming less formal now. Snacks have become popular, they can be eaten anywhere and at any time.

An even more convenient way to eat is to buy food from a "takeaway" (can be eaten either at home or in the takeaway shop). This is quicker than cooking a meal and cheaper than eating in a restaurant. The most common takeaway foods in Britain are fish and chips, hamburgers, and Chinese food.

More recently there has occurred a new change in the diet. As processed foods made in factories are believed to contain additives and be affected by chemical fertilizers, some people have turned their interest to natural foods. They would prefer a diet of nuts, honey, dried fruits, and naturally grown cereals and vegetables. Special "Health Food Stores", and even supermarkets now sell such natural health foods.

a. Read the passage carefully and then decide whether the following statements are true (T) or false (F).

1. In fact, much of the food eaten in Britain now is not traditional.
2. More and more people are interested in buying traditional food.
3. Fresh fruit is a natural convenience food, not available in winter.
4. Snacks can be eaten anywhere and at any time.
5. Hot food from a "takeaway" can be eaten either at home or in the takeaway shop.
6. Fish and chips, hamburgers, and Chinese foods are the most common takeaway foods in Britain.
7. Processed foods are thought to be affected by chemical fertilizers.
8. More recently, some people have turned their interest to processed foods.
9. Health foods are not available in supermarkets.
10. From the passage, we can conclude that people's interest in food has turned from the processed foods to natural health foods.

b. Fill the blanks with words given below, and charge the form when necessary.

| occur | process | disappear | contain | formal |
| conservative | popular | manufacture | traditional | convenience |

1. Shopping bags are provided for the customer's _____.
2. "Thanks" is slightly less _____ than "Thank you".
3. Chinese food is becoming _____ with Americans.
4. _____ foods made in factories are believed to have additives.
5. A number of changes _____ in subsequent years.
6. He is very _____ and does not like things to change.
7. His words do undoubtedly _____ a tremendous truth.
8. The sun _____ behind the clouds.
9. These are the _____ foods for Christmas.
10. They _____ televisions at the factory.

c. Complete the following dialogues by translating the Chinese into English.

1.

A：1) _____

（我代表我们公司请您参加今晚六点的晚宴，希望您能光临。）

B：I'd like to come. Thank you very much.

A：2) _____

（那我们六点钟在餐厅等你。）

B：All right. See you then.

A：See you.

2.

A：3) _____

（史密斯先生，您喝什么，雪碧还是葡萄酒？）

B：I'd like to have some wine.

A：4) _____

（让我们为远道而来的客人的健康干杯。）

B：Cheers!

3.

A：5) _____

（格林先生，让我为您夹点鱼。）

B: Thank you, but only a small piece.

A: 6) _____

(您还没有吃过鸡呢，吃一点吧。)

B: I'm afraid I have had more than enough.

Vocabulary List

additive	[ˈædətɪv]	n. 添加剂
occur	[əˈkɜː]	v. 发生
conservative	[kənˈsɜːvətɪv]	adj. 保守的
contain	[kənˈteɪn]	v. 包括
cereal	[ˈsɪəriəl]	n. 谷物
fertilizer	[ˈfɜːtəlaɪzə]	n. 肥料
manufacture	[ˌmænjuˈfæktʃə]	v. 生产/加工
nut	[nʌt]	n. 坚果
snack	[snæk]	n. 快餐
takeaway	[ˈteɪkəweɪ]	n. 外卖餐馆
supermarket	[ˈsuːpəmɑːkɪt]	n. 超级市场

 **Writing**

Invitation

Task 1　Writing Skills

在旅游行业中，经常需要邀请客人参加宴会、晚会、舞会及观看节目等，因此常要用到请柬。请柬分为正式和非正式两种。正式的请柬用于参加大型正式的社交场合，如宴会、开幕式、大型会议等，有固定的撰写格式，其特点如下：

(1) 一般要用艺术字。

(2) 高、宽分别为 10.5 厘米和 14.5 厘米左右。

(3) 用第三人称写，要写全名，不能缩写。

(4) 以总经理或经理的名义发邀请。

(5) 要使客人有足够的时间准备和答复。

(6) 如果要求客人答复，需在请柬上写明"R.S.V.P."，意思是"请回复"(please reply)。

Task 2　Sample Writing

Sample 1

正式请柬

Mr. and Mrs. Zhang Liang

Request the pleasure of

Mr. and Mrs. John

The presence at Beijing Opera

On Friday, August 22nd

At seven P.M.

Peace Theater

R.S.V.P.　　　　Telephone: 010-68965432

President Gu Binglin

Tsinghua University

Requests the pleasure of the company of Mr. Luis Brankurt,

At a New Year's Party

On December 30th, 2024, Monday at 7:00 P.M.

In Room 201, Guest House

R.S.V.P.
Telephone: 010-62780011
December 30th, 2024

Dress: Formal

　　从上面的请柬中我们注意到，正式请柬的书写格式不是普通书信那样一行接一行，而是以中线为准，以左右均匀的形式出现。

Sample 2

非正式请柬

Dear Mr. and Mrs. John,

　　Will you please go with us to see a farewell performance of Tom Waker on Sunday August 24th, at 7:00 P.M. at Peace Theater?

　　It has been a long time since we met in Shanghai last year. We do hope you will find it possible to go with us.

                                                  Sincerely yours,

                                                  Zhang Ming

Dear Mr. and Mrs. Brown,   July 5th, 2024

    We shall be pleased if you can be present for dinner in our apartment at 7:00 P.M. this Tuesday, July 30th in honor of Dr. Zhang Jie and his colleagues who are visiting us from Zhejiang University.

    Please let us have an early reply. Tel: 83364455

                                                  Sincerely yours,

                                                  Xiao Hong

Task 3   Writing Practice

a. Match the following groups of words and phrases.

1. distinguished guest   a. 音乐会
2. opera   b. 要求
3. pleasure   c. 表演
4. concert   d. 贵宾
5. theater   e. 出席
6. performance   f. 荣幸
7. presence   g. 剧院
8. request   h. 歌剧

b. Write two invitations, one formal and the other informal, using the information given in Chinese below. Add some information when necessary.

代表学校邀请 Mr. Henry King 参加水利工程实验室的开幕仪式,时间是 8 月 5 日,星期二下午 4:00;地点是主楼 501 房间。

Vocabulary Development

Words and Expressions

boiled   煮的
deep-fried   炸的
marinated   腌制的, 卤的

steamed	蒸的
rare	半熟的，半生的，一分熟的
medium	五分熟的
appetizer	开胃的食物、酒
sandwich	三明治
fried peanut	油炸花生米
pickled cucumber	腌黄瓜
salted vegetable	咸菜
clear soup of three delicious ingredients	三鲜汤
hot and sour soup	酸辣汤
braised pork	扣肉
pork braised in brown sauce	红烧肉
roast mutton	烤羊肉
diced chicken with cashew nuts	腰果鸡丁
smoked duck	熏鸭
fish and seafood	鱼与海鲜
blanched prawn	白灼海虾
braised carp in brown sauce	红烧鲤鱼
fried egg	煎蛋
preserved egg	皮蛋
walnut seeds with mushrooms	桃仁冬菇
kidney bean	四季豆
sweet dumplings	汤圆
rice noodles	粉条
steamed meat dumpling	小笼包
buttered toast	涂了黄油的烤面包
continental breakfast	欧洲大陆式早餐
soft drink	软饮料
mineral water	矿泉水
alcoholic beverage	含酒精饮料
main course	主菜

Useful Sentences

请给我菜单。May I have a menu, please?

是否有中文菜单？Do you have a menu in Chinese?

餐厅有哪些餐前酒？What kind of drinks do you have for an aperitif?

可否让我看看酒单？May I see the wine list?

我想点当地出产的酒 / 菜。I'd like to have some local wine/dishes.

是否可推荐一些不错的酒？Could you recommend some good wine?

我可以点餐了吗？May I order, please?

有哪些特色菜？What is the speciality of the house?

我想要一份开胃菜与肉菜 (鱼餐)。I'd like an appetizer and meat (fish) dish.

你想要几分熟的牛排？How do you like your steak?

全熟 (五分熟 / 一分熟)。Well-done (medium/rare), please.

请把盐 (胡椒) 传给我。Could you pass me the salt (pepper)?

请给我一杯水。I'd like a glass of water, please.

请再给我一些面包。May I have some more bread, please?

请给我一些甜点。I'd like a dessert, please.

甜点有哪几种？What do you have for dessert?

可不可以不要甜点、改要水果？Can I have some fruit instead of dessert?

可以抽烟吗？May I smoke?

我点的食物还没来。My order hasn't come yet.

这不是我点的食物。This is not what I ordered.

请结账。Check, please.

可以用这张信用卡付账吗？Can I pay with this credit card?

请给我收据。May I have the receipt, please?

我想去一家价位合理的餐厅。I want a restaurant with reasonable prices.

我想去一家不会嘈杂的餐厅。I'd like a quiet restaurant.

我想去一家气氛欢乐、活跃的餐厅。I'd like a restaurant with cheerful atmosphere.

是否可建议这一类的餐厅？Could you recommend that kind of restaurant?

此地餐厅多集中在哪一区？Where is the main area for restaurants?

这附近是否有中餐厅？Is there a Chinese restaurant around here?

这附近是否有价位不贵的餐厅？Are there any inexpensive restaurants near here?

你知道现在哪里还有餐厅是营业的吗？Do you know of any restaurants open now?

我想尝试一下当地的食物。I'd like to have some local food.

最近的意大利餐厅在哪里？Where is the nearest Italian restaurant?

Unit 5

Communication Services
通信服务

Unit Objectives

After learning this unit, you should

- know how to ask for different kinds of communication service, such as how to make telephone calls, post letters and parcels, etc.;
- master the basic words and expressions about communication services;
- get some practical knowledge about communication services;
- find ways to improve your writing skills about E-mail.

Background Knowledge

When traveling, people are bound to use some means of communication to send and receive messages, or search for some useful information. Today's communication choices are varied: telephones, mobile phones, mails, E-mail, fax, Internet and more. They are very convenient and become an indispensable part of people's life.

Types of phone

1. local call (市内电话): a telephone call made within a local calling area.

2. IDD and DDD: International direct-dialed phone (国际长途直拨电话) and domestic direct-dialed phone (国内长途直拨电话). They are long-distance telephone calls in which the caller dials the number directly without the help of an operator.

3. the operator call (接线员辅助呼叫): the call in which a caller telephones the operator for help instead of dialing the intended telephone number directly.

4. collect call (对方付费电话): a telephone call in which the calling party wants to place a call at the called party's expense.

5. person-to-person call (叫人电话): an operator-assisted call in which the calling party wants to speak to a specific party and not simply to anyone who answers. The caller is not charged for the call unless the requested party can be reached. This method was popular when telephone calls were relatively expensive.

6. station-to-station call (叫号电话): a method of placing a telephone call, with or without assistance, in which the calling party agrees to talk to whoever answers the telephone.

Practice Materials

Listening

Dialogue 1

a. Listen to Dialogue 1 and decide whether each of the following sentences is true (T) or false (F).

1. _____ The woman knows how to make an overseas call.
2. _____ The cheapest call is a person-to-person call.
3. _____ The caller's name is Xu Lili.
4. _____ The woman wants to make a call from China to Chicago.
5. _____ The woman will pay for the call.

b. Listen to the dialogue and answer the following questions.

1. How many types of calls are mentioned?

_____

2. Does the charge vary accordingly to the operator?

_____

3. Which type of call did the woman make?

_____

4. What's the number of Xu Lili?

_____

5. Will Mr. Xu accept the charges?

_____

c. Listen to the dialogue again and supply the missing words.

1. I'd like to make an _____ call to China.

2. The mini charge will apply for _____ minutes, then each additional minute will be charged.

3. ...Please tell me whom you are calling.

   ...It's _____ . Mr. Xu.

4. Area code 27, and the number is _____ .

5. _____ , please, and I'll call you back in a few minutes.

Notes

1. operator	（机器、设备等的）操作员；电话接线员
2. overseas call	越洋电话
3. vary	呈现不同；（使）变化，改变
4. mini	同类中最小型的东西
5. charge	收费，要价
6. apply	申请，请求；适用
7. additional	增加的，额外的，另外的
8. area code	区号

Dialogue 2

a. Listen to Dialogue 2 and decide whether each of the following sentences is true (T) or false (F).

1. _____ Susan wants to chat with her parents online.

2. _____ It's free of charge to go online in the hotel where they stayed.

3. _____ Richard and Susan have been to Hubei.

4. _____ Richard bought a map of Hubei.

5. _____ Susan will search some information about Hubei before she sends the photos to her parents.

b. Listen to the dialogue and answer the following questions.

1. Which room is Internet available?

   _____

2. Is Richard an attendant of the hotel?

   _____

3. Will they go to Hubei the day after tomorrow?

_____

4. What did Richard do on the Internet?

_____

5. What is Wuhan cuisine famous for?

_____

c. Listen to the dialogue again and supply the missing words.

1. I _____ Internet there last night.

2. I was going to the _____ last night and found some very interesting places in Hubei.

3. Have you searched some information about _____ in Hubei?

4. Oh, so many _____ .

5. You can put _____ in Google and search, and you may get more interesting information you want.

Notes

1.	surf	冲浪
2.	Yellow Crane Tower	黄鹤楼
3.	Yangtze Gorges	长江三峡
4.	http://www.chinatravelguide.com	中国旅游指南（网站）
5.	cuisine	烹饪艺术；菜肴
6.	vegetable bolts	菜苔
7.	key word	关键词
8.	Google	谷歌

Speaking

Dialogue 1

Making a Telephone Call

A: Assistant   B: Linda Hu   C: Tony Franklin

A: ABC Company. Can I help you?

B: Hello! Can I speak to Mr. Franklin, please?

A: Which Franklin? There are two Franklins here.

B: Tony Franklin, the marketing manager.

A: OK. Hold the line, please. I'll put you through. (After a while) Sorry, Mr. Franklin is not available now. He is at a meeting.

B: Can I leave a message for him?

A: Of course.

B: Could you tell him that Linda Hu from China called him and ask him to call back as soon as possible?

A: What's your number, please?

B: My telephone number is 347-780-7556.

A: OK. Can I confirm the information? Linda Hu from China called and asked Mr. Franklin to call her back as soon as possible. Her telephone number is 347-780-7556. Right?

B: That's right.

A: I've taken them down and I'll let him know, Ms. Hu.

B: Thank you very much. Bye.

A: Bye.

(After some time)

C: Hello, is that Linda?

B: Yes. Who is it? ...Aha, Tony! I recognized your voice right away.

C: Yes. Linda. I just got your message. What a surprise! Didn't you tell me you would come here next week?

B: Yes, but I changed my plan. Tony, I can't believe I get hold of you at last. I tried to contact you by phone several times, but you were not in.

C: I'm sorry. I'm a bit busy recently. Where are you now? Shall we meet each other after work?

B: Yes, I'm staying at the Time Hotel. We can meet each other if you are free then.

C: Can you find my place? If you can't, I shall be very glad to pick you up.

B: No, thank you. I can find the place. See you then.

C: See you.

Notes

1. available	可用的或可得到的；可会见的；可与之交谈的
2. confirm	确认，证实
3. the Time Hotel	时代饭店

Dialogue 2

Booking a Taxi

A：Airport Employee   **S**：Mr. Smith

A：Hello. Airway Transit Reservation Service. How can I help you?

S：Hi. I'm calling to reserve a taxi. I need a cab this Saturday morning.

A：All right. Please give me your name, address and phone number.

S：Okay. My name is Robert Smith. My address is 468 Steels Ave, North, Catharine. And my phone number is 289-908-1234.

A：Thanks. I got it.

S：How much will it cost?

A：Well. We charge by the mile. It will be about $60 from St. Catharine.

S：That's fair.

A：What kind of vehicle do you need, small car or a minivan?

S：A small car will be fine. By the way, can I pay by credit card?

A：I'm sorry. We can't accept credit cards. The only way you can pay is by cash.

S：Okay. That's fine.

A：What time will you want us to pick you up?

S：Seven o'clock in the morning on Saturday.

A：All right. Your cab will be at your home at 7 A.M. on Saturday morning. Thank you for your call.

Notes

1. Airway Transit Reservation Service　机场通勤预约服务
2. reserve　　　　　　　　　　　　预约，预订
3. cab　　　　　　　　　　　　　　出租车
4. 468 Steels Ave, North, Catharine　凯瑟琳市北斯蒂尔斯大街468号
5. charge　　　　　　　　　　　　收费，计费
6. by the mile　　　　　　　　　　按照里程
7. fair　　　　　　　　　　　　　公平的，合理的
8. vehicle　　　　　　　　　　　　车辆，交通工具
9. minivan　　　　　　　　　　　　（可乘坐六至八人的）小客车，小面包车
10. by the way　　　　　　　　　　顺便问一下，顺便说一声
11. credit card　　　　　　　　　　信用卡
12. pick sb. up　　　　　　　　　　接（某人）

Dialogue 3

At the Post Office

(Bob wants to deliver a parcel to Shanghai. Now he comes to the post office.)

Postal clerk 1: Hello, may I help you?

Bob: Yes, I'd like to have this parcel and letter delivered to Shanghai.

Postal clerk 1: Oh, we only carry out remittance business. For parcels, please go to the next counter.

Bob: Thank you! ... Hello, I have a parcel and a letter to deliver.

Postal clerk 2: Where do you need them to be delivered to?

Bob: I want to post them to Shanghai.

Postal clerk 2: How would you like to send them?

Bob: I'd like to send them by express.

Postal clerk 2: What is inside the parcel? Is there anything breakable?

Bob: They are all just some clothes and tea. There's nothing breakable.

Postal clerk 2: OK, please fill out this form and indicate the value of the content.

Bob: Sure... What's the postage, please?

Postal clerk 2: Hold on, let me put the parcel on the scale... It weighs up to 15kg, and that will be RMB 217 yuan. The letter is RMB 6 yuan. So it's RMB 223 yuan in total, please.

Bob: Here is 300 yuan.

Postal clerk 2: Here is your change and receipt. Please check it.

Bob: Thank you. By the way, can you tell me how long it takes to send the parcel to Shanghai?

Postal clerk 2: About 4 days.

Bob: OK. Thanks.

Postal clerk 2: You are welcome.

Notes

1. deliver a parcel —— 邮寄包裹
2. remittance business —— 汇款业务
3. express mail —— 快件，特快专递
4. breakable —— 易碎的
5. indicate —— 标示，指示，指出
6. postage —— 邮费，邮资
7. receipt —— 收据，发票

 Reading

The Future of Social Networking: Mobile Phones

Picture A: A girl goes to college. The first day she doesn't know anybody in the classroom but it's OK because she has her mobile with her. Only a few clicks and she accesses the profiles of eight students in the classroom, including their pictures. Luckily, two of them came from the same city where she lives. She messages them and they start to chat.

Picture B: An entrepreneur is on the lookout for a new marketing director on a conference. Within minutes he has identified nine people in the hall with the right CV, three of whom are looking forward to changing jobs. His mobile tells him one of them is standing 15 feet away. That evening, a record of all the people he has met is automatically displayed with their profiles on his home computer.

This is not science fiction—it is the future of social networking and it is just around the corner. After the explosion in internet-based social networking (MySpace, Facebook), doing the same thing in real life instead of in front of a computer becomes an obvious next step. Much of it is already happening on a small scale.

So how does it work? The key is the coming together of Internet-connected mobile phones and location or proximity technology.

You can browse the Internet quickly and easily on most new phones. Phones know where they are, thanks to in-built GPS satellite technology or triangulation from mobile phone masts. They can then tell if other phones are in the same area. Bluetooth short-range radio technology is also standard on most mobiles and with this, phones can pick up the presence of other Bluetooth-enabled phones within about 20 meters.

Effectively, by linking these two developments, your phone can tell if someone is near you and can access lots of information about them—the perfect ingredients for real social interaction.

The possibilities are endless. Can't ever put names to faces? Want to avoid all accountants, lawyers or journalists? Keep seeing that handsome man at the bar and need a common interest to get the ball rolling? All these scenarios are being solved by the new wave of mobile applications.

One company based in Berlin has just gone live with its mobile social network. More than 3,000 young Germans have signed up to the aka-aki service in just over a month.

Users of the service download an application onto their mobile phones free. The software uses Bluetooth, and when another member's phone comes within range, it pings.

The user can then check who it is and choose to access that person's profile, message them and, if they want, go over and have a chat.

Stefanie Hoffman, 30, one of aka-aki's founders, said that although she met her boyfriend through aka-aki, it was not just about dating. "The business applications are real," she said. "I went to a conference the other day—one girl and 80 guys—and usually I would feel very reluctant to go up to someone to talk. But my phone told me there were half a dozen aka-aki members there and so I could introduce myself."

That privileged sense of belonging is both the key to the success of mobile social networking and the greatest barrier. People will want to join because they can be part of a connected community. But until enough people join, these mobile networks will not take off. It is probably going to take one of the big beasts of Internet social networks such as Facebook, which already has many millions of members, to achieve this.

The other big question mark is privacy. Why would people want total strangers to have access to their details?

In the Mitte district of Berlin, Sehnaz Sensan, 27, is a student and aka-aki member. After I had messaged her to ask if we could talk, she said that she "encountered" mainly men (early adopters of new technology tend to be young men). "I can control what is on my profile and what people can know about me," she said. "They message me to say hello and I can message back and we can meet up or I can ignore it. It is a way of breaking the ice."

What about being bothered by strangers? "Men can come up to you anyway without knowing anything about you," Ms. Sensan said. "That's much more insulting. If I don't want an encounter then I don't switch it on."

Michael Arrington, one of the most influential technology bloggers in the world, says that the days when people are not happy to broadcast their CV or personal life electronically are over. "People always trade off privacy for removal of friction," he said. "A few years from now, we will use our mobile devices to help us to remember details of people we know. It will help us to meet new people for dating, business and friendship. Using your phone to create or enhance real world interactions is a killer application, but no one has cracked the nut yet. Once it happens, look out."

Arrington has blogged that Apple's hugely successful iPhone would be a great place to start. He has seen an "awesome" application being developed and says that iPhone users are the perfect group for a mobile social network—they are technological, elitist and identify with their brand.

Analysts and commentators are predicting huge growth in the sector. Aka-aki, which was developed from a university diploma project, now has serious funding from a leading

German venture capitalist.

It is not difficult to see how networks like aka-aki might make money. Anyone who has watched the film *Minority Report* by Tom Cruise will have seen how shops could message those on the network with offers when they pass by.

In another scenario, businesses such as restaurants could pay to access the service and when a member walks in, the store's profile appears. The member chooses to add the restaurant to a list of favored brands and the next week receives a two-for-one meal offer. The restaurant gets targeted "permission" advertising and more diners on a slow night.

But in the end are mobile social networks, not just a replacement for people simply talking to each other? Roman Hansler, another aka-aki cofounder, says that seeing other people's details on your mobile in real life is a conversation-starter, not a replacement. "This is about opening doors for real communication, not sitting in a virtual chat room," he said.

a. Answer the following questions according to the passage.

1. What is the next step after the explosion in Internet-based social networking?
___

2. How does social networking work?
___

3. What about being bothered by strangers?
___

4. How does business such as restaurants benefit from the network service?
___

5. Are mobile social networks not just a nearby replacement for people simply talking to each other?
___

b. Translate the expressions into Chinese or English.

1. seek to hide my views ___
   ___ 寻求，探索；追求；寻找
   seek shelter from rain ___
   Nothing seek, nothing find. ___
2. ___ 增强我们的竞争力
   enhance teachers' professionalism ___
   enhance the effect ___
   enhance one's political consciousness ___

3. mass communications media　_____

_____　世界性通信网

communication gap　_____

be in communication with　_____

4. _____　远距离；远程

in the range of　_____

a wide range of knowledge　_____

the annual range of temperature　_____

c. Choose an appropriate word to fill in each blank to make each sentence meaningful, and change its form when necessary.

ignore	scale	privacy	encounter
application	exploit	device	replacement
access	community		

1. The factory launched on the production of mobile phones on a large _____ .

2. We _____ the enemies' fierce resistance in that battle.

3. The _____ is small enough to wear on your wrist.

4. _____ is considered important in Britain.

5. He tried to _____ my remarks.

6. The people who speak English today make up the largest speech _____ in the world with the exception of speakers of Chinese.

7. We shall _____ our rich resource to expand the economy.

8. You have to enter your password to _____ your account.

9. He advocated (主张) the _____ of a new process to industry.

10. John got a _____ while he was away on holiday.

d. Translate the following sentences into English with words given in the brackets.

1. 进入这座建筑物的唯一通道是一条泥泞的小路。(access)

2. 我花了几个小时翻阅她书架上的书。(browse)

3. 为了保护这些令人叹为观止的奇观，政府在1890年修建了国家公园。(awesome)

4. 出色的交流技巧会增加你找到工作的机会。(enhance)

_____

5. 戴口罩是阻断呼吸道分泌物传播的有效手段。(effective)

_____

Vocabulary List

access	[ˈækses]	vt. 进入；访问，存取；接近，使用
accountant	[əˈkaʊntənt]	n. 会计 (员)，会计师
adopter	[əˈdɒptə(r)]	n. 采用者，采纳者
advertising	[ˈædvətaɪzɪŋ]	n. 广告业，广告
		adj. 广告的，广告宣传的
application	[ˌæplɪˈkeɪʃn]	n. 应用，运用，应用软件；申请，申请表
automatically	[ˌɔːtəˈmætɪkli]	adv. 自动地，机械地
awesome	[ˈɔːsəm]	adj. 使人畏惧的；可怕的；棒极了
barrier	[ˈbæriə(r)]	n. 障碍，隔阂；栅栏，关卡
blog	[blɒg]	n. 博客；网络日记；
		vi. 写/维护博客
blogger	[ˈblɒgə]	n. 写博客的人
brand	[brænd]	n. 商标，牌子
broadcast	[ˈbrɔːdkɑːst]	vt. & vi. 广播，播放；传播，乱传 (消息等)
browse	[braʊz]	v.& n. 随意翻阅，浏览
capitalist	[ˈkæpɪtəlɪst]	n. 资本家；拥有或控制雄厚资产的人
circumstance	[ˈsɜːkəmstəns]	n. 环境，条件，情况；境遇，经济状况
click	[klɪk]	n. 咔嗒声，咔嚓声
cofounder	[kəʊˈfaʊndə]	n. 共同创办人，共同创始人
commentator	[ˈkɒmənteɪtə]	n. 评论员，注释者；实况广播员
community	[kəˈmjuːnəti]	n. 社区，社会，团体大众，(生物) 群落
communication	[kəˌmjuːnɪˈkeɪʃn]	n. 交流，交际；通信，交通
crack	[kræk]	vt. 打开，砸开，裂纹，(使) 爆裂
device	[dɪˈvaɪs]	n. 装置，设备，器具；手段，策略
diploma	[dɪˈpləʊmə]	n. 文凭，毕业证书；执照
display	[dɪˈspleɪ]	n. & vt. 陈列，展览
effectively	[ɪˈfektɪvli]	adv. 有效地；有力地；实际上，事实上
electronically	[ɪˌlekˈtrɒnɪkli]	adv. 电子地
elitist	[ɪˈliːtɪst]	adj. 优秀人才的，杰出者的

enhance	[ɪnˈhɑːns]	vt. 提高，增加，加强
encounter	[ɪnˈkaʊntə]	vt. 遇到，遭遇；偶然碰到，邂逅
entrepreneur	[ˌɒntrəprəˈnɜː]	n. <法> 企业家，主办人
exploit	[ɪkˈsplɔɪt]	vt. 开发；开采；利用
explosion	[ɪkˈspləʊʒn]	n. 爆炸；爆发；激增，扩大
friction	[ˈfrɪkʃn]	n. 摩擦；摩擦力；冲突，不和
guy	[gaɪ]	n. 家伙，人，伙计
identify	[aɪˈdentɪfaɪ]	vt. 识别，鉴别，认出；把……和……看成一样
ignore	[ɪgˈnɔː]	vt. 不顾，不理，忽视
influential	[ˌɪnfluˈenʃl]	adj. 有影响的，有势力的，有权势的
ingredient	[ɪnˈgriːdiənt]	n. 成分，因素
insulting	[ɪnˈsʌltɪŋ]	adj. 出言不逊的，侮辱的，无礼的
interaction	[ˌɪntərˈækʃn]	n. 一起活动；合作，配合；交互作用
journalist	[ˈdʒɜːnəlɪst]	n. 新闻记者，从事新闻杂志业的人
mast	[mɑːst]	n. 桅，桅杆，柱，旗杆，天线杆
network	[ˈnetwɜːk]	n. 网络，网状系统
ping	[pɪŋ]	vi. 发出砰或咻的声音
predict	[prɪˈdɪkt]	vt. & vi. 预言；预测；预示
privacy	[ˈprɪvəsi]	n. 私事，隐私，秘密
privileged	[ˈprɪvəlɪdʒd]	adj. 保密的，秘密的；享有特权的
profile	[ˈprəʊfaɪl]	n. 简介，概况；轮廓，外形
range	[reɪndʒ]	n. 射程，距离；一系列；变化幅度，范围
reluctant	[rɪˈlʌktənt]	adj. 不情愿的，勉强的
replacement	[rɪˈpleɪsmənt]	n. 代替，替换，更换；取代物；代替者
removal	[rɪˈmuːvl]	n. 移走，移动，脱掉
scale	[skeɪl]	n. 规模；程度；范围；等级；级别
scenario	[səˈnɑːriəʊ]	n. (电影等的) 剧情说明；描述，推测
sector	[ˈsektə]	n. 部门；领域
seek	[siːk]	vt. 找寻，寻求；设法，企图，试图，尝试
social	[ˈsəʊʃl]	adj. 社会的；爱交际的，社交的；群居的
standard	[ˈstændəd]	adj. 标准的，权威的，第一流的 n. 标准，水准，规范；旗帜，标杆；支柱
targeted	[ˈtɑːgɪtɪd]	adj. 有针对性的；目标的
technological	[ˌteknəˈlɒdʒɪkl]	adj. 技术上的，科技的

triangulation	[trʌɪæŋjʊˈleɪʃn]	n. 三角测量，分成三角形
venture	[ˈventʃə]	n. 冒险，投机，风险
		vt. & vi. 敢于，冒险
virtual	[ˈvɜːtʃuəl]	adj. 实质上的，事实上的，实际上的

Phrases

be/feel reluctant to	不情愿；勉强
burial ground	坟场，公墓
marketing director	营销总监
science fiction	科幻
social networking	社交网络
proximity technology	感应技术
the new wave of	新一轮
short-range	短程的，短距离的
sense of belonging	归属感
break the ice	破冰
killer application	杀手锏应用
diploma project	毕业设计
venture capitalist	风险投资商
two-for-one	买一送一
chat room	聊天室
get the ball rolling	[俚语] 让球滚起来（动起手来）；开始
sign up	签约；签署
switch on	开；打开；接通
just around the corner	指日可待；临近
in-built	内置
on a small scale	小规模
on a slow night	（生意等）清淡的、不忙碌的夜晚
on the lookout	瞭望着；注视着；警惕

Terms

CV	（"curriculum vitae"的缩写），简历（书），个人履历；(AmE) resume
Mitte	米特（德国柏林的一个地名）

Notes

aka-aki	德国柏林艺术大学一批学生所成立的移动服务公司
Apple	(美国)苹果计算机公司
Bluetooth	蓝牙
MySpace, Facebook	美国最大的两家社交网络服务网站，提供人与人之间的互动，使用者可以完全自定义自己的朋友圈子。其中还提供个人档案页面、博客、群组、照片、音乐和视频影片的分享与存放
GPS satellite technology	全球卫星定位系统技术
iPhone	苹果手机
Minority Report	《少数派报告》，一部带有哲学意味的科幻电影

 Writing

E-mail 电子邮件

Task 1　Writing Skills

电子邮件(E-mail，electronic mail 的缩写)是一种常用的互联网服务，是一种用电子手段进行信息交换的通信方式。与传统信函相比，电子邮件具有传输速度快(几秒钟之内可以发送到世界上任何指定的目的地)、使用费用较低(不管发送到哪里，都只需负担电话费和网费即可)、开放性广、便捷(即写即发，不用跑邮局)等优势，因此受到人们的广泛欢迎。日常生活和工作中的各种信函往来、旅行中的各种预订等都可以通过电子邮件完成。

虽然不同的电子邮件系统提供的用户界面千差万别，但是标准的电子邮件一般由以下几个部分组成。

信头 (Heading)

信头包括以下内容。

(1) From (发自)：记录发件人邮箱地址。但电脑常自动默认，因此这点可忽略。

(2) To (发往)：记录收件人邮箱地址，不同于商业信/传真，收信者的头衔可忽略。

(3) Subject (主题)：为邮件的概括介绍，收件人能在其信箱的邮件列表中清晰浏览此内容。它一般为短句、短语或单词。它要求简洁明了、具有概括性，切忌笼统或含糊不清，如 "About tomorrow's meeting" 就不如 "Tomorrow's meeting canceled." 明确。当然根据 E-mail 内容的重要程度及相关情况还可以在前面添上 URGENT, FYI(for your information)。主题的书写规范和文章标题的一样。

(4) Cc（抄送）：carbon copy 的缩写。在有几个收件人时，把其他地址打到 CC 项下。收件人都获悉后以便沟通讨论。

(5) Bcc（暗送/隐匿抄送）：blind carbon copy 的缩写。同抄送有同样功能，但是保密的，每个其他收件人不知道另外的收件人是谁。

(6) Attachment（附件）：邮件附带的信息。附件的功能非常强大，通过它，可以发出各类电子文件，如图文、影像、录音等。

(7) Re（关于/回答）：在使用"回复"功能时，大多会引用来信的主题作为回信的主题，这时主题句子前会出现"Re:"（当然该主题可以自由修改）。如"Subject: Re: Question About Agenda for Oct. 1"。这里就是回复对方询问"Question About Agenda for Oct. 1"的一份邮件。"Re:"即指 Reply。

(8) Date（日期）：显示当时的时间和日期。

在以上几项中，不可或缺的是"To:"和"Subject:"两项，其他的可视需要进行增删。

正文 (Text)

正文由开头敬语、主体、结尾敬语和署名四部分组成。电子邮件的正文风格与传统的英语书信没多大差别，但要注意以下几点。

1) 称呼 (Salutation)

朋友、同事、同辈之间可以直呼其名，如"Hello, Peter"，"Hi, Linda"；使用"Dear"显得更加正式和委婉，如"Dear Liu Ying"；对上级或长辈最好使用头衔加姓，如"Dear Professor Smith"，"Dear Mr. Wang"；当不知道对方的姓名时可以用"Dear Sir/Madam"，"To whom it may concern"，"Dear Personnel Manager"等。

2) 主体 (Body)

邮件的主体力求简洁明了，便于阅读，太长的内容可以以附件的方式发出。因此，不要写不必要的事；语言上要尽量使用简单的单词和句子，一些动词的缩写形式，如 He's, We're, He'd 也可使用。主体的开头可采用倒金字塔的写作方式，即重要内容写在前面，随着叙述的一步步展开，重要性渐渐减弱。

3) 结尾敬语 (Complimentary Close)

结尾通常也很简明，常常只需一个词，如："Thanks"（甚至用缩略语 thx），"Best"，"Regards"，不需要用一般信函中的"sincerely yours"或"best regards"。

4) 署名 (Signature)

写完信后，人们一般习惯在信尾附上发件人的姓名（正式商务信函还可署上职务及公司名称等信息）。

注意：

回复别人邮件时，应该删除所有不需要的信息，这样可以给你的读者节省读邮件的时间。

电子邮件中流行的缩略语和符号

1) 缩略语

ASAP：as soon as possible
BFN：by for now
BRB：I'll be right back
BTW：by the way
C U：see you
KIT：keep in touch
FYI：for your information
YR/ur：your
HAGO：have a good one
HHOK：ha, ha, only kidding

IOW：in other words
NOYB：none of your business
OIC：Oh, I see
OTOH：on the other hand
Thx：thanks
TIA：thanks in advance
TTYL：talk to you later
YHBT：you have been trolled
IMHO：in my humble opinion
IMO：in my opinion

2) 表示情感的小符号

：-) 代表 "I'm smiling at this"
；-) 代表 wink; sly grin
：-/ 代表 resigned; so-so; disappointed, but what can you do?

：-(代表 "I'm sad about this"
：-0 代表 shocked; amazed

这些符号一般在句末(即在该句的标点符号之后)。

Task 2　Sample Writing

Sample 1

From："John Smith" <johnsmith@hotmail.com>
To：Michael2369@yahoo.com
Subject：Room reservation
Date：Tues, Oct 15th, 2024

Hi! Michael,

I will go to Beijing next week. If you are not too busy, will you book a single room at Crown Hotel for me? I'm leaving for Beijing on November 6th and will stay there for one week.

I'm looking forward to ur reply. :)

TIA,
John

Sample 2

> To：Terrencekb25@go2map.com
> From："David"<davidwh@126.com>
> Subject：Tell me your flight number, date and the time
>
> Dear Terrence,
>
> I'm glad to hear that you are coming to Shanghai. Have you booked the flight yet? Once you confirm the flight number, date and the time you are expecting to arrive, please let me know. I'll pick you up at the airport. See you soon.
>
> Best regards,
> David

邮件常用语

Glad to have got your E-mail from...

Thank you for your E-mail.

Did you receive the E-mail I sent a few days ago?

My new E-mail address is...

I forwarded your E-mail to...

Write back when you get a chance and let me know what's new.

Let me know if you have received the attachment.

I think you might have sent the wrong attachment.

Please try sending the attachment again.

Task 3 Writing Practice

a. Fill the following E-mail by translating the Chinese in the brackets.

Dear Mr. Black,

  Christmas and New Year are around the corner. We are planning an English party to celebrate them and we would like to invite you to participate in it. It will be held on December 23rd, 2024 in the club from 6:30 P.M. to 9:00 P.M.. We do hope you can make it as we are looking forward with great pleasure to seeing you. _____

_____. （我已将节目单发在附件里，请查收。）By the way, I have a new E-mail address. If you want to contact me, _____

_____. （您可以往我的新邮箱 Chenhui@sina.com 里发邮件。）

Warmest regards,

Chenhui

b. Write an E-mail according to the situation below. Add some more information if necessary.

由于天气原因和旅游线路的调整，你不得不取消 4 月 18 日在白玫瑰酒店预订的 4 月 20~24 日的 2 间双人房，请给酒店发一封电子邮件告知他们，并致歉。

Vocabulary Development

telephone book (directory)	电话簿
mobile phone, cell phone	手机
public phone	公用电话
pay phone	(投币式) 公用电话
telephone booth(box)	公用电话亭
extension	电话 (内线) 分机
outside line	电话外线
international code	国际冠码
country code	国家代码
area code	区号
yellow page	黄页 (分类部)
white page	白页 (住宅部)
directory assistance	查号台
pin number	密码
post office	邮局
mailbox	邮箱
pillar box	[英] (圆柱形) 邮箱
envelope	信封
addressee	收信人，收件人
surface mail	普通邮件
registered letter	挂号信
aerogram	(Br.E) 航空邮件，无线电报；(Am.E) airmail
printed matter	印刷品
stamps counter	售邮票处
parcel service counter	寄包裹处
certified mail	挂号邮件
return receipt	回执

surcharge	附加费
declare	说明，申报
express mail	特快专递
special delivery	限时专递
forward	转递
zip code	邮政编码
Room (R)	室
Floor (FL/F)	楼
Number (No.)	号
Alley	弄
Lane	巷
Street (St.) / Road (Rd.) / Boulevard (Blvd.)	街、路、大道
Township/City/District	乡、镇 / 市 / 区
County	县
urgent	紧急的
printer	打印机
surfing	冲浪
a room with Internet service	能上网的房间
desktop computer	台式电脑
laptop computer, portable computer	便携式电脑
palmtop	掌上电脑
wireless skipping Internet	无线宽带上网

一些主要电子邮箱：
网易邮箱 163.com / 126.com
QQ 邮箱 qq.com
新浪邮箱 sina.com
搜狐邮箱 sohu.com

Meeting Services
会议服务

Unit Objectives

After learning this unit, you should

- understand what is meeting service;
- master the basic words and expressions about meeting service;
- get some cultural knowledge about meeting service;
- find ways to improve your writing skills about Booking Form for Conference Rooms;
- be familiar with business English;
- be able to hold meetings in English.

Background Knowledge

Meeting service means that agents and operators provide the services in meeting planning, organization, inspecting, reception and supporting services during the meeting.

The overall meeting services

1. Communication with conference organizers (telephone/Internet/interview)

2. Developing a comprehensive meeting plan (A/B/C/...) for the meeting side and provide rationalized recommendations

3. Helping customers study

4. Determination of the program (nature/request/schedule)

5. Submitting budget

6. Signing of the contract, deposit

7. Booking hotels/session sites/vehicles according to the request

8. Preparation to meeting articles: representative card/emblem/meeting data/pens and paper/souvenirs, etc.

9. Arrangement to meeting place: welcome brands/banners/signs/testing equipment

10. Pre-negotiation

In the meeting

11. Pre-prepared: the required meeting information/conference articles/meeting speeches, and other related items in place

12. Meeting places: hotels, conference rooms, welcome banners/signs in place and so on

13. Conference equipments: laptop/projector/lighting/sound/recording equipment in place

14. Engagement: engaged in airport and station by cars/formal services

15. Registration: on behalf of the permit process/fees/hard materials, and so on

16. Accommodation: responsible for the distribution work of the room

17. Conference dining: the dining and banquet arrangements

18. Conference entertainment: entertainment form / consumption standards / confirmation of entertainment sites

19. Other meeting services: photos and DV/public relations/secretarial services/translation and related services

20. Tickets: offering return air tickets/booking service of train tickets

21. Logistics and external coordination

After the meeting

22. Travel arrangements after the meeting

23. Checkout: setting out the cost in the process of meeting in detail and check out

24. Data: data collection, according to the customer's requests to produce contact or meeting roster

25. Feedback of the customer / follow-up services

26. Summing up the meeting

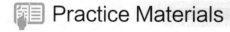

Practice Materials

Listening

Dialogue 1

a. Listen to Dialogue 1 and decide whether each of the following sentences is true (T) or false (F).

1. _____ The client is named Patricia Mitchell.
2. _____ The client is a Personal Manager of Tea Cooperation Ltd.
3. _____ It's about 30 people to have the meeting.
4. _____ The conference will last for two days.
5. _____ The client would invite their general manager to have an Opening Speech.

b. Listen to the dialogue and answer the following questions.

1. When does the client plan to have the conference?
_____

2. Who would the client invite to have the Opening Speech?
_____

3. How many experts would the client like to invite to give speeches?
_____

4. What size of meeting room does the client suggest to rent?
_____

5. Does the client go to check the meeting room?
_____

c. Listen to the dialogue again and supply the missing words.

1. I'm Patricia Mitchell, the _____ of Tea Cooperation Ltd.
2. I'd like to _____ the conference.
3. And we would like to invite two experts to give speeches about _____ and _____.
4. In that case, _____ is enough.
5. I suggest that you would have _____ for the Opening Speech on Monday morning.

Notes

1. layout manager   企划经理
2. cooperation   合作，协作
3. pre-professional   职前的
4. education   教育
5. staff   职员
6. make the arrangement for 安排

7. last	持续
8. opening speech	开幕词
9. culture	文化
10. technology innovation	科技创新

Dialogue 2

a. Listen to Dialogue 2 and decide whether each of the following sentences is true (T) or false (F).

1. _____ The client wants to rent a meeting room.
2. _____ It's about 13 people to have the meeting.
3. _____ The client wants to have coffee, tea and some roll bread for the morning break.
4. _____ The client comes from ABC Company.
5. _____ The client chooses Chinese style food for their lunch.

b. Listen to the dialogue and answer the following questions.

1. Which company does the client call for?
   _____

2. When does the client plan to rent the meeting room?
   _____

3. How long does the client want to rent the meeting room?
   _____

4. Which does the client prefer, Chinese style, the Western style or buffet?
   _____

5. Which style would the client like for the room setup?
   _____

c. Listen to the dialogue again and supply the missing words.

1. Do you have a _____ for holding a meeting the day after tomorrow?
2. We'd like to rent the meeting room from _____ to _____.
3. Classroom style with _____ on each desk.
4. Our meeting room is equipped with _____, an _____, an LCD, a whiteboard easel and _____, etc.
5. We also need some fresh flowers on the _____ table and the _____.

Notes

1. book a meeting	预定会议室
2. Convention Center	会议中心
3. facility	设备，工具
4. hold a meeting	召开会议
5. setup	机构，设置
6. stationery	文具，信纸
7. equipment	装备，设备
8. be equipped with	装备
9. beam projector	光束投影仪
10. an overhead projector	高射投影仪
11. LCD	液晶显示器
12. whiteboard easel	白板架
13. cable mikes	有线话筒
14. the reception desk	接待处
15. buffet	自助餐
16. roll bread	圆面包
17. tightly	紧紧地，坚固地

Background Information

Designing and Planning of a Conference

Designing conference plays an important role in the success of holding a wonderful meeting. Travel agents and tour operators should pay attention to the following aspects:

— the plan process

— preparation for meeting room in engineering and other aspects

— inviting experts

— booking hotels

— diet

— special framework programme

— organization of secretarial work

The distinctive conference planning is the prerequisite for the success of a meeting. Planning includes the following: selecting a theme, positioning mode, agenda, organization and coordination, public relations, media reported etc.

Travel agents and tour operators must make sure that the tone of a meeting theme is serious or lively. Then they should make the arrangements of agenda according to different patterns of meetings, including the meeting venue and the needs of clients, providing and installing the necessary equipments of conferences ahead of time to ensure the smooth progress of a meeting.

In course of a meeting, if clients have any changes or necessary needs, travel agents and tour operators will provide related programmes in accordance with clients' request so as to achieve the desired objectives of the meeting.

For major conferences, travel agents and tour operators will invite the relevant media to enlarge visibility of meeting, so as to achieve the entire success of conferences.

 Speaking

Dialogue 1

Booking a Meeting

A: Good afternoon. I'm Lisa Avon. Is Mr. Liu Fei here? I have invited him to mastermind a conference for our staff.

B: Yes. I'm Liu Fei. It's very nice to finally meet you, Ms. Avon, after so many phone calls and faxes. I'd like you to have my business card.

A: Thanks very much, Mr. Liu. Please accept mine. May we talk about the arrangement for the conference?

B: Of course. I think we can draw up a tentative plan now. If you want to make any changes, minor alternations can be made then.

A: All right.

B: When do you plan to have the conference?

A: From 9:00 A.M. to 11:00 A.M., this Friday.

B: For how many people?

A: We have eighty people in hand.

B: Then you may need a large-sized meeting room or a multi-function hall.

A: I think a large-sized meeting room is all right.

B: How would you like the room setup?

A: Classroom style. What kinds of facilities do you have for the meeting?

B: We have multi-media projector, white board, white marker pen, sound system, microphone and DVD.

A: Yes, very good. Thank you very much for your help.

B: You are welcome. We look forward to your coming. Goodbye.

> **Notes**
>
> 1. mastermind 策划
> 2. draw up 草拟
> 3. tentative 暂定的
> 4. minor 较小的，次要的
> 5. alternation 变换
> 6. multi-function hall 多功能厅
> 7. sign up 报名（或签约）参加
> 8. multi-media projector 多媒体投影仪
> 9. white marker pen 白板笔
> 10. sound system 扩音设备
> 11. microphone 扩音器，麦克风

Dialogue 2

Introduction of Hotel Meeting Facilities

(Mr. Scott is going to have a meeting in the hotel. He comes to the Business Center to ask about the meeting facilities.)

B: Business Clerk   S: Mr. Scott

B: Good morning, sir. May I help you?

S: Yes. I'm Henry Scott, in Room 1322. I'm here to ask you about holding a meeting at your property.

B: Happy to be of any help to you. We have a fully-equipped convention center that provides complete secretarial service, two multi-function halls with excellent audiovisual equipments, and three meeting rooms. Here is our support facilities list with prices.

S: Thank you. Let me see. Well, we will have an annual convention of the International Trading Association. The attendees are top businessmen across the world.

B: Can I see the name list of the attendees?

S: Certainly. Here it is.

B: Oh, I see. There are 150 attendees. I think our medium-sized room can serve your purpose.

S: Great. Do you have sufficient number of breakout rooms? We have several seminars after the plenary session.

B: At this time of peak season, we'll use public space if necessary. Here are convention brochures showing the details about meeting facilities.

S: Thank you. I shall consult with the president of the association. I'll let you know as soon as we have decided.

B: Thank you for coming. We look forward to seeing you again soon.

Notes

1. property	房产，地产，建筑物，房子
2. fully-equipped	设施齐全的，设施完备的
3. convention center	会议中心
4. secretarial service	文秘服务
5. multi-function hall	多功能厅
6. audiovisual	视听的
7. annual	每年的，年度的
8. International Trading Association	国际贸易协会
9. attendee	与会者，参与者
10. medium-sized	中型的，中等大小的
11. serve your purpose	满足你的需要，达到你的目的
12. sufficient	足够的
13. breakout room	小组讨论室，分会议室
14. seminar	研讨会
15. plenary session	全体会议，全体大会
16. peak season	旺季
17. public space	公共空间，公共场所
18. brochure	介绍手册，小册子
19. consult	咨询，请教，商讨
20. president	主席

Dialogue 3

Negotiation of Signing Conference Contract

Office Assistant: Good morning, Odyssey Convention Center. May I help you?

Nick: Hello, this is Nick Delwin from Communication. Could I speak to Helen Turner, please?

Office Assistant: Just a moment, please.

Office Assistant: I have Nick Delwin on the line for you.

Helen: Thank you... Hi, Nick. Nice to hear from you. How's the weather in New York?

Nick: It's pretty good for the time of year. What's it like in Shanghai?

Helen: Not good, I'm afraid.

Nick: That's a pity because I'm planning to go to Shanghai next week.

Helen: Really? Well, you'll come by to see us while you're here, I hope?

Nick: That's what I'm phoning about. I've got a meeting with a customer in Shanghai on Tuesday next week. I was hoping we could arrange to meet up to discuss the affairs about the conference contract, if it is convenient for you then.

Helen: Great. That would give us a chance to show you the convention centre, and we could also drop in at Caesar's Restaurant where Gregg has arranged your reception.

Nick: That's what I was thinking.

Helen: So you said you have to be in Shanghai on Tuesday? That's the 8th?

Nick: That's right. Would that be possible?

Helen: All right. See you then. Goodbye.

Notes

1. Odyssey — 奥德赛
2. communication — 传达；信息；交通；通信
3. just a moment — 请稍等
4. on the line — 在线
5. come by — 顺便拜访，顺便看望
6. meet up — 偶遇
7. contract — 合同
8. drop in — 顺便走访
9. Caesar — 凯撒（古罗马的将军、政治家、历史学家，公元前 100—公元前 44）
10. reception — 接待；招待会；接收；接人

 Reading

Business English: Holding Meetings in English

The Structure of a Meeting

One of the most common requirements of business English is holding meetings in English. The following sections provide useful phrases and sentences for conducting meetings and making contributions to a meeting. Meetings generally follow a more or less similar structure and can be divided into the following parts:

1. Introduction

Opening the Meeting

Welcoming and Introducing Participants

Stating the Principal Objectives of the Meeting

Giving Apologies for Someone Who is Absent

2. Reviewing Past Business

Reading the Minutes (notes) of the Last Meeting

Dealing with Recent Developments

3. Beginning the Meeting

Introducing the Agenda

Allocating Roles (secretary, participants)

Agreeing on the Ground Rules for the Meeting (contributions, timing, decision-making, etc.)

4. Discussing Items

Introducing the First Item on the Agenda

Closing an Item

Next Item

Giving Control to the Next Participant

5. Finishing the Meeting

Summarizing

Finishing Up

Suggesting and Agreeing on Time, Date and Place for the Next Meeting

Thanking Participants for Attending

Closing the Meeting

The following pages focus on each part of the meeting and the appropriate language for each situation.

Running a Meeting

The following phrases are used to conduct a meeting. These phrases are useful if you are called on to conduct a meeting.

1. Opening

Good morning/afternoon, everyone.

If we are all here, let's get started/start the meeting/start.

2. Welcoming and Introducing

Please join me in welcoming (names of participants)

We're pleased to welcome (names of participants)

I'd like to extend a warm welcome to (names of participants)

It's a pleasure to welcome (names of participants)

I'd like to introduce (names of participants)

3. Stating the Principal Objectives

We're here today to...

I'd like to make sure that we...

Our main aim today is to...

I've called this meeting in order to...

4. Giving Apologies for Someone Who is Absent

I'm afraid (name of participant) can't be with us today. She is in...

Unfortunately, (name of participant) will not be with us today because he...

I have received apologies for absence from (name of participant), who is in (place).

5. Reading the Minutes (notes) of the Last Meeting

To begin with, I'd like to quickly go through the minutes of our last meeting.

First, let's go over the report from the last meeting, which was held on (date).

Here are the minutes from our last meeting, which was on (date).

6. Dealing with Recent Developments

Jack, can you tell us how the XYZ project is progressing?

Jack, how is the XYZ project coming along?

John, have you completed the report on the new accounting package?

Has everyone received a copy of the Tate Foundation report on current marketing trends?

7. Moving Forward

So, if there is nothing else we need to discuss, let's move on to today's agenda.

Shall we get down to business?

If there are no further developments, I'd like to move on to today's topic.

8. Introducing the Agenda

Have you all received a copy of the agenda?

There are X items on the agenda. First, ... second, ... third, ... last, ...

Shall we take the points in this order?

If you don't mind, I'd like to go in order today.

Skip Item 1 and move on to Item 3.

I suggest we take Item 2 at last.

9. Allocating Roles (secretary, participants)

(name of participant) has agreed to take the minutes.

(name of participant), would you mind taking the minutes?

(name of participantt) has kindly agreed to give us a report on...

(name of participantt) will lead Point 1, (name of participant) Point 2, and (name of participant) Point 3.

(name of participant), would you mind taking notes today?

10. Agreeing on the Ground Rules for the Meeting (contributions, timing, decision-making, etc.)

We will hear a short report on each point first, followed by a discussion of...

I suggest we go round the table first.

Let's make sure we finish by...

I'd suggest we...

There will be five minutes for each item.

We'll have to keep each item to 15 minutes. Otherwise we'll never get through.

11. Introducing the First Item on the Agenda

So, let's start with...

I'd suggest we start with...

Why don't we start with...?

So, the first item on the agenda is...

Peter, would you like to kick off?

Shall we start with... ?

(name of participant), would you like to introduce this item?

12. Closing an Item

Shall we leave that item?

Why don't we move on to...?

If nobody has anything else to add, let's...

13. Next Item

Let's move onto the next item.

Now that we've discussed X, let's now...

The next item on today's agenda is...

Now we come to the question of...

14. Giving Control to the Next Participant

I'd like to hand over to (name of participant), who is going to lead the next point.

Next, (name of participant) is going to take us through...

Now, I'd like to introduce (name of participant) who is going to...

15. Summarizing

Before we close today's meeting, let me just summarize the main points.

Let me quickly go over today's main points. To sum up, ...

OK, why don't we quickly summarize what we've done today?

In brief, ...

Shall I go over the main points?

16. Finishing Up

Right, it looks as though we've covered the main items.

If there are no other comments, I'd like to wrap this meeting up.

Let's bring this to a close for today.

17. Suggesting and Agreeing on Time, Date and Place for the Next Meeting

Can we set the date for the next meeting, please?

So, the next meeting will be on... (day), the... (date) of... (month) at...

Let's next meet on... (day), the... (date) of... (month) at... What about the following Wednesday? How is that?

18. Thanking Participants for Attending

I'd like to thank Marianne and Jeremy for coming over from London.

Thank you all for attending.

Thanks for your participation.

19. Closing the Meeting

The meeting is finished, we'll see each other next...

The meeting is closed.

I declare the meeting closed.

a. Answer the following questions according to the passage.

1. What is one of the most common requirements of business English?

2. How many sections are there for holding a meeting? What are they?
_____

3. What are "the Ground Rules for the Meeting"?
_____

4. What does it mean by "Giving Control to the Next Participant"?
_____

b. Translate the expressions into Chinese or English.

1. Opening the Meeting　　　　　宣布会议开始
   _____　　　主持会议
   the Principal Objectives　　　_____
   the Minutes of a Meeting　　　_____
2. Recent Developments　　　　　_____
   _____　　　转向下一个议题
   Introducing the Agenda　　　　_____
   Allocating Roles　　　　　　　_____
3. decision-making　　　　　　　_____
   _____　　　达成一致
   the Ground Rules　　　　　　　_____
   Closing an Item　　　　　　　 _____
4. Giving Control to sb.　　　　_____
   _____　　　总结
   _____　　　结束今日议题
   Closing the Meeting　　　　　 _____

c. Choose an appropriate word or phrase to fill in each blank to make each sentence meaningful, and change its form when necessary.

agenda	requirement	conduct	similar
give apologies for	allocate	summarize	principal
state	be divided into		

1. They share with them _____ beyond the immediate goal of democratization of the electoral process.

2. The busmen _____ that the strike will continue until general agreement is reached about pay and working conditions.

3. That space _____ for a new hospital.

4. My aunt _____ her business very successfully.

5. I _____ him _____ my conduct.

6. He _____ the hero's life of one sentence "Weightier than Mount Tai or lighter than a feather."

7. The class _____ two groups by the teacher.

8. If you have any _____, ask me.

9. My new dress is _____ to the one you have.

10. Once the _____ contradiction is grasped, all the problems will be readily solved.

d. Translate the following sentences into English with words or phrases given in the brackets.

1. 增加薪金问题是今天下午会议的重要议程。(agenda)
_____

2. 他对公司的成功做出了重要的贡献。(contribution)
_____

3. 所有的与会者都被告知要在会议室入口处签字。(participant)
_____

4. 她用几句话概括了新方案的宗旨。(summarize)
_____

5. 他们把会议日期从 20 日提前到 18 日。(move forward)
_____

Vocabulary

agenda	[əˈdʒendə]	n. 议程
allocate	[ˈæləkeɪt]	vt. 分配
appropriate	[əˈprəʊpriət]	adj. 适当的
conduct	[kənˈdʌkt]	n./v. 行为，操行；引导；管理
contribution	[ˌkɒntrɪˈbjuːʃn]	n. 捐献，贡献
declare	[dɪˈkleə]	vt. 断言，宣布
development	[dɪˈveləpmənt]	n. 发展
generally	[ˈdʒenrəli]	adv. 一般，通常
introduction	[ˌɪntrəˈdʌkʃn]	n. 介绍，导言，绪论
minute	[ˈmɪnɪt]	n./vt. 备忘录，笔记，记录，摘录

objective	[əb'dʒektɪv]	n./adj. 目标；客观的
participant	[pɑːˈtɪsɪpənt]	n. 参与者
principal	[ˈprɪnsəpl]	n./adj. 负责人，首长，校长；主要的，首要的
requirement	[rɪˈkwaɪəmənt]	n. 要求，必要条件
review	[rɪˈvjuː]	n./vt. 回顾，复习
section	[sekʃn]	n. 部分；项；区
similar	[ˈsɪmələ]	adj. 相似的，类似的
situation	[ˌsɪtʃuˈeɪʃn]	n. 情形，(建筑物等的) 位置
state	[steɪt]	vt. 声明，陈述，规定
summarize	[ˈsʌməraɪz]	v. 概述，总结，摘要
trend	[trend]	n./vi. 倾向，趋势

Phrases

decision-making	决策
recent development	近期发展
the ground rule	基本规则
the minutes of a meeting	会议纪要
the principal objectives	会议主要议题
warm welcome	热烈欢迎
agree on	达成一致
close an item	结束一个议题
close the meeting	宣布散会
conduct a meeting	组织会议
divide into	分成
finish up	结束，完成；用光
focus on	集中
give apologies for	道歉
give control to	请……发言
hold a meeting	召开会议
make contribution	贡献
move forward	转向下一个议题
open the meeting	宣布会议开始
run a meeting	主持会议
more or less	或多或少

 **Writing**

Booking Form for Conference Rooms

Task 1 Writing Skills

会议预定单可对会议要素（会议室、时间、地点、议题、预定单位、参加人数）、会议准备（会议室安排、会议资料准备、设备准备）、会议餐饮等进行全面规划和管理。实现从会议协调、会议准备、会议服务、会议总结到文件归档整个过程的管理，能对协调会议安排、提高会议质量起到良好作用。填写会议预订单通常包括：

(1) 会议预订人姓名。

(2) 会议主办单位名称、联络人姓名、头衔、地址、联络电话、传真。

(3) 会议类型（学术会议、各种研讨会、商品展销会、新产品发布会、记者招待会、新茶话会和其他商业会议等）。

(4) 会议日期、会议开始时间及计划安排的会议厅名称。

(5) 出席人数。

(6) 付款方式（现金、信用卡、支票）。

(7) 预定金额。

(8) 会议各项费用开支和总计额。

(9) 会议厅的布置要求。

(10) 会后餐饮菜单项目及酒水要求。

(11) 接受预订的日期、经办人姓名。

(12) 编号。

Task 2 Sample Writing

1) Conference Room Booking Form

HAFFA Conference Room Booking Form

To：Alice Liu – HAFFA

Enquiry：2796 3121   Fax：2796 3719

Name of Applicant：_____

(Member's Company Name)

Contact Person：_____

Telephone No.：_____

Fax No.：_____

In Case of Emergency/Typhoon Situation:

Person in Charge：_____

Mobile Phone: _____
Event Title: _____
Date of Use: _____
Period (XX: 00-XX: 00): _____
No. of Users: _____
Equipment (Please " √ " the appropriate box.)

Overhead Projector		Television + Video Cassette Player	
Slide Projector		Whiteboard with Markers	
LCD Projector		Laser Pointer	

Attached please find our Company Cheque # _____ in the amount of HK$ _____ (including HK$ _____ Room Rental Fee & HK$ _____ LCD Projector Rental Fee) in favour of "HAFFA".

Please also find our Company Cheque # _____ in the amount of HK$_____ which accounts for the rental deposit.

On behalf of the hirer, I, the undersigned, agree to abide by the conditions/regulations of use of HAFFA Conference Room as contained in the HAFFA News.

Authorized Signature_____

(With Company Chop)

2) Booking Form for Conference Rooms

AUDIO–VISUAL AND OTHER REQUIREMENTS

The room hire rate includes an AV technician and the following audio-visual facilities. Please indicate your requirements.

- ☐ Data projector (speaker to provide lap-top)
- ☐ Lectern & table top microphones
- ☐ Multi-standard video player/DVD player
- ☐ Overhead projector
- ☐ Data projector (PC not provided)
- ☐ Hand-held microphone
- ☐ Tie-clip microphone
- ☐ Flip chart
- ☐ Multi-standard video player
- ☐ Lectern microphone
- ☐ Cabaret Style Set-up-additional charge of £150 (only applicable to the Rutherford Theatre)

ADDITIONAL REQUIREMENTS

Please indicate your requirements.

- ☐ Laptop with full Office XP @ £100 per day

☐ Extra microphones-price on request

☐ Wireless Internet connection £50 (multiple lines)

☐ Extra Flip chart @ £25 each

☐ LCD Television £80

☐ Cloakroom attendant/Receptionist @ £120 per day

☐ Exhibitor tables (6ft Trestle with cloth) £10

☐ Poster boards-price on request

☐ Fax @ £1.50 per page

☐ Photocopying @ A4 10p, A3 15p per page

N.B. All prices exclude VAT

I hereby accept the terms and conditions above.

Signature： Date：

76 Portland Place • London W1B 1NT • Tel +44020 7470 4884 • Fax +44 020 7470 4931

E-mail：enquiries@76portlandplace.com

IOP Enterprises Ltd is registered in England (No.： 347 1563)

Common Sentence Patterns in Meetings

1. Let's call the meeting to order.

我宣布会议开始。

2. Well, ladies and gentlemen, I think we should begin.

女士们、先生们，会议开始。

3. Good morning. It looks like everyone's here, so let's get started.

早上好。人都到齐了，会议正式开始。

4. Let me bring your attention to (what I see as) the main issues.

让我们进入主要问题。

5. Let's focus on the main issues.

让我们关注主要问题。

6. To discuss this matter, I'd like to call on Mr. Zhang.

关于这个问题，请张先生来发言。

7. I'm sorry, but I don't agree with you.

抱歉，我不同意你的看法。

8. The meeting is now closed.

宣布会议结束。

Task 3 Writing Practice

a. Translate the following form into Chinese.

CONFERENCE CENTRE AND MEETING ROOM BOOKING FORM 2021

PERSONAL DETAILS　　　　　Booking Reference：＿＿＿＿＿＿

Name and Address of Organization：＿＿＿＿＿＿＿＿＿＿＿＿＿＿

Contact(s)：＿＿＿＿＿＿＿＿　　E-mail：＿＿＿＿＿＿＿＿＿＿＿

Telephone No.：＿＿＿＿＿＿　　Fax No.：＿＿＿＿＿＿＿＿＿＿

Date Required：＿＿＿＿＿＿＿＿＿＿＿＿＿＿＿＿＿＿＿＿＿＿

Time Required From ＿＿＿＿＿＿ To ＿＿＿＿＿＿＿＿＿＿＿＿

Number Attending：to be confirmed at least 48 hours in advance (72 hours for fine dining)：

Room Required：＿＿＿＿＿＿＿＿＿＿＿＿＿＿＿＿＿＿＿＿＿＿

Room Layout Required (board/theatre/cabaret)：＿＿＿＿＿＿＿＿

Title of Meeting (for foyer notice)：＿＿＿＿＿＿＿＿＿＿＿＿＿

b. You are a staff in the convention center in Dublin Writers Museum. You should fill in a convention form for Mr. Bruce Ward, who wants to book a conference room for 40 people to have a English Teaching Symposium on Monday morning from 9:00 A.M. to 11:00 A.M. on behalf of a dean in Central China Software College. He needs Top Table, PA system, Signing-in table and Overhead Projector. His E-mail: kitty@sina.com and telephone number: 139××××8765.

CONFERENCE ROOM BOOKING FORM

Beckett Room

DUBLIN WRITERS MUSEUM

18 PARNELL SQUARE, DUBLIN

WWW.WRITERSMUSEUM.COM

WRITERS@DUBLINTOURISM.IE

The Beckett Room (29 × 40 feet) is a bright and comfortable conference room ideal for business meetings, launches, seminars, workshops or any informal occasion.

If you would like to view our facilities please contact the Manager at the above address or telephone 01-8722077.

Hire Options：Theatre style meeting capacity：100

Boardroom style meeting capacity：40

Contact Name：＿＿＿＿＿＿＿＿＿＿＿＿＿＿＿＿＿＿＿＿＿＿＿

Company: _____
Address: _____
Telephone: _____ Fax: _____
E-mail: _____
Hire Option: _____
Day: _____ Date: _____ Year: _____
Time: Start _____ Finish _____
Number of attendees: _____

FACILITIES REQUIRED

Seating Arrangement:
(Tick items required below)
Top Table: _____ Signing-in Table: _____
1 PA System: _____ 1 Lectern: _____
1 Television/Video: _____ 1 Overhead Projector: _____
1 Slide Projector: _____ 1 Flip Chart: _____
1 LCD Projector: _____ 1 Screen: _____
(This projector can display resolution 640 × 480 to 1024 × 768)
Other (please specify): _____
The above equipment is subject to availability and may incur extra charges.
Please check with the Manager in advance for further information.

Vocabulary Development

advisory committee	顾问委员会，咨询委员会
agenda	议程
assembly	大会
banquet	酒宴
board of directors	董事会
box supper	慈善餐会
cocktail party	鸡尾酒会
closing speech	闭幕词
closure	闭幕
committee of experts	专家委员会
congress	代表大会

constitution	宪法，章程
statute	法令，法规
convention	会议
fancy ball	化妆舞会
farewell party	欢送会
final sitting	闭幕会
general committee, general officers	总务委员会
item on the agenda	议程项目
notice board	布告牌
opening	开幕
opening sitting	开幕会
other business	其他事项
plenary meeting	全会
procedure	程序
public gallery	旁听席
rules of procedure	议事规则
seat	席位
secretariat	秘书处
session	会期，会议期间（美：meeting）
speaker	报告人
standing orders, by-laws	议事程序
timetable, schedule	日程表，时刻表
the sitting is open	会议开幕
place on the agenda	列入议程
make a speech, deliver a speech	发表演讲
welcome meeting	欢迎会

Banquet Services
宴会服务

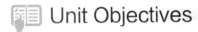 Unit Objectives

After learning this unit, you should

- understand the types of banquet service;
- master the basic words and expressions about banquet service;
- get some cultural knowledge about banquet service;
- find ways to improve your writing skills about Note Writing;
- be familiar with some Chinese & Western dishes.

Background Knowledge

Types of Banquet Service

It's important to decide on the type of service used at a banquet. Each service costs differently from one another.

1. Plate service (also known as American service): It is the most common form of banquet service. The food is at the kitchen and waiters send the plates to the table from the left to the guest. At the end of the course, the plates are picked up from the right.

2. Russian service: It is also called platter service. Food is served from platters and waiters work as teams. They place food items on the diners' plates.

3. French service: It requires much space between tables for waiters to move around. With this service, a gueridon (餐厅里上菜服务用的小桌子) is set at the table side and food is prepared on the gueridon.

4. Preset service: It is a faster service that is often for lunches. The first course of soup, salad or appetizer is set on the table before the guest arrives.

5. Buffet service: It is a display of food items on table stations, so that attendees can select food for their own. This service may combine with other styles. For example, a banquet may begin with a buffet and then a sit-down dinner in plate service style; or the first and reserved courses are served by the waiter and the main dishes in buffet style.

Practice Materials

Listening

Dialogue 1

a. Listen to Dialogue 1 and decide whether each of the following sentences is true (T) or false (F).

1. _____ Li Hua is a tour guide of China International Travel Agency.
2. _____ The tour guide made the call and wanted to make a reservation yesterday.
3. _____ It is already past the normal lunch-serving time when the tour group arrive.
4. _____ The tourists get their rice by themselves.
5. _____ The tour guide pays the bill after the meal.

b. Listen to the dialogue and answer the following questions.

1. How many people does the group consist of?
_____
2. Why are the tables free when the group arrive?
_____
3. What kind of meal would the tourists like to have?
_____
4. How many bottles of beer would they like to order?
_____
5. What time will the group have their supper that evening?
_____

c. Listen to the dialogue again and supply the missing words.

1. I made a call and reserved _____ tables for a tour group.
2. You can sit at _____ you like.

3. We are sorry to have _____.

4. Shall we put it on your _____?

5. Would you please sign your name here and put down your _____?

> **Notes**
>
> 1. China Travel Agency   中国旅行社
> 2. green bean   青豆
> 3. sweet and sour ribs   糖醋排骨
> 4. saute chicken cubes   炒鸡丁
> 5. sign   签字

Dialogue 2

a. Listen to Dialogue 2 and decide whether each of the following sentences is true (T) or false (F).

1. It's Frank who invites some friends to dinner at a restaurant.
2. They order six cold dishes and four hot dishes.
3. The ladies prefer some orange juice to wine.
4. Two persons want to have some beer instead of wine.
5. A Chinese dinner usually starts with a soup.

b. Listen to the dialogue and answer the following questions.

1. How many foreigners are involved in the dialogue?

_____

2. Who orders the dishes for them?

_____

3. How many bottles of beer do they order?

_____

4. What does a Chinese dinner usually finish up with?

_____

5. Who shows others how to eat Beijing Roast Duck?

_____

c. Listen to the dialogue again and supply the missing words.

1. We'll have a bottle of _____ and two bottles of _____.
2. Following the shark's fin soup, there will be _____.

3. That's really a big _____.

4. Finally, there's some dim sum for _____.

5. Please help yourselves to _____ you like.

Notes

1. lightly fried prawns	轻炸大虾
2. sweet and sour pork ribs	糖醋排骨
3. steamed mandarin fish	清蒸鳜鱼
4. clear chicken soup	清鸡汤
5. cold dishes	凉菜
6. jelly fish	海蜇皮
7. sliced boiled chicken	白切鸡
8. braised fresh mushrooms	油焖鲜蘑
9. green French beans with ginger sauce	姜汁扁豆
10. poultry	家禽
11. staple food	主食
12. feast	筵席，宴会
13. dim sum	点心
14. specialty	特色菜
15. crepe	薄饼
16. dip	蘸
17. sauce	酱
18. spring onion	小葱

Background Information

The Culinary Arts of China

Cooking in China has an age-long history. It specializes in its own ways of processing various kinds of dishes of local tastes and characteristics.

According to books on cooking, the total number of ancient and modern Chinese dishes is about 8,000, taking only the famous dishes! The ingredients may be classified into some 600 broad categories. There are 48 basic ways of cooking, including roasting, frying and boiling, all of which bring out the best ingredients.

Chinese cooking is subdivided into a great number of schools notable for their local flavors. Among them are the more popular and well-known eight schools—Shandong,

Sichuan, Jiangsu, Zhejiang, Guangdong, Hunan, Fujian and Anhui. There are also more than twenty other outstanding local dishes like Beijing dishes and Shanghai dishes. Vegetarians and Buddhists have their own particular tastes. In big cities like Beijing, Shanghai and Guangzhou, restaurants of a certain local flavor of its own style or after a certain school can easily be found.

The art of cooking in China gives much attention to the colors, the flavors, the tastes and the appearances of cooked dishes. Even the arranging of the cooked pieces in the dish is done in such utmost care as to make the whole dish present an artistic look. In a word, Chinese cooking has won worldwide reputation.

Notes

1. culinary	烹调的
2. schools	（这里指）菜系
3. flavor	风味
4. vegetarian	素食者
5. buddhist	佛教徒
6. give attention...to	把(重点等)放在

Speaking

Dialogue 1

Preparing a Banquet Menu

S: Mr. Stool **H**: Hotelier

S: What is the menu for your standard banquet?

H: We don't have a standard menu, we create one for our clients.

S: OK. What do you suggest?

H: We start the meal with meat starters and soup.

S: That's good.

H: Then we serve the main dishes.

S: What is in the main dishes?

H: We serve pork, beef, lamb, chicken, vegetables and rice.

S: Can you serve fish as well?

H: Yes, we can serve anything you want.

S: Good. What do you serve for dessert?

H: We serve cake.

S: Everyone likes cake.

H: Yes, that's true.

S: What about after the cake?

H: After the cake we will serve drinks so that the guests can have toasts.

Notes

1. banquet	宴会
2. menu	菜单
3. hotelier	旅馆老板，宾馆（酒店）经理
4. standard banquet	标准宴会
5. client	顾客，客户
6. starter	（一餐中的）第一道菜，开胃小吃
7. main dish	主菜
8. pork	猪肉
9. beef	牛肉
10. lamb	羊肉
11. serve	上（菜），提供，服务
12. dessert	（餐后）甜食，甜点
13. toast	吐司面包；干杯，敬酒

Dialogue 2

Serving the Western Style Banquet

(*The waiting staff is serving a Western style banquet.*)

Staff: You're at Table 18. Here we are. Take your seat, please.

Customer: I'm nearly late. Listen, our host is making the speech.

Staff: Yes. Let me fill brandy in your cup. The host is raising his cup for a toast.

Host: Ladies and gentlemen, may I propose a toast to the health of you all? Cheers!

Customer: Hey, this dish looks like a squirrel. What on earth is it?

Staff: This is the Squirrel-Shaped Mandarin Fish. Not only is it in the shape of a squirrel, it will sound like a squirrel crying when I pour the broth on it.

Customer: Isn't it that wonderful?

Staff: Yes. Please stay a little bit far away from the plate. When the broth is poured, it might splash.

Customer: How does it taste?

Staff: It tastes crispy, with sour and sweet flavors. Here is one portion for you. Would you try the flavors for yourself?

Customer: Hum, well, it is so soft inside.

Staff: May I take this plate away?

Customer: OK. What desserts do we have tonight?

Staff: Mango pudding and homemade cheese cake.

Customer: When will fruits come?

Staff: Just a minute, please. Here is your fruit knife. Do be careful.

Host: Ladies and gentlemen, thank you for your coming this evening.

Staff: Is everything all right?

Customer: Yes, everything is fine.

Staff: Thank you. This is your coat, Sir. Good night.

Notes

1. host	主持人，主办人
2. brandy	白兰地
3. broth	肉汤
4. splash	溅
5. crispy	脆的
6. flavor	味道
7. portion	（一）份
8. raise one's cup for a toast	举杯祝酒
9. homemade cheese cake	自制奶酪蛋糕

Dialogue 3

Serving the Buffet Dinner

At the Pacific Restaurant, a new buffet has been opened to attract customers. Now a server (S) is assisting a customer (C).

S: What can I do for you, Sir?

C: Excuse me, but what is included in the price?

S: Well, our "All You Can Eat" salad bar allows you get as much food as you like. New plates are provided at the far end of the bar.

C: How about drinks?

S: Only 6 yuan extra, and you can get a bottomless cup of soft drink. May I also recommend this month's "Happy Hour" meal for drinks between 5:00 P.M. and 7:00 P.M.?

C: OK, we'll have a try. Where is the sauce?

S: You can find sauces, dressings and condiments near the fruit section of the salad bar.

C: This dish doesn't have an English name. Could you tell me what this is in English?

S: All right. This dish is the popular turkey sausages with turnip.

C: Sounds OK to me. Where could I find a serving spoon?

S: Here you are. Is this big enough?

C: Sure. Thanks.

S: My pleasure. Anything else I can do for you?

C: No, thanks.

S: Sure. Let me know if I could be of further help. Please enjoy your buffet.

Notes

1. bottomless	无限的
2. sauce	调味酱，沙司
3. dressing	调料
4. condiment	调味品
5. sausage	香肠
6. turnip	萝卜，芜菁
7. "All You Can Eat"	"请君选用"
8. salad bar	沙拉吧台

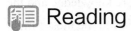

Reading

Table Manners

Different countries have different table manners, it is wise to understand them before you go. Here're some top tips.

Don't make noises with your mouth. Close your mouth when eating. People make mouth noises because they eat without closing their mouths. When you drink your soup, don't sip it, but swallow it all in one mouthful.

Don't talk with your mouth full. If someone talks to you, wait until your mouth is empty before answering.

Imagine you are eating with someone you have just met. He spits bones onto the table.

He wipes his mouth on his sleeve. He rushes for the best piece of food that is served. He does not have good table manners.

Fortunately, most of us eat neatly and are not greedy. These two points are the basic rules of good table manners.

Different cultures of the world have different table manners because of the serving of their food, utensils and national customs. By knowing and using the table manners of different cultures, we show that we are willing to learn from them. That is a sure way to make friends.

There is not much call for a complete working knowledge of table manners in America today. Many families only gather all at once around the dinner table at holiday feasts, and most restaurants are too casual to require, or even to allow for, more than basic good table manners. If, having dropped his napkin, a diner at a bistro were to attempt to practice proper etiquette by signaling a member of the staff to bring a fresh one, he would probably have to do without a napkin at all. Try as he might to make eye contact and indicate the nature of the problem with a subtle wiggle of the eyebrow and downward flicker of the glance, he is likely to succeed only in causing his date to think he is making a play for the server. Although strict good manners forbid placing a used eating utensil back on the table, the server removing a plate on which a fork has quite properly been positioned "pointing at 11 o'clock" might just plop that item back where it started, making more of a clatter than if the diner had simply done it herself.

From time to time—perhaps at an important business dinner, a romantic date at an expensive restaurant, or a first dinner with the family of the person who may be "the One"—it is necessary to display a more sophisticated knowledge of table etiquette. This is not difficult, once you have mastered the basics. Anyone armed with his core knowledge and the ability to adapt smoothly to the situation at hand will be able to handle even the most formal event. The goal is not, after all, to demonstrate utter mastery of the most arcane details of etiquette (which would be quite difficult considering the wide variations of customs in different cultures and from generation to generation), but rather to behave with graciousness and poise at the table.

Posture

Proper posture at the table is very important. Sit up straight, with your arms held near your body. You should neither lean on the back of the chair nor bend forward to place the elbows on the table. It is permissible to lean forward slightly every now and then and press the elbows very lightly against the edge of the table, if it is obvious that you are not using them for support.

Eating Soup

Dip the spoon into the soup, moving it away from the body, until it is about two-thirds full, then sip the liquid (without slurping) from the side of the spoon (without inserting the whole bowl of the spoon into the mouth). The theory behind this is that a diner who scoops the spoon toward himself is more likely to slosh soup onto his lap, although it is difficult to imagine what sort of eater would stroke the spoon so forcefully through the liquid that he creates waves. It is perfectly fine to tilt the bowl slightly again away from the body to get the last spoonful or two of soup.

Offering Food

Take note, when you are the host of a party, of the way you offer additional servings to your guests. Urging someone to "have another (or a second or third) helping" can be seen as an unpleasant insinuation that the guest has eaten too much. It is best to phrase each offer of food as if the dish has just been brought out for the first time.

"Please Pass the Salt"

The proper response to this very simple request is to pick up both the salt and the pepper and place them on the table within reach of the person next to you, who will do the same, and so on, until they reach the person who asked for them. They are not passed from hand to hand, nor should anyone other than the original requester sprinkle her food when she has the shakers in her possession. The reason for this is that American etiquette is not about efficiency. Often, the most refined action is that which requires the greatest number of steps to carry it out (as in, for example, the zigzag method of handling a fork and knife).

a. Answer the following questions according to the passage.

1. Why do people make mouth noises while eating?
___

2. How do you drink your soup?
___

3. What are those two basic rules of good table manners?
___

4. If you are the host of a party, what is the best way to offer additional servings to your guests?
___

5. What's the proper response to the request "Please pass the salt"?
___

b. *Translate the expressions into Chinese or English.*

1. table manners　　　　_____
   _____　　举止良好
   in a manner　　　　_____
   have no manners　　_____
2. formal event　　　　_____
   _____　　时事
   _____　　团体赛
   at all events　　　　_____
3. make a play for　　　_____
   _____　　在……中起一份作用，参与
   come into play　　　_____
   _____　　公平的竞赛
4. at hand　　　　　　_____
   _____　　把……传下去
   at sb.'s hand(s)　　　_____
   _____　　给予(某人)帮助

c. *Choose an appropriate word or phrase to fill in each blank to make each sentence meaningful, and change its form when necessary.*

custom	casual	forbid	adapt	demonstrate
lean	make a play for	sip	greedy	sophisticated

1. It's a species that has _____ well to winter climes.
2. It's well-known that the living _____ vary from country to country.
3. The guest took a _____ of brandy and turned to chat with the lady next to him.
4. The doctor _____ the old man to smoke, but he failed to follow it.
5. Tom was such a _____ businessman that nearly nobody trusted him.
6. His girlfriend was very angry when she found out that he was _____ another pretty girl.
7. The young man's mother always asks him to wear a suit, but he prefers wearing _____ clothes.
8. Everybody says that Dick is a very _____ man although he is just in his early twenties.

9. The engineer is surprised to find out the post _____ a little bit.

10. The contestants not only spoke fluent English but also _____ excellent body language.

d. Translate the following sentences into English with words or phrases given in the brackets.

1. 这位导游总是很幽默。(manner)

_____

2. 昨天人们很少外出，因为迷雾笼罩了全城。(swallow up)

_____

3. 幸运的是，大雨在我们动身前往北京之前停了。(fortunately)

_____

4. 他最后一段话证明他对这个话题一无所知。(demonstrate)

_____

5. 由于时间不够，现在不能深入讨论这个问题。(forbid)

_____

Vocabulary List

adapt	[əˈdæpt]	v. 使适应
arcane	[ɑːˈkeɪn]	adj. 神秘的；不可思议的
bistro	[ˈbiːstrəʊ]	n. <俗> 小酒馆，小咖啡店
casual	[ˈkæʒuəl]	adj. 偶然的，不经意的
clatter	[ˈklætə]	n. 咔嗒，哗啦声；嘈杂的谈笑声
core	[kɔː]	n. 果核；中心，核心
date	[deɪt]	n. 约会对象
demonstrate	[ˈdemənstreɪt]	v. 示范，证明
downward	[ˈdaʊnwəd]	adj. 向下的
efficiency	[ɪˈfɪʃnsi]	n. 效率，功效
elbow	[ˈelbəʊ]	n. 肘
etiquette	[ˈetɪkət]	n. 礼节
feast	[fiːst]	n. 节日；盛宴，筵席
flicker	[ˈflɪkə]	n. 扑动；闪烁；颤动
forbid	[fəˈbɪd]	v. 禁止，不许
forcefully	[ˈfɔːsfəli]	adv. 强有力地，激烈地
glance	[glɑːns]	n. 一瞥；眼光；匆匆一看
gracious	[ˈgreɪʃəs]	adj. 亲切的
greedy	[ˈgriːdi]	adj. 贪吃的；贪婪的；渴望的

insinuation	[ɪnsɪnjʊ'eɪʃn]	*n.* 暗示，暗讽
lap	[læp]	*n.* (坐时的) 大腿前部，膝盖；下摆
lean	[liːn]	*v.* 倚靠；倾斜；倾向
mastery	['mɑːstəri]	*n.* 掌握
mouthful	['maʊθfʊl]	*n.* 一口，满口
napkin	['næpkɪn]	*n.* 餐巾，餐巾纸
neatly	[niːtli]	*adv.* 整洁地，优美地
pepper	['pepə]	*n.* 胡椒粉
plop	[plɒp]	*v.* 使掉下，扑通落下
poise	[pɔɪz]	*n.* 平衡；姿势；镇静
position	[pə'zɪʃn]	*v.* 安置；决定……的位置
posture	['pɒstʃə]	*n.* (身体的) 姿势，体态
qualification	[ˌkwɒlɪfɪ'keɪʃn]	*n.* 资格，条件
refined	[rɪ'faɪnd]	*adj.* 精制的；优雅的；精确的
romantic	[rəʊ'mæntɪk]	*adj.* 传奇式的；浪漫的
scoop	[skuːp]	*v.* 掘，挖
shaker	['ʃeɪkə]	*n.* 摇动者，混合器
signal	['sɪgnəl]	*v.* 打信号，发信号
sip	[sɪp]	*v.* 吸吮
slosh	[slɒʃ]	*v.* 溅，泼
slurp	[slɜːp]	*v.* 啧啧吃，啜食
sophisticated	[sə'fɪstɪkeɪtɪd]	*adj.* 老练的，久经世故的
spit	[spɪt]	*v.* 吐 (唾沫)，吐出
sprinkle	['sprɪŋkl]	*v.* 撒 (某物) 于 (某物之表面), 洒, 喷撒
subtle	['sʌtl]	*adj.* 敏感的；微妙的；精细的
swallow	['swɒləʊ]	*v.* 吞咽
tilt	[tɪlt]	*v.* (使) 倾斜；(使) 翘起
urge	[ɜːdʒ]	*v.* 催促；力劝；极力主张
utensil	[juː'tensl]	*n.* 器具
utter	['ʌtə]	*adj.* 全然的；绝对的
variation	[ˌveəri'eɪʃn]	*n.* 变更，变化，变异
wiggle	['wɪgl]	*n.* 踌躇，摆动
wipe	[waɪp]	*v.* 擦，揩
zigzag	['zɪgzæg]	*adj.* 曲折的；齿形的；Z 字形的

Phrases

attempt to	尝试做……，企图做……
be armed with	用……武装
be willing to	愿意做……
carry out	进行，实施
make a noise	制造噪声
make a play for	挖空心思吸引……，想尽办法获得……
make friends	交朋友
pick up	拾起，捡起
point at	指向
after all	毕竟
at hand	在手边，在附近
from generation to generation	一代代，世世代代
from time to time	有时，不时
in the possession of sb.	为某人所有
now and then	时而，不时

 # Writing

Note Writing

Task 1 Writing Skills

便条是我们日常生活和学习中广泛使用的一种简单书信。与普通书信相比，它形式简约、内容简短、语言直接、接近口语，且无需邮寄，通常几句话就能将最新的信息、通知、要求或者活动的事项等转告给对方。常见的便条有收条、欠条、留言和请假条等。

(1) 便条的结构

便条由四部分组成：① Date：便条日期；② Salutation：称呼；③ Body：正文；④ Signature：署名。

1) Date：日期

即写便条的时间，它一般位于右上角 (也可写在右下角)。由于写和读相隔时间较近，日期的书写形式比较随便，既可以写为月日，也可以写为周几，还可以写为几点钟等具体时间。日期的书写形式与书信中的相似，如：July 10, 2022；6:30 P.M.。

2) Salutation：称呼

便条开篇须有称呼语，但称呼可以较为随便，有时 Dear 也可略去，如：Lucy, Miss Yang, Professor Zhang。

3) Body：正文

正文部分要言简意赅、通俗易懂，多采用口语语言。由于留条人和收条人彼此情况一般都比较熟悉，因此客套话常常都可以省略。但如果读者是上级、长辈，或关系较疏远，或谈的事情较正式，便条的语气应该庄重、谦恭些，表达要客气委婉些。如：Would it be possible for you to see me sometime next week?

结尾处表示祝福祝贺等的客套话一般可以省略。

4) Signature：署名

便条结尾须署上留条人的姓名，位置在正文的右下角。如果与对方关系较熟，可以只写姓或名，如：Jack, Brown, Gao 等。

(2) 便条的种类

便条可以分为两大类：说明性便条和凭证性便条。前者旨在说明某种事情或情况，如请假条、留言条等。后者是可以作为凭证的书面条子，因此具有一定的约束力或某种法律效力，如借条、收条等。这里我们主要谈谈留言条、请假条、借条和收条的写法。

1) 留言条 (message)

留言条是在有急事需告诉别人而又不能面谈时留给他人的一些信息，如辞行留言、借物还物留言、求助留言、临时通知等。

2) 请假条 (note asking for leave)

请假条可自己写，也可由他人代写。写请假条时，要说明请假的原因和时间，并对由请假带来的不便表示歉意，语气要诚恳。如有医生出具的证明(或其他证明)最好一起附上。

3) 收条和借条 (receipt/IOU)

当向他人借钱借物或收到他人的欠款欠物时，常常需要写一份借条或收条。借条应写明何时向何人借何物；收条应写明何时收到何物、何人接收。

Task 2　Sample Writing

(1) 留言条 (message)

Sample 1　Note for saying good-bye

May 8, 2022

Dear Richard,

　　I'm leaving for home by air at six this evening. It is a pity that I can't see you to say good-bye before leaving. I have enjoyed my stay here. Thank you very much for your hospitality and the trouble you have taken on my behalf. Please remember me to your parents.

Yours,
Bill

Sample 2 Transmitting a telephone message

11:00 A.M.

Chen Wei,

    Miss Wu, your classmate, has just rung up, saying that she has arrived this morning by train and is staying at Ramada Hotel (Room 509). She wants you to go there to discuss the schedule tomorrow and ring her back as soon as possible.

Liu Yang

(2) 请假条 (note asking for leave)

April 10

Dear Professor Brown,

    I am very sorry that I shall be unable to attend class today owing to a bad cold and high fever. I'm enclosing a certificate from my doctor who said I must stay in bed for two days. I ask you for two days sick leave. I shall be much obliged if I can get your permission.

Yours respectfully,
Wang Xiaopeng

Encl.：a certificate from my doctor

(3) 收条 (receipt)

December 15, 2021

    Received from Mr. Hill the following things：One typewriter, One tape-recorder, RMB 2000 Yuan only.

Bruce

Common Sentence Patterns of Notes

    (1) Will you please excuse my absence for... 我因……不能到场，望见谅。

    (2) I shall be much obliged if you will grant me my application for three days' leave of absence. 如果您能批准我三天的假期，我将感激不尽。

    (3) Because of..., I'm unable to come... 因为……我不能前来。

    (4) Please come this afternoon if possible. 如果可能，今天下午务请光临。

    (5) I hope there will be no much trouble to you if... 如果您能……我希望这不至于给您带来太多麻烦。

    (6) Received/borrowed from... 今收到 / 借到……

Task 3　Writing Practice

a. Finish the following reservation letter by translating the Chinese in the brackets into English.

Mr. Liang,

_____ (你不在时，中国旅行社的导游来过电话). It seemed that he wanted to talk with you about something really urgent. _____ (他要你尽快给他办公室回电话).

Yours sincerely,
Han Meimei

b. Suppose you are Henry. You have received a telephone saying that your grandfather is seriously ill. You want to go home to see him. Please write a note to ask Mr. White the Director, for a business leave of a week beginning on April 9.

Vocabulary Development

Menu

1. Kung Pao Chicken　　　　　　　　　　宫保鸡丁
2. Sliced Chicken with Curry Sauce　　　　咖喱鸡片
3. Tender Boiled Chicken with Soy Sauce　 白斩鸡
4. Baked Chicken with Salt　　　　　　　 盐焗鸡
5. Beijing Roast Duck　　　　　　　　　 北京烤鸭
6. Braised Duck with Brown Sauce　　　　 酱鸭
7. Fragrant Crisp Duck　　　　　　　　　香酥鸭
8. Stewed Duck　　　　　　　　　　　　清炖鸭子
9. Sweet and Sour Pork　　　　　　　　　糖醋咕咾肉
10. Twice Cooked Pork　　　　　　　　　回锅肉
11. Steamed Pork with Rice Flour　　　　　粉蒸肉
12. Fish-flavored Pork Slices　　　　　　　鱼香肉丝
13. Braised Meat Balls in Brown Sauce　　　红烧狮子头
14. Pork Slices with Gravy　　　　　　　　滑溜里脊
15. Fride Spare Ribs with Spiced Salt　　　 椒盐排骨
16. Roast Suckling Pig　　　　　　　　　 烤乳猪

17. Grilled Beef Steak 铁扒牛排
18. Quick Fried Beef with Scallion 葱爆牛肉
19. Roast Mutton Chops 烤羊排
20. Instant Boiled Sliced Mutton 涮羊肉
21. Dry Fried Mandarin Fish in Chili Sauce 干烧鳜鱼
22. Fish Slices in Vinegar Gravy 醋溜鱼片
23. Fish slices with egg white 芙蓉鱼片
24. Steamed Perch in Ginger and Scallion 清蒸鲈鱼
25. Fried Shredded Squid 炒鱿鱼丝
26. Braised Abalone with Mushroom 扒鲍鱼
27. Stewed Shark's Fin in Brown Sauce 烧鱼翅
28. Sautéed Shrimp Meat 清炒虾仁
29. Baked Lobster with Sesame Sauce 香汁烤龙虾
30. Sea Blubber Combination 海蜇拌三丝
31. Hot and Sour Soup 酸辣汤
32. Wonton Egg Drop Soup 云吞蛋花汤
33. Bird's Nest Soup 燕窝汤
34. Three Fresh Delicacies Soup 三鲜汤
35. Sliced Ham and Wax Gourd Soup 火腿冬瓜汤

Other terms for banquet dinner

tablecloth	桌布
dining table	餐桌
knife and fork	刀叉
wine glasses	玻璃酒杯
table decoration	桌上饰物
serving trolley	上菜手推车
fruit bowl	水果钵
head table	主桌
event order	宴会订单
aperitif	开胃酒
portion (of food)	一份（食物）

Unit 8

Recreation and Entertainment Services
消遣服务

 Unit Objectives

After learning this unit, you should

- understand how to give information about recreation and entertainment;
- master the basic words and expressions about travel recreation and entertainment;
- get some cultural knowledge about recreation and entertainment;
- find ways to improve your writing skills about writing Poster;
- be familiar with some ways of recreation and entertainment.

 Background Knowledge

Types of Recreation

After a busy sightseeing day, we may be exhausted physically, yet excited mentally. Therefore, during the process of our tour, the travel agency usually arranges some leisure time when we can participate in some activities which may consume less energy, such as playing golf, going to famous local bars, enjoying and appreciating Chinese traditional opera, going to the cinema, and so forth.

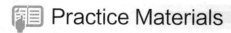

Practice Materials

Listening

Dialogue 1

a. Listen to Dialogue 1 and decide whether each of the following sentences is true (T) or false (F).

1. There are ballets, dramas, concerts and opera on that night.
2. The *Butterfly Lovers* is sort of a tragedy.
3. The man will sit in the dress circle with his fellows.
4. The ticket he booked is 400 yuan each.
5. The man will pay by his credit card.

b. Listen to the dialogue and answer the following questions.

1. What's the name of the place the man is calling?

_____

2. When does the man want to watch?

_____

3. Where are the seats in the stall?

_____

4. What's the man's credit card number?

_____

5. What's the expiry date of the man's card?

_____

c. Listen to the dialogue again and supply the missing words.

1. I think I am more willing to _____ a Chinese one.
2. It is a Yueju opera, which is _____ and prevalent in Zhejiang Province.
3. We have seats in the stalls, and in the dress circle as well _____.
4. For those in the dress circle, which are _____, 400 yuan each.
5. You can pick up your tickets at the _____ before 7:00 P.M. tonight.

> **Notes**
>
> | | |
> |---|---|
> | 1. National Centre for the Performing Arts | 国家大剧院 |
> | 2. consult | 咨询 |
> | 3. ballet | 芭蕾舞 |
> | 4. orchestra | 管弦乐队 |
> | 5. the *Peony Pavilion* | 《牡丹亭》 |
> | 6. the *Red Detachment of Women* | 《红色娘子军》 |
> | 7. the *Butterfly Lovers* | 《梁山伯与祝英台》 |
> | 8. brilliant | 非凡的 |
> | 9. originate | 起源 |
> | 10. prevalent | 流行的 |
> | 11. stalls | 正厅 |
> | 12. dress circle | 二楼正座 |
> | 13. on hand | 现有的，在手边的 |
> | 14. expiry date | 有效期限 |

Dialogue 2

a. Listen to Dialogue 2 and decide whether each of the following sentences is true (T) or false (F).

1. The weather is good that night.

2. The young woman is excited after a day of sightseeing.

3. In a packaged tour, they can not always do what they want.

4. The other man takes jogging to keep healthy.

5. The young woman may also try some ball games.

b. Listen to the dialogue and answer the following questions.

1. Why doesn't the young woman go out?

_____

2. Why doesn't the man go out?

_____

3. What does the young woman do in her spare time?

_____

4. Why does the man suggest the young woman take some ball games?

_____

5. Where are they going the next day?
_____

c. Listen to the dialogue again and supply the missing words.

1. The views are _____, but I cannot bear to walk for long.

2. Anyway, the view is worth _____.

3. Does it really _____ you?

4. When you grow older, you will _____ your health.

5. I may simply attend _____.

Notes

1. starry   繁星满天的
2. amazing   令人惊奇的
3. marvelous   了不起的，极好的
4. packaged tour 随团旅行
5. worthwhile 值得的
6. commodity   商品
7. shopwindow 橱窗
8. jogging   慢跑
9. awesome   可怕的；让人惊叹的
10. badminton 羽毛球
11. tennis   网球
12. violent   剧烈的
13. Fragrant Hill 香山

Speaking

Dialogue 1

Asking about Swimming Facilities

(Mrs. Smith is in the Hilton Hotel on vacation. She comes to the Front Desk to ask about the swimming facilities. R：Receptionist S：Mrs. Smith)

R：Hello, can I help you?

S：Hi. Do you have a swimming pool?

R：Yes, there is an indoor swimming pool in the basement.

M: Great. Can my children use it?

R: Yes, children can use the pool under adult supervision.

M: Is there a lifeguard to supervise the children?

R: There is a lifeguard on duty from 10 A.M. until 6 P.M.

M: OK, are there any other rules for the children?

R: They need to wear swimming costumes.

M: I'll make sure they keep their trunks on. Is there a diving board?

R: Yes, there is diving board and also swimming lanes.

M: Do you have changing rooms?

R: Yes, we have changing rooms and showers in the basement.

M: OK, thanks for your help.

R: No problem. Enjoy your swimming.

Notes

1. indoor	室内的
2. swimming pool	游泳池
3. on vacation	在度假
4. basement	地下室，地下层
5. under adult supervision	在成年人的监护之下
6. lifeguard	救生员
7. supervise	监督，管理，指导
8. on duty	值班，上班
9. swimming costume	游泳衣
10. trunk	（男式）游泳裤
11. diving board	跳（水）板
12. swimming lane	泳道
13. changing room	（体育中心等的）更衣室

Dialogue 2

Windsurfing on the Ocean

A: This place serves terrific breakfasts, don't you think?

B: Yes, nothing better. I was absolutely amazed by the various names and their mouthwatering appearance.

A: So was I. It was my first time to see the wonton noodles, sliced noodles, sesame paste noodles and flat noodles.

B: And clay oven rolls, fried bread stick, steamed sandwich... Umm, really tasty!

A: Hey, hey, hey, come back here! What are you planning to do today?

B: I saw yesterday that some tourists rent windsurfers at the beach. I want to rent one, too.

A: Have you done windsurfing before?

B: No, but it looks fun. I am always longing for trying it.

A: Well, can you take a little advice from a friend?

B: Sure, what?

A: Don't waste your money. Windsurfing is not so easy as you imagined. And it will be windy today, you won't be able to do it. You will fall and fall and fall. Moreover, they will charge you fifty dollars for a half hour.

B: Well, I will see.

(30 minutes later)

A: Hey, you are wet all over. Didn't you go windsurfing?

B: I tried for a half hour. It was interesting, but... well... I couldn't do it.

A: See? I've told you. It's very hard.

B: I couldn't even stand on it and hold the sail. I probably fell down fifty times.

A: Fifty times?

B: Yes, it was really stupid.

A: Well, that's not too bad then.

B: What do you mean? It's expensive!

A: Yes, but you have to calculate a little. You paid fifty dollars and you fell down fifty times. So you only spent one dollar per fall. That's cheap!

Notes

1. windsurf — 帆板运动
2. terrific — 非常棒的
3. absolutely — 绝对地
4. amaze — 使吃惊
5. mouthwatering — 令人垂涎的
6. wonton noodle — 云吞面
7. sliced noodle — 刀削面
8. sesame paste noodle — 麻酱面
9. flat noodle — 板面

10. clay oven roll　　　　　　　烧饼
11. fried bread stick　　　　　　油条
12. calculate　　　　　　　　　计算

Dialogue 3

In the Pub

(During the tour to Beijing, Mike and Joe want to freshen themselves up, and they go to a pub.)

Mike: How is the night life in Beijing, Joe?

Joe: I heard from some natives that it is wonderful.

Mike: Really? How about going to have fun in this ancient but modern city?

Joe: That would be fantastic.

Mike: But where shall we go?

Joe: Don't worry. The guide told me there was a pub called Angel nearby. It is quite famous.

Mike: Great! Let's go!

(In the pub)

Waiter: Welcome! Where would you like to sit, please? The bottommost charge is different according to the seats.

Joe: OK. What's the difference?

Waiter: If you sit at a table, the charge will be 100 yuan for each table. That of the box is 300 yuan. But if you sit around the bar, that will be 20 yuan for each person.

Mike: Well, where do you like to sit, Joe?

Joe: How about at a table? That's neither too crowded nor too expensive.

Mike: Fine.

Waiter: This way, please.

(After they get seated)

Waiter: May I have your order, please?

Joe: I'd like a cup of cider. How about you?

Mike: A pint of lager, and a packet of crisps, please. Here is the money.

Waiter: Thank you very much.

Joe: See, the music is really crazy, and so are the people around.

Mike: Yeah, this could be the most swinging place in the whole of Asia.

Joe: I couldn't agree more. Let's join them.

Mike: Let's go!

Notes

1. incentive	激励
2. pub	酒吧
3. native	本地人
4. fantastic	美妙的
5. bottommost charge	最低消费
6. box	包间
7. bar	吧台
8. cider	苹果酒
9. pint	品脱
10. lager	淡啤酒
11. crisp	薯片

Reading

Beijing Opera

Beijing Opera or Peking opera is a kind of Chinese opera which arose in the mid-19th century and was extremely popular in the Qing Dynasty court. It is widely regarded as one of the cultural treasures of China. Beijing and Tianjin are respected as the base cities of Beijing Opera in the north while Shanghai is the base in the south.

Although it is called Beijing Opera, its origins are not in Beijing but in the Chinese provinces of Anhui and Hubei. Beijing Opera got its two main melodies, Xipi and Erhuang, from Anhui and Hubei operas. Much dialogue is also carried out in an archaic dialect originating partially from those regions. It also absorbed music and arias from other operas and musical arts such as the historic Qinqiang as well as being very strongly influenced by Kunqu, the form that preceded it as court art. It is regarded that Beijing Opera was born when the Four Great Anhui Troupes came to Beijing in 1790. Beijing Opera was originally staged for the court and came into the public later. In 1828, some famous Hubei troupes came to Beijing. They often jointly performed in the stage with Anhui troupes. The combination gradually formed Beijing Opera's main melodies.

There are four main roles in Beijing Opera：Sheng (生 , Male role), Dan (旦 , Female role), Jing (净 , Painted face, male role), Chou (丑 , Clown role). The three roles other than the second role represent male characters. There is an explanation about why the roles take the names above. It is said that they were chosen to have opposite meanings to their Chinese characters. Sheng in Chinese may mean "strange" or "rare", but the chief male role is a well-known character. Dan, which means "morning" or "masculine", is contrary to the feminine nature of the characters. Jing means "clean", but in fact the paintings on their faces make the characters look unclean but colorful. And Chou in Chinese sometimes represents the animal "ox", which, in some senses, is slow and silent—in contrast, the Chou characters are usually quick and talkative.

When it comes to types of facial makeup in Beijing Opera, it is a national cosmetic with special feature. As each historical figure or a certain type of person has a certain type, just like we should sing and perform according to the score, so they are called "types of facial makeup in operas". It is reported to originate from mask.

Types of facial makeup in Beijing Opera are based on certain personality, temperament or some special types of figures for the use of certain colors. Red expresses the warriors of strong personae in operas such as Guan Yu, Jiang Wei, Chang Yuchun; black facial makeup in opera is for people with the character of integrity, bravery and even recklessness, such as Bao Zheng, Zhang Fei, and Li Kui; yellow ones represent vicious brutality, such as Yuwen Chengdu and Dian Wei; blue or green ones represent irritable characters, such as Dou Erdun, Ma Wu; white ones symbolize general treacherous court officials, such as Cao Cao, Zhao Gao.

Color painting methods of facial makeup in Beijing Opera are basically divided into three categories: kneaded face, smeared face and thickened face. Initial role of facial makeup in opera is to facilitate the development of the plot, by exaggerating the role with striking appearance, and personage's personality, psychological and physiological characteristics. Later types of facial makeup in opera become more complex, delicate, and profound. Itself becomes a national pictorial art which manifests facial expressions.

a. Answer the following questions according to the passage.

1. Exemplify the source of Beijing Opera.

_____

2. What are the characteristics of Beijing Opera?

_____

3. Give a brief introduction to the facial makeup in Beijing Opera.

_____

4. How many color painting methods are there in Beijing Opera?

_____

5. What is the function of facial makeup?
_____

b. *Translate the expressions into Chinese or English.*

1. cultural treasure　　　　　_____
　 culture shock　　　　　　_____
　 _____　　文化传播
　 cultural documentary　　　_____
2. _____　　最早的居民
　 an original idea　　　　　_____
　 an original thinker　　　　_____
　 _____　　原稿
3. an integral to human body　_____
　 _____　　完整的设计
　 an integrated transport scheme　_____
　 _____　　综合性格
4. take a profound interest in　_____
　 _____　　一声长叹
5. profound ignorance　　　_____
　 _____　　难解之谜

c. *Choose an appropriate word to fill in each blank to make each sentence meaningful, and change its form when necessary.*

| symbolize | integrity | precede | absorb | figure |
| originate | treasure | reckless | warrior | temperament |

1. The rich man always _____ the memory of the days spent with the poor but kind boy.
2. To be a champion, skill is not enough, you have to have the right _____.
3. The poet _____ his lover with a flower.
4. She _____ conspicuously in the public debate about the issue.
5. He is a man of _____ ; he never breaks his promises.
6. The floor is dry, for the water _____ by the sponge.
7. The young man has been fined for 100 dollars for _____ driving.
8. This point has been dealt with in the _____ chapters.

9. The Mongolian is a _____ nation.
10. This style of writing _____ from France.

d. Translate the following sentences into English with words given in the brackets.

1. 如果你是一个易怒的人，你可以尝试着打太极，它可以让你变得平静。(irritable)
_____

2. 新建的人民广场将使老年人的晨练变得更方便。(facilitate)
_____

3. 板球起源于英国，一度被称为"绅士的运动"。(originate)
_____

4. 国家剧院下月将演出《李尔王》。(present)
_____

5. 一个人是否能成为一个好导游很大程度上取决于他的气质。(temperament)
_____

Vocabulary List

absorb	[əbˈzɔːb]	v. 吸收
archaic	[ɑːˈkeɪɪk]	adj. 古老的，陈旧的
aria	[ˈɑːrɪə]	n. 咏叹调
brutality	[bruːˈtæləti]	n. 残忍，野蛮的行为
complex	[ˈkɒmpleks]	adj. 复杂的；合成的，综合的
cosmetic	[kɒzˈmetɪk]	adj. 化妆用的
court	[kɔːt]	n. 宫廷，朝廷
facilitate	[fəˈsɪlɪteɪt]	v. 使容易，使便利，帮助，促进
feminine	[ˈfemənɪn]	adj. 女性的
figure	[ˈfɪɡə]	n. 外形，轮廓，体形；图形；数字；身份 v. 表示，象征，认为
integrity	[ɪnˈteɡrəti]	n. 正直，诚实
irritable	[ˈɪrɪtəbl]	adj. 易怒的，急躁的
manifest	[ˈmænɪfest]	v. 表明，证明
masculine	[ˈmæskjəlɪn]	adj. 男性的，男子气概的
melody	[ˈmelədi]	n. 旋律，曲调
origin	[ˈɒrɪdʒɪn]	n. 起源，由来；起因；出身，血统

originate	[əˈrɪdʒɪneɪt]	v. 发起，起源，发生
partially	[ˈpɑːʃəli]	adv. 部分地
persona	[pəˈsəʊnə]	n. 人，戏剧中的角色 (pl. personae [pəˈsəʊnaɪ])
physiological	[ˌfɪziəˈlɒdʒɪk(ə)l]	adj. 生理学的，生理学上的
precede	[prɪˈsiːd]	v. 领先（于），在……之前
present	[ˈpreznt]	v. 赠给，呈现，提出
profound	[prəˈfaʊnd]	adj. 深刻的，意义深远的；渊博的；造诣深的
psychological	[ˌsaɪkəˈlɒdʒɪkl]	adj. 心理（上）的
reckless	[ˈrekləs]	adj. 不计后果的
represent	[ˌreprɪˈzent]	v. 表现，象征，提出异议
score	[skɔː]	n. 乐谱
symbolize	[ˈsɪmbəlaɪz]	v. 象征，作为……的象征
temperament	[ˈtemprəmənt]	n. 气质，性情
treacherous	[ˈtretʃərəs]	adj. 背叛的，奸诈的
treasure	[ˈtreʒə]	n. 财宝，财富 v. 珍爱，珍惜；储藏，珍藏
troupe	[truːp]	n. 剧团
vicious	[ˈvɪʃəs]	adj. 不道德的，堕落的，恶意的，品行不端的
warrior	[ˈwɒriə]	n. 战士，勇士，武士

Phrases

be regarded as	被看作……
originate from	起源于……
contrary to	与……相反
in contrast	相反

Terms

kneaded face	揉脸
smeared face	抹脸
thickened face	勾脸

Writing

Poster

Task 1 Writing Skills

海报是人们日常生活中极为常见的一种招贴形式，多用于电影、戏曲、比赛、文艺演出等活动。海报中通常要写清楚活动的性质，活动的主办单位、时间、地点等内容。海报的语言要求简明扼要，形式要做到新颖美观。

海报的格式，通常由三部分组成，即标题、正文与落款。

海报的标题对于海报的宣传极为重要，因此标题的撰写要做到简洁明快、新颖醒目，抓住读者的注意力。海报的标题形式通常有两种：一是直接使用"海报"（Poster）一词；另一种则是根据海报的内容撰写标题。

海报正文是海报的核心部分，它是对海报标题的具体描述。语言要求形象生动、简明扼要，要做到既有鼓动性，又不夸大其词。正文的常见表现形式有简介说明式和描述式两种。

落款写在最后，是活动的主办单位。

Task 2 Sample Writing

Sample 1

篮球赛的海报（简洁说明式）

Friendly Basketball Match

All Are Welcome

Organized by the Students' Union of our school, a friendly basketball match will be held between No. 3 Middle School team and ours on the basketball court on Saturday, June 5, at 4 P.M.

The School Students' Union

Tuesday, June 1st.

【译文】

篮球友谊赛

欢迎大家观看由我们学校学生会组织的我校篮球队和第三中学篮球队的友谊赛。

比赛时间：6月5日周六下午4点

校学生会

6月1日 周二

Sample 2

英语电影海报（描述式）

This Week's Film

Name：Modern Times

Time：7 P.M. Saturday, April 10th

Place：the Meeting Hall

Price：3 yuan

Ticket office：the school gate house

The School Students' Union

【译文】

本周电影

片名：摩登时代

放映时间：4月10日周六晚7点

地点：学生会堂

票价：3元

售票地点：学校门房

校学生会

Task 3　Writing Practice

Write two posters according to the information given.

1) 学术报告会

为纪念"五四"运动九十周年，特邀校友××博士来校作学术报告。

题目：知识经济时代的学习和工作

时间：5月4日14点

地点：校礼堂

欢迎全校师生踊跃参加

校学生会

2022年5月2日

2) 商品促销海报

好　消　息
夏季清仓物资处理

本店陈列商品一律八折出售。请顾客们仔细看货，认真挑选。商品一旦付款出门后不退不换，特此预先声明。如蒙惠顾，无比欢迎。

贝金森购物服务中心

Vocabulary Development

Words about Sports and hobbies

wrestling	摔跤
boxing	拳击
squash	壁球
golf	高尔夫
sailing	帆船
baseball	棒球
track and field	田径
rugby	英式橄榄球
cricket	板球
horse racing	赛马
motor racing	赛车
gardening	园艺
shooting	射击
knitting	编织
sewing	缝纫
cooking	烹饪
amateur dramatic performance	业余戏剧表演
painting	绘画

Words about Tour

China's category A travel agency	一类社
China's category B travel agency	二类社
China's category C travel agency	三类社
Clothes, wearing and appearance	服装仪表
guide book	旅游指南
guide practice	导游实践
international tourism	国际旅游
itinerary	旅行计划，节目
local guide	地陪，地方导游

local tourist organization	地方旅游组织
low season	淡季
tourist spots	旅游点
tourist trade	旅游业
travel	旅行
travel business	旅游业务
travel expert	旅游专家
travel industry	旅游业
travel journalist	旅游记者
travel press	旅游报纸
travel publication	旅游出版物
traveling	旅游
travel writer	旅游作家
trip	旅行
World Tourism Organization	世界旅游组织
Tourist Administration	旅游局
China's National Tourism Administration	中国国家旅游局
Provincial Tourism Administration	省旅游局
Autonomous Region Tourism Administration	自治区旅游局
Municipal Tourism Administration	市旅游局
Autonomous Prefecture Tourism Administration	自治州旅游局
County Tourism Administration	县旅游局

Unit 9

Local Tour Guide Services
地陪服务

Unit Objectives

After learning this unit, you should

- understand how to give local tour guide service;
- master the basic words and expressions about local tour guide service;
- get some cultural knowledge about local tour guide service;
- find ways to improve your writing skills about a Welcome Speech;
- be familiar with A Welcome Speech.

Background Knowledge

When we arrive at a tour destination, we will meet various types of tour attractions.

Types of Tour Attractions

1. natural attractions(自然景点): The natural beauty, recreation, such as landscape, seascape, parks, mountains, flora, coasts, islands, and so on.

2. commercial attractions(商业景点): Retail operations dealing in gifts, handcrafted goods, art, and souvenirs that attract tourists.

3. festival and events(节日和活动): Mega-events such as the Olympics, World Cup, and World Fairs or market, parade, celebration, anniversary, charitable endeavor, etc.

4. economic attractions(经济景点): Opportunities for the travelers to visit city facilities, but rarely attract foreign visitors.

5. cultural attractions(文化景点): The places in the country, either of architectural

value or associated with a particular person, family, or period.

6. man-made attractions（人造景点）：Such institutions as Disneyland.

Practice Materials

Listening

Dialogue 1

a. Listen to Dialogue 1 and decide whether each of the following sentences is true (T) or false (F).

1. _____ The woman wants to have a talk with the man.
2. _____ There are some changes for the tour itinerary.
3. _____ Millstone Hill is near East Lake.
4. _____ May Flower Hotel is a three-star hotel.
5. _____ The man will visit Yellow Crane Tower.

b. Listen to the dialogue and answer the following questions.

1. Where did the talk take place?

2. Which scenic spot will the man visit first?

3. Where will the man have lunch?

4. When will the man set off tomorrow morning?

5. What scenic spots will the man visit the next day?

Notes

1. itinerary   路线
2. spare   提供，付出
3. boast   自夸，以……为自豪
4. East Lake Scenic Area   东湖风景区
5. Millstone Hill   磨山
6. abundant   丰富的

7. Yellow Crane Tower	黄鹤楼	
8. Yangtze River	长江	
9. consideration	考虑	

Dialogue 2

Listen to the passage and supply the missing words.

Mt. Huangshan is the _____ of the two rivers of the Yangtze and Qiantang. It has long been famous for its _____, fantastically shaped rocks, sea of clouds and _____.

Mt. Huangshan pines are very special. Instead of taking roots in soil, they _____, showing the _____. The ancient Guest-Greeting Pine, rising high into the sky with its right hand _____ branches extending to _____, has long been the _____ of the mountain.

Clouds on this mountain swirl around _____, forming a "sea of clouds". The clouds on the mountain, according to its location, can be divided into East Sea, West Sea, South Sea, North Sea and _____.

Notes

1. watershed	分水岭	
2. odd	奇怪的，古怪的	
3. fantastically	奇异地，古怪地	
4. vigor	活力，精力	
5. pine	松树	
6. symbol	象征	

Background Information

元旦	New Year's Day (Jan. 1)
国际劳动妇女节	International Working Women's Day (Women's Day) (Mar. 8)
国际劳动节	International Labor Day (May Day) (May 1)
中国青年节	Chinese Youth Day (May 4)
国际儿童节	International Children's Day (Children's Day) (June 1)
中国共产党诞生纪念日	Anniversary of the Founding of the Communist Party of China (July 1)
建军节	Army Day (Aug. 1)

教师节	Teachers' Day (Sept. 10)
国庆节	National Day (Oct. 1)
春节 (农历正月初一)	the Spring Festival (New Year's Day of the Chinese lunar calendar)
元宵节 (农历正月十五)	the Lantern Festival
清明节 (四月五日前后)	the Qing Ming Festival (Tomb-sweeping Festival)
端午节 (农历五月初五)	the Dragon Boat Festival
中秋节 (农历八月十五)	the Mid-Autumn Festival (the Moon Festival)
重阳节 (农历九月初九)	the Double Ninth Festival

Speaking

Dialogue 1

A Bus Tour of London

A: Amy   **B**: Benjamin

A: We are on our way. I think our first stop is Buckingham Palace.

B: That's right. I can already see the Palace Garden on the left.

A: And here is Buckingham Palace! Look, isn't it beautiful? It is much bigger than I imagined.

B: The bus is turning right to Buckingham Gate. And now we are joining Victoria Street.

A: Yes we are going towards Westminster Abbey. I can see it now! Look at your right.

B: I can see it. The bus is stopping. I think we will be able to go inside.

A: This is amazing. I'm glad we decided to take this bus tour. So where next?

B: I guess we should see Big Ben soon.

A: Yes. It is just round the corner. Oh, can you see the London Eye? Look straight and to your right.

B: Look at this bridge. We will soon be crossing the Thames.

A: This is Lambeth Bridge. We will then loop back and cross the river again on Westminster Bridge.

B: Wonderful.

> **Notes**
>
> | | | |
> |---|---|---|
> | 1. | stop | 停靠站 |
> | 2. | Buckingham Palace | 白金汉宫（英国王宫） |
> | 3. | Palace Garden | 御花园，皇宫花园 |
> | 4. | Buckingham Gate | 白金汉门 |
> | 5. | Victoria Street | 维多利亚街 |
> | 6. | Westminster Abbey | 威斯敏斯特大教堂（英国名人墓地） |
> | 7. | bus tour | 巴士旅游 |
> | 8. | amazing | 令人惊讶的，惊人的 |
> | 9. | Big Ben | 大本钟 |
> | 10. | the London Eye | 伦敦眼（摩天轮） |
> | 11. | the Thames | 泰晤士河 |
> | 12. | Lambeth Bridge | 拉姆贝斯桥 |
> | 13. | loop back | 返回，转回头 |
> | 14. | Westminster Bridge | 威斯敏斯特桥 |

Dialogue 2

Walking on the Fifth Avenue

A: Isn't it wonderful to take a walk here?

B: What do you mean?

A: I mean one can look at all these magnificent tall buildings around him.

B: You mean the skyscrapers? Do you really think you like them? Don't you think it's a bit suffocating standing under them?

A: Not as an occasional visitor. It'd be a different story, of course, if one should have to be here every day.

B: Look at that building across the street from us. That's the Empire State. It stands at 102 stories high.

A: I know the name. It's quite famous but don't you think it looks a bit old-fashioned as compared with some others?

B: You're right and it's no longer the tallest building in New York now.

A: What other important buildings are we going to see on the Fifth Avenue?

B: Quite a number. Actually every skyscraper has a history. A few blocks ahead we'll see St. Patrick's Cathedral at E 50th Street and just across the street will be the world-renowned Rockefeller Center. It's a landmark in the history of architecture.

A: What's there after that?

B: We'll then be standing at where the Central Park begins. Facing the park on the Fifth Avenue are probably the most expensive apartments in the world.

A: I don't think we'll be able to visit the inside of those apartments. But what are all these skyscrapers for?

B: Mostly they are office buildings and huge department stores. New York is financial center of the world, isn't it?

Notes

1. the Fifth Avenue	第五大道
2. magnificent	宏伟的，壮丽的，令人印象深刻的
3. skyscraper	摩天大楼
4. suffocating	令人窒息的
5. occasional	偶尔的，不经常的
6. the Empire State	帝国大厦
7. a bit	稍微，有点儿
8. old-fashioned	老式的，过时的，不时髦的
9. no longer	不再
10. block	街区
11. St. Patrick's Cathedral	圣帕特里克教堂
12. world-renowned	举世闻名的
13. Rockefeller Center	洛克菲勒中心
14. landmark	地标
15. architecture	建筑学，建筑风格，建筑式样
16. the Central Park	中央公园
17. apartment	公寓（套房）
18. what (...) for	为了什么目的，（某物）有何用
19. office building	办公楼
20. department store	百货商店
21. financial center	金融中心

Dialogue 3

Visiting the Imperial Palace

Tourist: Mr. Li, could you tell us why the Palace Museum has another name—the

Forbidden City?

Guide: Sure. The Palace Museum is the official name given by the Government of New China to the imperial palace of the Ming and Qing Dynasties. It was where the emperors lived. Common people were not permitted to approach it, so it is called the Forbidden City.

Tourist: I heard that the gardens and buildings were numerous. How did the emperors arrange those palaces, halls, houses and towers?

Guide: The palace is divided into two main sections. The southern part is the outer court for holding ceremonies; while the northern one, the inner court, was used as the living quarters for the emperor and his family.

Tourist: Look, what a brilliant building it is!

Guide: The Hall of Supreme Harmony is the largest hall in the Forbidden City. Many important ceremonies were held in this hall, for example, the celebration of the Spring Festival, the enthronement of an emperor or the celebration of the emperor's birthday.

Tourist: We're now in the inner court, right? The bulletin tells us that this building is called the Palace of Heavenly Purity.

Guide: Yes. This is the central building in the inner court where the Ming emperors used to live. And here is the Palace of Earthly Tranquility where the emperor and the empress had to spend their wedding night.

Tourist: Where did Empress Dowager Cixi hold court from behind a screen?

Guide: It is in the chamber of the Hall of Mental Cultivation. Ladies and gentlemen, we're going to take a rest in the Imperial Garden. And you can also find pavilions, rare flowers and ancient pines and cypresses.

Notes

1. Forbidden City	紫禁城
2. numerous	无数的
3. brilliant	辉煌的，壮丽的
4. Hall of Supreme Harmony	太和殿
5. enthronement	即位，登基典礼
6. Palace of Heavenly Purity	乾清宫
7. the Palace of Earthly Tranquility	坤宁宫
8. Empress Dowager Cixi	慈禧太后
9. Hall of Mental Cultivation	养心殿

10. Imperial Garden 御花园
11. pavilion 亭，阁
12. cypress 柏树

Task Practice

Make a dialogue of introducing a scenic spot with your classmates.

 Reading

Passage 1

A Welcome Speech

Good morning, ladies and gentlemen!

Welcome to Wuhan! We are leaving the airport for May Flower Hotel where you will stay tonight. Now we are on our way to the hotel. Please sit back and relax. Your luggage will be sent to the hotel by another coach, so you don't have to worry about it.

First, let me introduce my colleague. This is Mr. Li, our driver. He has more than 20 years of driving experience. My name is Liu Yan, and my English name is Amy. You can just call me Amy or Xiao Liu. We are from China Wuhan International Travel Service. On behalf of the travel service and my colleague, I'd like to extend a warm-hearted welcome to all of you. During your stay in Wuhan, I will be your local guide. We'll try our best to make your visit go smoothly. If you have any problems, please don't hesitate to tell us. My mobile phone number is 139×××× 6458. I'll have it switched on for 24 hours. Don't hesitate to contact me whenever you need to.

Now, we are on the way to our hotel. It is a three-star hotel in the downtown areas of Wuchang. Now, to your left, we are driving across the famous Wuhan Yangtze River Bridge, which was built up in 1957 and is the earliest highway-railway bridge over the Yangtze River. Our dear Chairman Mao once wrote a poem praising for it, for it links Wuchang to Hanyang and turns a huge natural channel into a man-made broad way. From the bridge, you can see the rolling water run to the east with ships going back and forth on it. Attention, please! There are two magnificent buildings setting at the two ends of the bridge. They are Yellow Crane Tower and Guishan Television Tower. They are all landmarks of Wuhan and respectively represent the brilliant history and thriving present of Wuhan.

Ladies and gentlemen! Wuhan is a city with a long history and bright culture. It is one of the famous historical and cultural cities ratified by the State Council. So you will feast your eyes on both cultural sites and natural sites. The well-known scenic spots you're going to visit include East Lake Scenic Area, Millstone Hill, Yellow Crane Tower, Guiyuan Buddhist Temple, just to name a few. "I like to eat the delicious hot-and-dry noodles; I like to wear the cotton jacket I bought on Han Zheng Street; I like to live near the flourishing Liuduqiao area; I like to cross each bridge over the Yangtze," writes a Chinese Wuhan resident. The saying exactly summarizes the features of Wuhan. Now we are arriving at Yuema Square. Can you see a statue in the square? It's over there, a big statue of Dr. Sun Yat-sen, a great figure in the earlier twentieth century in China.

As an old Chinese saying goes, "Isn't it delightful to meet friends from afar?" I am very happy to see you from the other side of the Pacific Ocean—the United States of America. I shall do my best to make tour trip pleasant. Tonight we shall hold a welcome party for you. I hope you will enjoy the wonderful Wuhan snacks. At the party, I shall tell you the itinerary of your one-day tour in Wuhan.

Oh, the coach is so fast. We have arrived at May Flower Hotel. Now, please get off one by one, and follow me to check in.

Thank you for your cooperation!

a. Answer the following questions according to the passage.

1. Exemplify some famous scenic spots in Wuhan.

   _____

2. What characteristics does Wuhan have?

   _____

3. Give a brief introduction to the Wuhan Yangtze River Bridge.

   _____

4. Which building represents the brilliant history of Wuhan?

   _____

5. When will the guide announce the tour itinerary?

   _____

b. Translate the expressions into Chinese.

1. China Wuhan International Travel Service _____
2. on behalf of   _____
3. a warm-hearted welcome   _____
4. go smoothly   _____

5. switch on _____

6. Guiyuan Buddhist Temple _____

7. Isn't it delightful to meet friends from afar? _____

c. Choose an appropriate word to fill in each blank to make each sentence meaningful, and change its form when necessary.

| hesitate | rolling | landmark | thrive | ratify |
| summarize | extend | downtown | represent | flourish |

1. It may be briefly _____ in the following outline.
2. He orientated himself by finding a familiar _____.
3. You can _____ your knowledge by reading books.
4. Their business flourished when they moved _____.
5. Phonetic symbols _____ sounds.
6. The heads of the two governments met to _____ the treaty.
7. This species of flower _____ in a warm climate.
8. Our country is _____ and prospering day by day.
9. The coin _____ underneath the piano.
10. He _____ over the choice between the two suits.

d. Translate the following sentences into English with words or phrases given in the brackets.

1. 这家旅馆欢迎乘旅游车来的旅游团。(coach)
_____

2. 几乎没有动植物能在沙漠中生长得很好。(thrive)
_____

3. 我们去罗马前必须把事情安排得妥当些。(leave for)
_____

4. 旅途中我们饱览了美景。(feast one's eyes on)
_____

5. 看着电视上被日益破坏的生态环境而不采取行动是很困难的。(sit back)
_____

Vocabulary List

coach	[kəʊtʃ]	n./v. 四轮大马车；长途汽车
downtown	[ˈdaʊntaʊn]	adv./adj. 在市区，住市区；市区的
extend	[ɪkˈstend]	v. 扩充，延伸；给予，提供
figure	[ˈfɪgə]	n. 身份；人物
itinerary	[aɪˈtɪnərəri]	n. 路线
landmark	[ˈlændmɑːk]	n. (航海)陆标，地界标；里程碑，划时代的事
luggage	[ˈlʌgɪdʒ]	n. 行李，皮箱
magnificent	[mægˈnɪfɪsnt]	adj. 华丽的；高尚的；宏伟的
ratify	[ˈrætɪfaɪ]	vt. 批准，认可
rolling	[ˈrəʊlɪŋ]	adj./n. 转动的，摇摆的，起伏的；旋转，翻滚，动摇
snack	[snæk]	n./v. 小吃，快餐；一份；吃快餐(小吃)
summarize	[ˈsʌməraɪz]	v. 概述，总结
thrive	[θraɪv]	v. 兴旺，繁荣；茁壮成长，旺盛

Phrases

sit back	不采取行动；休息一下
switch on	接通
build up	逐步建立，逐步形成
feast one's eyes on	饱眼福

Terms

Guishan Television Tower	龟山电视塔
Guiyuan Buddhist Temple	归元寺
Han Zheng Street	汉正街
Liuduqiao area	六渡桥
Hot-and-dry noodles	热干面
Wuhan Yangtze River Bridge	武汉长江大桥
Yuema Square	阅马场

Passage 2

Visiting Badaling Great Wall

The Great Wall is a symbol of Chinese civilization, and one of the wonders that the Chinese people have created. Badaling Great Wall, the most representative part, was promoted as a key national cultural relic, protected under the approval of the State Council in 1961. In 1988, it was enlisted in the World Cultural Heritage Directory by UNESCO. July 7, 2007 has once again witnessed the worldwide reputation that the Great Wall gained—it was listed among the New Seven Wonders of the World.

Guide: We are heading for a place called Badaling. You'll be able to get a very clear view of the Wall from there. Badaling is a mountain about 1,000 meters above sea level. The Great Wall runs along its ridge.

Tourist: How far is it from Beijing?

Guide: 75 kilometers to the northwest of Beijing. We're almost there now. We've been climbing for the past thirty minutes.

Tourist: So I noticed.

Guide: The car will take us right to the foot of the Wall—here we are.

Tourist: So this is the famous Wall. How high is it?

Guide: The average height is about 7.5 meters and at this point it's 5.4 meters wide at the top. These steps will take us up there.

Tourist: Let's go. Oh, what a marvelous sight, just like a giant serpent winding its way over the mountains! It's really breath-taking. How long is the Wall? I wonder.

Guide: It runs all the way across the eastern half of China. The length is about 12,000 li or 6,000 kilometers. That's why we call it "Wan Li Chang Cheng" in Chinese, which literally means "The Ten-Thousand-li-Long Wall".

Tourist: 6,000 kilometers! No wonder it's said that this Wall is the only building that could be seen from the moon.

Guide: Exactly! It's the pride of Chinese people, and a precious world cultural heritage.

Tourist: What are these towers on the wall spaced at regular distances from each other?

Guide: They're fortresses.

Tourist: I can see lots of people going up there. Can we go up, too?

Guide: Certainly. Let's walk to the fortress on that peak... You know, the guards used to light bonfires when they were being attacked. The troops stationed along the Wall would then know where to consolidate their defenses.

Tourist: I see. Look at these huge stone slabs! I wonder how they were moved up the hills without machinery.

Guide: It's amazing, isn't it? It really shows the ingenuity of the working people in ancient times.

Tourist: The wall was really a tremendous engineering feat. The amount of labor that went into it must have been enormous. Now tell me again, when was the Wall built and how long did it take to do it?

Guide: The Wall was first started about 2,300 years ago.

Tourist: That's a long time ago.

Guide: Yes, it is. You see, China is a country with many nationalities. At that time China was not unified but consisted of a number of vassal states. They often fought among themselves. The rival states in central China built walls to protect themselves from each other.

Tourist: I see. So there were different walls originally, all disconnected and separating the various vassal states.

Guide: That's right. It was only after Qin Shi Huang brought these states under a unified rule that the separate walls were linked into one.

Tourist: Who was that?

Guide: Qin Shi Huang, the first emperor of the Qin Dynasty.

Tourist: Now I recall having read something about him. Wasn't he the first man who had succeeded in unifying China?

Guide: Yes, he was. China has had a long history as a unified nation since his time.

Tourist: Ha, a good memory I have. Now, let's get back to the Great Wall.

Guide: Well, we aren't too far off the track. After the unification of China, Qin Shi Huang erected a long wall, by linking up and adding to the separate walls already existing. The work took more than ten years to finish. Actually, the new walls added for the joining were even greater than that of the original walls.

Tourist: Really?

Guide: Now, this is the farthest point we can go. We haven't restored the whole length of the wall, and from here, the going gets rather rough. Let's sit down here and rest for a while before we turn back. You must be rather tired after the climb.

Tourist: Yes, it's steeper than it looks.

Guide: After our lunch we'll go on to the Ming Tombs.

a. Answer the following questions according to the passage.

1. Why is the Great Wall called "Wan Li Chang Cheng" in Chinese?

_____

2. What were the fortresses used for?

_____

3. Give a brief introduction to the history of the Great Wall.
_____

4. How long did it take to finish the Qin Great Wall?
_____

5. What is the average height of Badaling Great Wall?
_____

b. Translate the expressions into English.

1. _____   国家重点文化遗址
2. _____   国务院
3. _____   世界文化遗产名录
4. _____   联合国教科文组织
5. _____   新世界七大奇迹
6. _____   诸侯国

c. Choose an appropriate word or phrase to fill in each blank to make each sentence meaningful, and change its form when necessary.

| consolidate | ingenuity | run | off the track | restore | head for |
| wind one's way | no wonder | protect...from | | recall | link up |

1. Clouds are gathering, I think we'd better _____ the zoo in case it starts to rain.
2. The road _____ through the mountains.
3. The stream _____ through the woods.
4. But I really can't _____ your name at this moment.
5. You'll never work it out by that method, you are _____ altogether.
6. Arrangements were well advanced for _____ this newly operated length of motorway with the Lancaster bypass.
7. It's _____ that the children love to visit the farm.
8. You'd better wear dark glasses to _____ your eyes _____ the sun.
9. She _____ her power during her first year in office.
10. The boy showed _____ in making toys.
11. The government planned to _____ the ruined abbey.

d. Translate the following sentences into English with words or phrases given in the brackets.

1. 我们拂晓时开航，直接驶向罗德岛。(head for)

_____

2. 这条路顺着河岸延伸。(run along)

_____

3. 这个纪念碑是为夏洛特女王而建立的。(erect)

_____

4. 这个山顶常年被白雪覆盖。(peak)

_____

5. 作为旅游中心，它不亚于欧洲的任何一个地方。(rival)

_____

Vocabulary List

bonfire	[ˈbɒnfaɪə]	n. 大篝火，营火
breath-taking	[ˈbreθˈteɪkɪŋ]	adj. 惊人的
consolidate	[kənˈsɒlɪdeɪt]	v. 巩固
dynasty	[ˈdɪnəsti]	n. 朝代，王朝
erect	[ɪˈrekt]	adj. 直立的，竖立的；v. 盖，使竖立，使直立；树立，建立
feat	[fiːt]	n. 技艺，功绩，武艺，壮举，技艺表演
fortress	[ˈfɔːtrəs]	n. 堡垒，要塞
ingenuity	[ˌɪndʒəˈnjuːəti]	n. 机灵，独创性
literally	[ˈlɪtərəli]	adv. 照字面意义，逐字地
machinery	[məˈʃiːnəri]	n. [总称] 机器，机械
originally	[əˈrɪdʒənəli]	adv. 最初，原先
peak	[piːk]	n. 山顶，顶点；(记录的) 最高峰
rival	[ˈraɪvl]	n. 竞争者，对手；v. 竞争，对抗，相匹敌
slab	[slæb]	n. 厚平板，厚片；混凝土路面；板层
serpent	[ˈsɜːpənt]	n. 大毒蛇，阴险的人
tremendous	[trəˈmendəs]	adj. 极大的，巨大的
unification	[ˌjuːnɪfɪˈkeɪʃn]	n. 统一，合一，一致
vassal	[ˈvæs(ə)l]	adj. 臣属的，诸侯的

Phrases

a tremendous engineering feat	一项庞大的工程（成就）
no wonder	难怪
stone slab	石板
head for	开往，前往（某地）
run along	沿着……延伸，延续
succeed in	在……方面成功
wind one's way	弯曲前进，迂回
off the track	离题，出轨

Terms

Badaling	八达岭
vassal states	诸侯国
the Ming Tombs	明十三陵
the Qin Dynasty	秦朝
the World Cultural Heritage Directory	世界文化遗产名录
UNESCO	联合国教科文组织

Writing

A Welcome Speech

Task 1 Writing Skills

"欢迎词"代表着一段旅行的开始，决定导游给游客留下怎样的第一印象。一篇好的欢迎词能很快地拉近导游和游客的距离，中外游客大都注重第一印象，因此致好欢迎词非常重要。一篇好的欢迎词应具备五个要素：

(1) 表示欢迎，即代表接待社、组团社向客人表达欢迎之意。

(2) 介绍人员，即介绍自己，介绍参加接待的领导、司机及所有人员。

(3) 预告项目，即介绍一下城市的概况和在当地将游览的项目。

(4) 表示态度，即愿意为大家热情服务、努力工作，确保大家满意。

(5) 预祝成功，即希望得到游客的支持与合作，努力使游览获得成功，祝大家愉快健康。

以下是概括上面所提及的五个要素的典型表达法：

Ladies and gentlemen,

Welcome to … ! May I introduce my Chinese colleagues to you? This is Mr. … from

China International Travel Service. He will travel with you throughout the trip in China. This is Mr. ..., our driver. His bus number is 235456. My name is Wang Feng. I am from ... city. My job is to smooth your way, care for your welfare, try my best to answer your questions, and be your guide during your stay in ... . If you have any special interest, please tell your tour leader and he will let us know. We'll try our best to make your stay in ... a pleasant one. We highly appreciate your understanding and cooperation.

欢迎词切忌死板、沉闷，如能风趣，自然会缩短与游客的距离，使大家成为朋友，很快熟悉起来。在以上五个基本要素的基础之上，导游还应根据游览景点、城市的类型和特点以及游客的身份、职业、国籍等情况，有针对性地、因地制宜地灵活展开自己的欢迎词。当然，如在欢迎词中加上一两句中国好客的谚语或格言，如"有朋自远方来，不亦乐乎"（Isn't it delightful to meet friends from afar？）或 We are so happy to have friends like you coming from afar.）、"有缘千里来相会"（No distance can prevent friends getting together.）等，将会增色不少。

Task 2 Sample Writing

Good morning, ladies and gentlemen,

Welcome to Wuhan! We are so happy to have friends like you coming from afar. First, please allow me to introduce myself. My name is Liu Yan. My surname is Liu, so you can call me Xiao Liu. And this is Mr. Li, our driver, who has had 20 years of driving experience. We come from Wuhan International Travel Service. On behalf of our company and our colleagues, we'd like to extend a warm welcome to you all.

I'll be your local tour guide during your two-day tour in this city and we'll be at your service at any time. We'll do everything possible to make your visit a pleasant experience. If you have any problems or suggestions, please don't hesitate to let us know.

Wuhan is the place to find both history and natural wonders. Its long history dates back to 3,500 years ago. It is the biggest hub city in Central China. Divided by the Yangtze, Wuhan has come to be known as the Three Towns of Wuhan with Hankou and Hanyang on the west bank, and Wuchang on the east. That is why Wuhan has the nickname of "city of river". Hubei Provincial Museum and Yellow Crane Tower are two places to appreciate ancient Chinese history and culture. Two famous places for local Wuhan snacks are Ji Qing Jie Night Street and Hu Bu Xiang breakfast street. Time-honored Han Zheng Street and the bustling walking street near Jiang Han Road are two choices for shopping lovers. They are all listed in your two-day tour itinerary. Put Wuhan on your itinerary and you will not be disappointed.

We have reserved two suits and eight twin beds for you at the May Flower Hotel. It is a three-star hotel in the downtown areas of Wuchang. We shall meet at the lobby at 7:30 A.M. for our first visit tomorrow. Please do remember the plate number of our bus. The number is 235645. Thank you.

We hope you'll enjoy your stay in this city.

Common Sentence Patterns of Tour Guides

1. Do you wish to put any changes into the itinerary?
你们想对旅游线路做改动吗?

2. We will start at 7:00 tomorrow morning from the hotel lobby.
我们明早七点从酒店大堂出发。

3. It takes an hour to arrive at the Yuyuan Garden.
到达豫园需一小时。

4. You'll have a good chance to feast your eyes on the lake.
你们将有机会饱览湖上美景。

5. May I have your attention to the mountains in the distance? What a view of grand scenery!
请大家注意远处的群山,一幅多么美丽的景象啊!

6. If you look in this direction, you can see the picture of a tiger on the cliff.
你们从这个方向看,可以看到老虎在悬崖上。

7. The place is famous (noted / well-known) for its silk and pottery.
此地以丝绸和陶器闻名。

8. This tower boasts the tallest building in Asia.
此塔以亚洲最高的建筑闻名。

9. Now we are at the center of the garden.
现在我们在花园中心。

10. Can any of you tell me the height of the pagoda?
谁能告诉我宝塔的高度是多少?

Task 3   Writing Practice

a. Finish the following welcome speech by translating the Chinese in the brackets into English.

_____ (大家好):

_____! (欢迎你们到北京来) _____! (有朋自远方来,不亦乐乎)

_____ (请允许我在这里做一下自我介绍) first. My name is

Tom Li, from Beijing International Travel Service. _____ (我代表)our company and colleagues, _____ (欢迎大家来我们地区旅游). In the days to follow, I'll be accompanying you to tour the beautiful lakes and mountains in this region. _____ (竭诚使你们一路游览愉快) unique from that of your previous tour. _____ (这位是我们的司机王师傅). _____ (我们的车号是) 34256. _____ (大家记好了) so that you might not get on the wrong bus. _____ (在旅途中大家如果有什么要求及困难，尽管提出来). We will try our best to help you and _____ (我们将随时为大家服务).

b. Write a welcome speech according to the situation below. Add more information if necessary.

假如你是一名英语导游，你要负责接待一个来自海外的旅游团，他们将在你所在的城市游览观光。在从机场到宾馆的路上你需给游客们致欢迎词，欢迎词的内容应包括五个基本要素。

Model

Good morning, ladies and gentlemen,

Welcome to Hangzhou! I'm Angela, the local guide of your tour in Hangzhou, and I'm from Hangzhou International Travel Service. This is Mr. Wang, our driver. He has 20 years of driving experience. Here we'd like to extend a warm welcome to you all.

There is a famous Chinese saying: "Just as there is a paradise in heaven, there are Suzhou and Hangzhou on earth". From the saying we can imagine how beautiful and special Hangzhou is! In the following two-day-tour, you are sure to have an exciting and unforgettable experience. Your included sightseeing tour features visits to Lingyin Temple, Yue Temple and the West Lake. You'll be fascinated by the historical sites and natural scenes of the city.

We hope you'll enjoy the tour. We'll be at your service at any time and do everything possible to make your visit a pleasant experience. If you have any problems or suggestions, please don't hesitate to let us know. My phone number is ... and our bus number is ... Once again, wish you enjoy your stay in Hangzhou.

Vocabulary Development

fort, fortress	堡垒
castle	城堡
long corridor	长廊

hall	殿
vault	拱顶
drum-tower	鼓楼
lotus pond	荷塘
lakeside rocks and rockeries	湖石假山
altar	祭坛
watchtower	角楼
Bridge of Nine Turnings	九曲桥
corridor	廊；回廊
emperor's mausoleum/tomb	陵墓
tower, mansion	楼
pailou, decorated archway	牌楼
bridge	桥
pavilion on the water	水榭
pagoda, tower	塔
terrace	台
staircase	梯
pavilion	亭阁
pavilions, terraces and towers (a general reference to the elaborate Chinese architecture)	亭台楼阁
stream	溪流
temporary imperial palace	行宫
bell-tower	钟楼
pillar, column, post	柱
inscriptions on a tablet	碑刻，碑文，碑铭
forest of steles, forest of tabtets	碑林
pedestal of the tablet	碑座
mural	壁画
fresco	湿壁画
mountain resort	避暑山庄
summer resort	避暑胜地
winter resort	冬季旅游胜地
holiday resort	度假胜地
Buddhist resort	佛教圣地
ski resort	滑雪胜地

iceberg	冰山
volcano	火山
green hill	青山
site, venue, locale, seat	场所
unearth	出土
Taoist temple	道观
Taoist mountain	道教名山
embankment	堤防
buried legion	地下军团
sculpture	雕塑
statue	雕像
summit	顶点
token of love	定情之物
cave, cavern	洞穴，岩洞
antique replica	仿古制品
replica	复制品
superior workmanship	高超工艺
lone cypress	孤柏
antique, antiquity, curio	古董
place of historical interest	古迹
ancient architectural / building complex	古建筑群
ancient tomb	古墓
age-old pine trees	古松
antique / curio shop	古玩店
national park	国家公园
sea level	海平面
rank first of the five great mountains in China	号称五岳之首
descendant	后裔
inscriptions on bones and tortoise shells	甲骨文
rockery	假山
architectural style	建筑风格
south of the lower reaches of the Yangtze River	江南水乡
spectacle	景象
appreciate the charms of natural landscape	领略自然景观的魅力
honeymoon resort	蜜月度假胜地

famous mountain / mountain resort	名山
famous mountains and great rivers	名山大川
carved out of a cliff	摩崖石刻
waterfall, fall	瀑布
cascade	小瀑布
plunging waterfall	飞瀑
Qufu	曲阜
winding path	曲径
places of historic figures and cultural heritage	人文景观
artifact	人造物品
sunrise	日出
sunset	日落
water-eroded cave	溶洞
Karst scenery	熔岩景色，喀斯特地貌
stone boat	石舫
calcified pond	石灰池
limestone cave	石灰岩洞
grotto	石窟
stone steles	石碑
stone bridge	石桥
stalagmite	石笋
portrait stone	石像
the eighth wonder of the world	世界第八大奇迹
seven wonders of the world	世界七大奇迹
World Heritage Sites (WHS)	世界文化遗产保护地
Window of the World	世界之窗
calligraphic relics	书法真迹
riverside scenery	水乡景色
private garden	私家园林
four wonders	四大奇观
miniature	缩影
the most spectacular cave unparalleled elsewhere in the world	天下第一洞
the finest spring under heaven	天下第一泉
Wudang martial arts	武当功夫

perilous peaks	险峰
Shangri-la (earthly paradise or utopia—generally secluded and peaceful)	香格里拉
inlay	镶嵌
renovate	修复
snow-topped peaks	雪峰
snow-capped mountain	雪山
glazed tile	釉面砖
imperial garden	御花园
garden architecture	园林建筑
virgin forest	原始森林
algae	藻类
botanical garden	植物园
theme park	主题公园
natural attraction / landscape / scenery	自然景观
building complex	综合建筑
sitting Buddha	坐佛

Visiting Places of Interest

参观游览

Unit Objectives

After learning this unit, you should

- understand how to give information about the places you are visiting;
- master the basic words and expressions about introducing places of interest;
- get some cultural knowledge about the places you are visiting;
- find ways to improve your writing skills about Travel Route;
- be familiar with some domestic famous places of interest.

Background Knowledge

Before traveling, it is quite essential for us to get some information about the places we are heading for voluntarily or through the travel agency. The places may be historic architectures, ancient relics, museums, theme parks, art galleries or even safari parks.

Types of Places of Interest

1. Ancient relics（古代遗迹）: the Ruins of Yin Dynasty...

2. Historic architectures: the Great Wall, the Yellow Crane Tower, the Great Wild Goose Pagoda ...

3. Museums: the Museum of Emperor Qin Shi Huang's Tomb Figures of Soldiers and Horses, the Palace Museum...

4. Parks and Gardens: the Summer Palace, Zhongshan Park...

5. Theme Parks: Disneyland, Happy Valley...

6. Safari Parks: Badaling Wild Animal Zoo...

7. Art Galleries: National Art Museum of China...

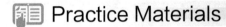 Practice Materials

Listening

Dialogue 1

a. Listen to Dialogue 1 and decide whether each of the following sentences is true (T) or false (F).

1. The man wants to go to the Badaling Great Wall.
2. They may reach there in about 75 minutes.
3. They need to turn right at the third crossing before they reach Qinghua Donglu.
4. They will be driving on the expressway for about 53 kilometers.
5. The route is really complex.

b. Listen to the dialogue and answer the following questions.

1. How are the man and his family traveling?

2. Does the local resident speak English?

3. How do they know when they should leave the expressway?

4. How long will they travel till they get to their destination?

5. Who can they turn to when they lost their way again?

c. Listen to the dialogue again and supply the missing words.

1. If there is _____, it will be around three quarters of an hour.
2. That will not be _____, but you have a long way to go.
3. That's not so _____. I have noted.
4. I will _____ to the tunnels.
5. There will be services provided in English by _____.

> **Notes**
>
> 1. fly-drive package tour   自驾游
> 2. Badaling Wild Animal Zoo   八达岭野生动物园
> 3. traffic jam   塞车
> 4. expressway   高速公路
> 5. tunnel   隧道
> 6. China Telecom   中国电信

Dialogue 2

a. Listen to Dialogue 2 and decide whether each of the following sentences is true (T) or false (F).

1. The trip will begin on October 24th.
2. The man will lose 20% of his money which he paid for the trip.
3. A copy of the ID card is needed to join the trip.
4. The travel agency will charge an extra for the transfer of the subscriber.
5. The staff will be on duty at 4:30 P.M. on Saturday.

b. Listen to the dialogue and answer the following questions.

1. What's the name of the travel agency?
   _____

2. What's the man's name?
   _____

3. What are the solutions if he doesn't want to cancel the trip?
   _____

4. Why is a copy of the ID card needed?
   _____

5. When is it OK for the man to go to the travel agency on Wednesday?
   _____

c. Listen to the dialogue again and supply the missing words.

1. I got registered in one of your _____ to Tibet last week.
2. I regret to tell you that if you cancel your _____, you will _____.
3. I am sorry that we can do nothing as it is _____.
4. A fee of 20 yuan will be charged for _____.
5. What time is suitable for us to carry out those _____?

Notes

1. China Travel Service	中国旅行社
2. register	注册，登记
3. escorted tour	全程陪同旅游
4. abrupt	突然地
5. cancel	取消
6. penalty	违约金
7. stipulate	规定
8. suspend	推迟
9. transfer	转让
10. departure	出发
11. accomplish	完成
12. with regard to	关于
13. accommodation	住宿
14. subscriber	签署者
15. procedure	手续

Speaking

Dialogue 1

Planning a Vacation

Alyssa: Hey Matt, how is your winter break so far?

Matthew: Oh, it's awesome! My parents are off to Cuba, and I'm free all the time.

Alyssa: Wow, lucky you. You know what? Why don't we go on a vacation?

Matthew: Great idea. But, wherever we are heading for, Cuba is not an option. Gees, what if my parents find out?

Alyssa: Too risky, eh? Umm, what about Hainan? China? It's a great place!

Matthew: Yeah, I have always been yearning to visit that place. Isn't it one of China's largest islands? I love coconuts. Think about it: the amazing beach, the delicate local food...

Alyssa: Oh my god, please, stop daydreaming already! We have to plan it! What are we supposed to bring? I mean, it's winter! We can't just bring like summer T-Shirt, bikini, chilling out at the beach!

Matthew: No way. Hainan is in the south, so I bet it's going to be scorching and hot all year long. I can't wait to swim there!

Alyssa: I am definitely bringing a jacket, a coat, some long-sleeved shirts, some tank tops and T-shirts. Oh ya, and my precious diary...

Matthew: A camera, swimming suit, definitely. I want to bring my little brother Ethan along, is that OK?

Alyssa: Sure, I was thinking of telling Julia and Brittany to join us as well! OK, now, we have to book a hotel.

Matthew: Leave it to me. I will go with Holiday Inn. Is that OK?

Alyssa: All right, thanks. So now, all the preparation work is done. I am going home and start packing. I've got to call Brittany and Julia. Phone me when you have booked the hotel, OK?

Matthew: No problem. I will get the packing done as well.

Alyssa: See you soon, Matt. I hope the vacation is going to be wonderful!

Matthew: I hope so, too. Bye.

Notes

1. winter break — 寒假
2. option — 选择
3. yearn for — 渴望
4. coconut — 椰子
5. delicate — 精致的
6. bikini — 比基尼
7. chill out — 放松
8. scorching — 灼热的
9. tank top — 背心
10. Holiday Inn — 假日酒店

Dialogue 2

Asking for Tourist Information

(Jenny is on an independent tour in Beijing. Now she is asking some information in a travel agency.)

Assistant: Do you need more information?

Jenny: Definitely, yes. I'd like to visit the Summer Palace. When is a good time to visit it?

Assistant: You can usually visit it between 9 A.M. and 6 P.M.

Jenny: I see. And what about the museums in Beijing?

Assistant: Yes, there are a few good museums. We have brochures about all of them. What kind of museums interests you?

Jenny: I like museums about history.

Assistant: Well, I think you would really like this one: the Palace Museum, the most famous at home and abroad, in which you can find many antiques.

Jenny: It sounds great. When is it open?

Assistant: At this time of year, it opens between 8:30 A.M. and 4:30 P.M.. But you must enter the museum before 3:30 P.M., for after that time you won't be able to finish your visiting.

Jenny: And how much does it cost?

Assistant: As it is in the peak season now, it is 60 yuan for adults and 20 yuan for children who are above 120 centimeters.

Jenny: Thank you.

Assistant: You're welcome.

Jenny: Oh, one last question: is there any special restaurant near there? You know, food always appeals to tourists.

Assistant: Of course! There are restaurants such as Quanjude, near the Front Door, which is one of China Time-honored Brands and famous for roast duck; Donglaishun, east to the plaza, which is famous for its rinsed mutton; and if you love hot food, we can go to Zeyuan near Xihuamen, not far away from Donghuamen. The courtyard is famous for its western food.

Jenny: Sounds good. Can you give me some advice? I am kind of lost. My dear, I don't know which one to choose.

Assistant: That depends on what you want to eat. How about the roast duck? You can also bring some back to your family and friends for there are vacuum packages to take out.

Jenny: That's great. OK, I will try that. Thanks very much.

Assistant: It is my pleasure. Wish you enjoy yourself. Bye!

Jenny: Goodbye!

Notes

1. foreign independent tour	外国散客旅游
2. Summer Palace	颐和园
3. brochure	小册子
4. Palace Museum	故宫博物院
5. antique	古董
6. peak season	旺季
7. appeal to	有吸引力
8. rinsed mutton	涮羊肉
9. vacuum package	真空包装

Dialogue 3

Visiting the Acropolis in Athens

(Jimmy is on his way to the Acropolis in Athens. Susan is introducing its information to him. Jimmy, a tourist. Susan, the tour guide)

J: I'm very glad. We'll see the Acropolis in Athens soon!

S: Yes. It's a good place.

J: Can you tell me something about the Acropolis in Athens?

S: Of course. It contains many buildings, such as Parthenon Temple, Hill Gate, Wisdom Goddess Temple. But the most famous one is Parthenon Temple.

J: I've heard that carvings in Parthenon Temple are very successful.

S: There you go. It was directed by a famous carver—Phidias.

J: Who's Phidias?

S: He was a statesman.

J: How about Wisdom Goddess Temple?

S: Wisdom Goddess was called "the giver of victory". She is very wise and clever. Her temple was damaged by Turk in 1686. In the nineteenth century it was restored.

Notes

1. Acropolis in Athens	雅典卫城
2. Parthenon Temple	帕特农神庙
3. Hill Gate	山门
4. Wisdom Goddess Temple	智慧女神庙

5. carving	雕刻品，雕刻图案
6. direct	指导
7. carver	雕刻师
8. Phidias	菲迪亚斯（古希腊的雕刻家）
9. statesman	政治家
10. the giver of victory	胜利的赐予者
11. wise	聪明的，充满智慧的
12. temple	庙宇，圣殿，寺院
13. damage	破坏，毁坏
14. Turk	土耳其人
15. restore	修复，使恢复

Reading

Shanghai Travel and Tours Guide

Located at the center of the mainland's coastline, Shanghai has long been a major hub of communications, transportation, and international exchange. The municipality covers an area of more than 6,340 square kilometers and has a population of nearly 24.9 million. Shanghai is China's largest economic comprehensive industrial base, and a famous historical and cultural city.

The city consistently attracts investment and is seen as an ideal venue for business gatherings. It is also a must on any agenda during a tour of China. Shanghai has fostered a comprehensive transportation network that incorporates land, sea, and air travel, as well as a convenient urban transportation system. More than 300 airlines serve the city, providing direct flights to more than 48 countries. The addition of the Shanghai Pudong International Airport, which went into operation in 1999, is expected to increase the annual passenger volume to some 76 million.

Special tourist trains running between Shanghai and the neighboring provinces of Jiangsu and Zhejiang, as well as tourist bus routes along newly-constructed expressways, offer great convenience for regional travel. Shanghai has more than 400 travel agencies to assist visitors, and the 127 star-rated hotels offer a total of 40,000 guest rooms.

Visitors to Shanghai are not only dazzled by the modern metropolis and the gateway to a developing China, but also able to immerse themselves in the unique Shanghai culture, a combination of Chinese and Western elements. Colorful festivals and celebrations dot the yearly Shanghai activities calendar, such as the Shanghai Nanhui Peach Blossoms Festival, Shanghai International Tea Culture Festival and Shanghai China International Art Festival.

Shanghai has also introduced special tour packages aimed at the different interests of visitors, such as bicycling tours, hiking tours, gourmet tours, rehabilitation and health care tours, study tours, Japanese young women's tours, honeymoon tours, and convention and exhibition tours.

The Bund

The well-known Bund is a must for visitors to Shanghai. 117 buildings lining the narrow shoreline of the Huangpu River offer a living exhibition of Gothic, Baroque, Roman, Classic Revival and Renaissance architectural styles, as well as combinations of Chinese and Western styles. They are also a condensation of the recent history of the city. The wide embankment offers ample room for strolling and is used by locals for morning exercises and evening gatherings. In the evening, colorful lights illuminate the area and create a shimmering image deserving the name Pearl of the Orient.

The Yu Garden

The Yu Garden is a classical landscape in the Southern Chinese style with a history of more than 400 years. Pavilions, halls, rockeries and ponds display the finest in landscaping from the southern style as seen in the Ming and Qing Dynasties. More than 40 landscapes were ingeniously separated by latticed walls, winding corridors and lattice windows.

People's Square

People's Square has become the political and cultural center in Shanghai since 1994, when it was rebuilt. In and around the square are a massive fountain named the Light of Huangpu River, 10,000 square meters of lawns, six groups of relief carvings that depict the history of Shanghai, the New Shanghai Museum, the offices of the municipal government, an underground shopping plaza, the Shanghai Grand Theater and the Shanghai Exhibition Center.

The Oriental Pearl Tower

The Oriental Pearl Tower is 468 meters high, the tallest in Asia and the third tallest in the world. It faces the Bund across the Huangpu River. When viewed from the Bund, the tower and the Nanpu and Yangpu bridges create a vivid imagery known as "two dragons playing with a pearl". The sphere at the top has a diameter of 45 meters and is 263 meters above ground. The observation deck in the sphere offers a sweeping view of the city. The revolving restaurant is set at 267 meters above Pudong New Area. The dance ball, piano bar and 20 karaoke rooms, at 271 meters, are also opened to the public. The penthouse, which sits at 350 meters, has an observation deck, meeting room, and coffee shop. The tower integrates broadcasting technologies with sightseeing, catering, shopping, amusement, and accommodations. It has become the symbol of the city and a major tourist attraction in Shanghai.

Cruise on the Huangpu River

Cruising on the Huangpu River, visitors can gaze at the mighty skyscrapers, the Monument to the People's Heroes, the famous Waibaidu Bridge and Huangpu Park on one bank, and the Oriental Pearl Tower, International Convention Center, Jin Mao Building and the newly rising Pudong New Area on the other. The Yangpu and Nanpu bridges span the river. From the river, visitors can also view the ruins of ancient cannon emplacements and fortifications at Wusong and the magnificent view of the Yangtze River as it empties into the sea.

Nanjing Road

East Nanjing Road, honored as "China's No. 1 Street", has become an all-weather pedestrian arcade. Shops and restaurants provide products and services with their own characteristics, making it an ideal place that integrates shopping, restaurants, amusement and sightseeing.

Luxun Park

The museum and tomb are located in Lu Xun Park. Lu Xun was an eminent man of letters. The museum exhibits Lu Xun's manuscripts, some of his personal effects, document, and photos. The headstone at the Tomb of Lu Xun is in the calligraphy of Mao Zedong and reads "The Tomb of Mr. Lu Xun".

Dr. Sun's Residence

Dr. Sun Yat-sen, the forerunner of the Chinese democratic revolution, and his widow Soong Ching Ling, lived in this building from 1918 to 1924. It was in the residence that Dr. Sun Yat-sen met representatives of the Communist Party and fostered the first cooperation between the Communist Party of China and the Kuomintang.

Soong Ching ling's Residence

This is the former residence of Soong Ching ling, an honorary chairwoman of the People's Republic of China and the widow of Dr. Sun Yat-sen. She lived, worked, and studied here for a long time of her life.

Shanghai Grand Theater

Located in the northwestern corner of People's Square, the Shanghai Grand Theater covers 70,000 square meters. It is actually composed of three theaters. The theater can accommodate performances of ballet opera, symphonies, chamber music, modern dramas, and musicals. It also owns the largest, fully automatic stage in Asia. The theater has become a symbol of modern culture in Shanghai.

a. Answer the following questions according to the passage.

1. What is the basic information of Shanghai?
_____

2. What about the transportation in Shanghai?
_____

3. Why is Shanghai a must on any agenda during a tour of China?
_____

4. What are the special festivals or celebrations on the yearly Shanghai activities calendar?
_____

5. Exemplify some famous scenic spots in Shanghai.
_____

b. Translate the expressions into Chinese or English.

1. economic development　　　_____
   economic geography　　　　_____
   an economical car　　　　　_____
   _____　　　　　　　简练的写作风格
2. a comprehensive description
   _____　　　　　　　综合性学校
   comprehensive insurance　　_____
3. a historic occasion　　　　_____
   a historical fact　　　　　　_____
   _____　　　　　　　历史人物
   _____　　　　　　　有历史记载的时间
4. the Tower of London　　　_____
   _____　　　　　　　象牙塔
   the towering dome of the cathedral _____
   _____　　　　　　　杰出的思想家

c. *Choose an appropriate word to fill in each blank to make each sentence meaningful, and change its form when necessary.*

agenda	venue	condensation	illuminate	honorary
foster	stroll	comprehensive	ingenious	immerse

1. He was sitting in the garden gazing at the moon, _____ in ecstasy.
2. As there is much pressure from her work, she cherishes the chance of _____ with her mother in the little park.
3. The report is a brilliant _____ of these years' effort.
4. As the train to the art centre was delayed, the engineer had to change his _____.
5. It is raining heavily outside, therefore, the host announced a last-minute change of___.
6. The effort made by the pioneers _____ us a resolute route to victory.
7. Nowadays, there are heated discussions about movie stars employed as _____ professors in universities.
8. Young as a child, Thomas is _____ at solving difficult crossword puzzles.
9. Each government _____ the growth of agriculture.
10. After years of hard work on her major, she has a _____ grasp of the subject.

d. *Translate the following sentences into English with words given in the brackets.*

1. 在许多正式场合，男人应该穿西装，这是惯例而已。(convention)
_____

2. 这对老夫妇非常享受这场令人眼花缭乱的技艺表演。(dazzle)
_____

3. 春节马上就要到了，街道上到处张灯结彩。(illuminate)
_____

4. 在漫长的一段旅程后，他躺在浴缸中，把身子浸泡在热水中。(immerse)
_____

5. 这群外国旅客对宏伟的天安门广场叹为观止。(magnificent)
_____

Vocabulary List

accommodate	[əˈkɒmədeɪt]	*v.* 供应，向……提供空间
agenda	[əˈdʒendə]	*n.* 议程
ample	[ˈæmpl]	*adj.* 充足的，丰富的

annual	[ˈænjuəl]	adj.	每年的
arcade	[ɑːˈkeɪd]	n.	拱廊，有拱廊的街道
calendar	[ˈkælɪndə]	n.	日历
calligraphy	[kəˈlɪgrəfi]	n.	书法
cannon	[ˈkænən]	n.	大炮
catering	[ˈkeɪtərɪŋ]	n.	饮食
comprehensive	[ˌkɒmprɪˈhensɪv]	adj.	全面的，广泛的；包容的
condensation	[ˌkɒndenˈseɪʃn]	n.	浓缩
convention	[kənˈvenʃn]	n.	大会；协定；习俗，惯例
cruise	[kruːz]	vi./n.	巡游，巡航
dazzle	[ˈdæzl]	v.	使……眼花，炫耀
diameter	[daɪˈæmɪtə]	n.	直径
dot	[dɒt]	v.	在……上打点
embankment	[ɪmˈbæŋkm(ə)nt]	n.	堤防
expressway	[ɪkˈsprɛsweɪ]	n.	高速公路
forerunner	[ˈfɔːrʌnə]	n.	先驱
fortification	[ˌfɔːtɪfɪˈkeɪʃ(ə)n]	n.	防御工事
foster	[ˈfɒstə]	v.	养育，培养；鼓励
gateway	[ˈgeɪtweɪ]	n.	门，通路
gourmet	[ˈgʊəmeɪ]	n.	美食家
headstone	[ˈhɛdstəʊn]	n.	墓石，基石
hiking	[ˈhaɪkɪŋ]	n.	徒步旅行
honorary	[ˈɒnərəri]	adj.	荣誉的，名誉的
hub	[hʌb]	n.	中心
illuminate	[ɪˈluːmɪneɪt]	v.	照亮，阐明
immerse	[ɪˈmɜːs]	v.	沉浸，使陷入
incorporate	[ɪnˈkɔːpəreɪt]	v.	合并
ingenious	[ɪnˈdʒiːniəs]	adj.	有独创性的
integrate	[ˈɪntɪgreɪt]	v.	使成整体
magnificent	[mægˈnɪfɪsnt]	adj.	华丽的，宏伟的，高尚的
massive	[ˈmæsɪv]	adj.	大块的；结实的
metropolis	[məˈtrɒpəlɪs]	n.	大城市
municipality	[mjuːˌnɪsɪˈpæləti]	n.	市政当局
newly-constructed	[ˈnjuːli-kənˈstrʌktɪd]	adj.	新建的

orient	[ˈɔːrient]	n. 东方
pavilion	[pəˈvɪliən]	n. 亭，阁
pedestrian	[pəˈdestriən]	n. 步行者
penthouse	[ˈpenthaʊs]	n. 顶层公寓；阁楼
rehabilitation	[riːəˌbɪlɪˈteɪʃn]	n. 复原
representative	[ˌreprɪˈzentətɪv]	n./adj. 代表；典型的，有代表性的
residence	[ˈrezɪdəns]	n. 居住，住处
revolve	[rɪˈvɒlv]	v. 使旋转
shimmer	[ˈʃɪmə]	n. 微光
sphere	[sfɪə]	n. 球体
star-rated	[ˈstɑːˈreɪtɪd]	星级的
stroll	[strəʊl]	v. 漫步，闲逛
symphony	[ˈsɪmfəni]	n. 交响乐
venue	[ˈvenjuː]	n. （事件的）发生地点
widow	[ˈwɪdəʊ]	n. 寡妇

Writing

Travel Route

Task 1　Writing Skills

旅行社在和游客洽谈旅游事宜的时候，旅行的行程安排是非常重要的，其中包括出发时间、乘坐的交通工具、游览地点及时间、饮食和住宿安排等。制定旅游路线应本着简洁、明了的原则。在制作中，一般没有标题和对象，因为这些内容多为默认的。一般将时间放在最显著的位置，可用具体时间，如 "×月×日" 或者 "第×天"，然后注明时间、地点或事件，多用短语。

Task 2　Sample Writing

Day 01：Arrival in Quanzhou

8:00 Visit Kaiyuan Temple, the Stone Tower.

12:00 Lunch at XX restaurant. After lunch, continue the tour to the Jimei district—the hometown of patriotic overseas Chinese Chen Jiageng.

18:00 Check in XX hotel. After that, have dinner. Tourists can have a rest at the hotel or go out to enjoy the nightlife in Quanzhou.

Day 02：

7:00 Morning call, have breakfast.

8:30 Check out and drive to Xiamen. Take a city tour to visit the Gulangyu Islet, the one and only Piano Museum in China and Egret Garden. In the evening, go shopping at Longtoulu Shopping Street, then go back to the hotel.

Day 03：After breakfast, visit the Stone Forest, then transfer to the shopping street for the free activities. In the afternoon drive back to Quanzhou. After dinner, the tour ends.

【译文】

第一天：到达泉州

8:00 游览开元寺，石塔。

12:00 于××饭店就餐，饭后游览集美区——爱国华侨陈嘉庚的家乡。

18:00 入住××酒店，然后就餐，游客可自行在酒店休息或外出享受泉州的夜生活。

第二天：

7:00 提供早晨叫醒服务并用早餐。

8:30 办理退房手续后乘车去厦门，游览鼓浪屿，中国唯一的钢琴博物馆和白鹭洲公园，晚上在龙头路购物街购物后返回酒店。

第三天：早餐后参观石林，然后至购物街自由活动。下午乘车返回泉州，晚餐后行程结束。

Task 3　Writing Practice

a. Finish the following route by translating the Chinese in the brackets into English.

6:30～8:00 Tourists gather at the gate of Wangfujing.

8:00 Visit the Palace Museum, also named the Imperial Palace, the biggest and most complete ancient architectures existed in the world.

10:30 Visit the Temple of Heaven, one of_____.(被联合国教科文组织确认为"世界文化遗产"。)

12:30 Lunch at ×× restaurant, then_____. (驱车去颐和园，世界上最大的皇家园林)

17:00 Drive back to Wangfujing.

b. Listed below is a 3-day travel route in East China, translate it into English.

第一天：到达杭州

8:00 游览西湖。

12:30 于××餐馆就餐，然后参观中国丝绸博物馆的丝绸时装表演。

16:00 乘车赴上海，入住××酒店，然后自由活动。
第二天：
7:30 集合，于酒店吃早餐。
8:30 泛舟黄浦江。
12:30 于城隍庙和上海小吃街就餐，然后游览东方明珠电视塔，南浦大桥，金茂大厦和孙中山故居。
18:00 于××餐厅就餐，然后在南京路（中华商业第一街）上自由活动。
第三天：早餐后各自乘飞机返回。

Vocabulary Development

中外景观

classical Chinese garden	中国古典园林
traditional Chinese garden	中国传统园林
ancient Chinese garden	中国古代园林
Chinese mountain and water garden	中国山水园
imperial palace garden	帝王宫苑
royal garden	皇家园林
private garden	私家园林
garden on the Yangtze Delta	江南园林
western classical garden	西方古典园林
English style garden	英国式园林
Anglo-Chinese style garden	中英混合式园林
Italian style garden	意大利式园林
Spanish style garden	西班牙式园林
French style garden	法兰西式园林
Le Notre's style garden	勒诺特尔式园林
Renaissance style garden	文艺复兴式庄园
Rococo style garden	洛可可式园林
Baroque style garden	巴洛克式园林
manor	庄园
villa garden	别墅花园
peristyle garden, patio	廊柱园
xystus	古希腊室内运动场

maze, labyrinth	迷阵
Ling You Hunting Garden	灵囿（周代）
Ling Zhao Water Garden	灵沼（周代）
Ling Tai Platform Garden	灵台（周代）
E-Pang Palace	阿房宫（秦代）
ShangLin Yuan	上林苑（汉代）
WeiYang Palace	未央宫（汉代）
Luoyang Palace	洛阳宫（魏代）
Hua-Qing Palace	华清宫（唐代）
Gen Yue Imperial Garden	艮岳（宋代）
Yuan-Ming Yuan Imperial Garden	圆明园
Yi-He Yuan Imperial Garden; Summer Palace	颐和园
Chengde Imperial Summer Resort	承德避暑山庄
Suzhou traditional garden	苏州园林
Hanging Garden	悬园，又称悬空园，架高园
Royal Botanical Garden; Kew garden	英国皇家植物园，又称邱园
Versailles Palace Park	凡尔赛宫苑
Fontainebleau Palace Garden	枫丹白露宫园

Scenic Spots Introduction
景 点 介 绍

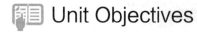

Unit Objectives

After learning this unit, you should

- understand how to introduce scenic spots;
- master the basic words and expressions about scenic spots introduction;
- find ways to improve your writing skills about On-the-way Introduction;
- be familiar with some domestic scenic spots.

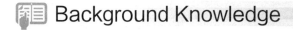

Background Knowledge

Tourist Attractions

Tourist attractions refer to those objects and events, existing both in nature and human society, which are of interest to tourists and pull them to travel. The tourism industry can take advantage of tourist attractions to produce benefits for the society and the environment. Tourist attractions include natural resources such as weather, landscapes and other natural sites as well as humanistic resources like historical relics, culture and customs. In China, tourist attractions often mean the same as tourism resources. The definition of tourism resources indicates that the natural and human factors which attract tourists may become tourism resources.

Tourism Resources in China

China is a vast land, rich in tourism resources. It has scenic spots and historical sites, spectacular landscapes, and colorful and varied national customs. China encompasses a great diversity of landscapes and a corresponding variety of natural resources and climate types.

A visitor to China is attracted by the green mountains and meandering rivers in the south such as the Yangtze River and by the grasslands and forests in north China. Touring the country, one seems to have entered a traditional Chinese landscape painting.

China is home to one of the world's four great civilizations. A history of 7,000 years has left behind great numbers of cultural relics and places of historical interest spread across the vast country.

The Chinese civilization has nurtured brilliant cultures and arts. Music, dances, opera, martial arts, calligraphy, painting, engraving, silk-weaving, porcelain-making, cuisine, architecture... all have a unique Chinese flavor and attractions.

China is a big family of 56 ethnic groups. Chinese music, dance and opera, and the culture and customs of ethnic minorities are treasure stores of tourism resources.

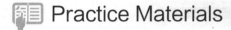 Practice Materials

Listening

Dialogue 1

a. Listen to Dialogue 1 and decide whether each of the following sentences is true (T) or false (F).

1. _____ The tour guide is a native in Pingyao.
2. _____ There are about 700 stores and shops in the bazaar, but most of them decline.
3. _____ Jack doesn't like forest.
4. _____ Rishengchang Exchange Shop is a famous souvenir shop.
5. _____ Pingyao is famous for the banking business.

b. Listen to the dialogue and answer the following questions.

1. Why does Jack travel with the tour guide instead of walking around by himself?

_____

2. What is available in those curiosity shops?

_____

3. What would Jack have bought if he had enough money, according to himself?

_____

4. What was the earliest bank that appeared in China?
_____

5. Where is Rishengchang Exchange Shop located?
_____

c. Listen to the dialogue again and supply the missing words.

1. But you're a _____, why not walk around Pingyao city by yourself?
2. It is one of the best places where you can _____ the ancient Chinese culture.
3. It seems to me they are all _____ shops.
4. The traditional buildings here are really _____.
5. Pingyao used to be the _____ center of China.

Notes

1. the ancient city of Pingyao	平遥古城
2. Nandajie Street	南大街
3. architecture	建筑
4. backpacker	背包客，背包旅行者
5. marvelous	不可思议的；极佳的
6. concrete	混凝土
7. bazaar	市场
8. thrive	兴旺；繁荣；成功；致富
9. available	可供雇用/出租/出售
10. curiosity shops	古玩店
11. dazzling	璀璨夺目，耀眼的
12. array	列队，排列；一排
13. antique	古董
14. jade ware	玉器
15. lacquer ware	漆器
16. souvenir	纪念品
17. attractive	有魅力的，吸引人的，令人感兴趣的
18. compound	大院，院子
19. magnificent	极棒的，华丽的
20. Rishengchang Exchange Shop	日升昌票号
21. financial	财政的，金融的，金融界的

Dialogue 2

a. Listen to Dialogue 2 and decide whether each of the following sentences is true (T) or false (F).

1. The complex of Rishengchang Exchange Shop is of great value.
2. The bank continues to thrive to this day.
3. Tongxinggong Armed Escort Company Museum is a Qing styled complex.
4. The armed escort firms played an important role in the development of Chinese commerce.
5. Jack is more interested in the Chinese architecture in Pingyao.

b. Listen to the dialogue and answer the following questions.

1. What happened to the bank one century ago?
_____
2. Why was Rishengchang Exchange Shop very important?
_____
3. Why did the people establish the escort firm in Pingyao?
_____
4. What is Pingyao popular for?
_____
5. Where is the Qiao's Compound?
_____

c. Listen to the dialogue again and supply the missing words.

1. This bank looks like a Chinese classic _____.
2. Unfortunately, the bank became _____ a century ago.
3. The banker must be an _____.
4. Why did the people _____ the escort firm here?
5. It is not far away from here, some 20 kilometers _____ of Pingyao.

Notes

1. glory — 荣誉，壮观
2. security company — 保安公司
3. deposit — 储蓄，保证金，押金
4. complex — 综合性建筑
5. bankrupt — n. 破产者 adj. 破产的 v. 使破产

6. mansion	宅邸
7. upstart	暴发户
8. Tongxinggong Armed Escort Company Museum	同兴公镖局博物馆
9. Tongxinggong Armed Escort Company	同兴公镖局
10. prosperous	繁荣的
11. Qiao's Compound	乔家大院

 Background Information

Ancient City of Pingyao

The old city of Pingyao is in Shanxi Province. It is a well-preserved historic city and also a prototype of ancient Chinese cities. It largely maintains its historical appearance of the Ming and Qing Dynasties (1368~1912). Built initially in King Xuan's reign (827 B.C.~782 B.C.) of the Western Zhou Dynasty, Pingyao has a history of over 2,700 years. Through this age-long developmental course, cultural remains come down to the present in a large number and great density, for which Pingyao is praised as a "major preserver county of cultural relics" in Shanxi, a province rich in ancient Chinese buildings. (The substantial cultural remains preserved in the old city not only represent the architectural styles, construction methods and material-using standards of ancient Chinese cities in various historical periods, but also mirror the artistic advances and aesthetic achievements of ancient China's ethnic groups in different regions.) The city is under national protection and included in the UNESCO World Heritage List in 1997.

 Speaking

Dialogue 1

Scenic Spots Introduction

(David, the tour guide, is showing a group of tourists around Mount Huangshan.
D: David, the guide   B: Mr. Black, a tourist   W: Mr. White, a tourist)
(At the gate of Mount Huangshan Scenic Spot)

D: (Counting the tourists) Are we all here?

B: Yes, let's go.

D: OK.

W: David, would you tell us what Mount Huangshan is famous for?

D: Sure. It is famous for its oddly shaped pines. On Mount Huangshan, towering cliffs are everywhere; every cliff has its pines and each pine has its unique posture. The other wonders are spectacular rocks, hot springs and its ever-changing sea of clouds. These are called the four wonders of Mount Huangshan.

W: Sounds great! I can't wait to get there.

(After a while)

D: Here we are, at the top of the hill. Come on. Look at the sea of clouds.

B: What a breathtaking view! The clouds and mists look like a sea, indeed. And the sea water is drifting like ten thousand horses galloping ahead.

D: Look, please. On your right is Tiandu Peak, one of the three main peaks of Mount Huangshan and also the steepest. It is 1,810 meters high. On the way up, you can see a cliff called Jiyu Bei, which means Carp's Backbone.

B: Oh, I see. Is it the highest peak?

D: No, the highest peak is on your left, named the Lotus Flower Peak, at a height of 1,864 meters. Famous pine trees, such as the "Flying Dragon" and the "Twin Dragons" are found there.

B: That's sounds very exciting. Shall we climb up the highest peak first, Sam?

W: That's a good suggestion. Let's go!

D: Please return here by 11:00, will you? We'll have lunch at Yuping Guesthouse.

B & W: All right. See you later.

Notes

1. scenic spots	景点
2. oddly	奇怪地，古怪地
3. pine	松树
4. towering cliff	悬崖峭壁
5. posture	姿势，姿态
6. spectacular	壮观的，雄伟的
7. breathtaking	非常激动人心的，壮观的
8. mist	薄雾
9. drift like ten thousand horses galloping ahead	像万马奔腾一样翻滚
10. steep	陡的，急剧上升的
11. Carp's Backbone	鲫鱼背
12. Lotus Flower Peak	莲花峰

13. summit　　　　　　　　　　　　峰顶，最高点
14. guesthouse　　　　　　　　　　上等旅社，宾馆

Dialogue 2

Going to a Botanical Garden

(Two friends are going to a Botanical Garden. They are at the entrance.)

A： Look at those crowds of people milling about just inside the gate. It seems that some public meetings are going on.

B： Oh, there must be some plays or acrobatics going on there. Let's go in and have a look.

A： Oh, look at those cute children. How happy they seem!

B： I can't help recalling my own childhood as I look at them. So innocent! So carefree!

A： Don't be so sentimental. Look at that old couple on that bench. Don't you think they are happy?

B： Oh, they are also enjoying themselves here. It's good for their health. Let's go a little faster.

A： All right. Let's go.

Notes

1. milling about / around　　　　成群结队、漫无目的地乱转乱挤
2. botanical　　　　　　　　　　植物（学）的
3. botanical garden　　　　　　　植物园
4. acrobatics　　　　　　　　　　杂技；特技
5. can't help doing　　　　　　　忍不住（要做某事）
6. recall　　　　　　　　　　　　记忆；回忆起
7. innocent　　　　　　　　　　　天真的，单纯的
8. carefree　　　　　　　　　　　无忧无虑的
9. sentimental　　　　　　　　　　易动感情的，多愁善感的

Dialogue 3

(Continue...)

A： Just look at those gorgeous tulips there.

B： They are beautiful, aren't they?

A: I think so.

B: What a wonderful time of the year! It's so restful. What are those small yellow and white flowers sprouting up on the lawn?

A: The yellow ones are buttercups and the white ones are daisies.

B: Aren't those azalea bushes beautiful?

A: Yes. Here's an interesting bed with a mixture of daffodils, violets, lilies of the valley and bluebells.

B: By the way, do you know much about how to grow flowers?

A: Oh, not much. But my mother grows a lot at my home.

B: It takes plenty of time to take care of them.

A: Of course. You've got to water them and see that they get enough bright sunlight. Sometimes you also have to give plant food.

B: It really takes a lot of knowledge.

A: Some flowers need special care. Others need special food.

B: That's too complicated. But the satisfaction out of the labor is incomparable.

Notes

1. gorgeous — 华丽的，灿烂的
2. tulip — 郁金香
3. sprout up — 发芽
4. lawn — 草坪；草地
5. buttercup — 毛茛科
6. daisy — 雏菊
7. azalea — 杜鹃花
8. daffodil — 水仙花
9. violet — 紫罗兰
10. lily of the valley — 铃兰
11. bluebell — 风信子
12. complicated — 复杂的，难解的
13. incomparable — 无与伦比的，不能比较的

 Reading

Gulangyu Island

Gulangyu Island, situated only five minutes by boat from Xiamen City, is really a Shangri-la-like tourist attraction. It is renowned for its delicate natural beauty, ancient relics and varied architecture and enjoys a laudatory title "Garden on the Sea". Its original name was "Yuanshazhou Island". During the Ming Dynasty, it was renamed Gulangyu because of the huge reef surrounding it. "Gu" in Chinese means drum; "lang" means waves and "yu" means island. When the tide comes in, the waves pound the reef and make a sound like the beating of a drum.

Gulangyu Island has about 16,000 permanent residents, all of whom live in a relaxing, healthy and placid lifestyle. The Dragon Head Hill, Hoisting Flag Hill and Hen Hill stand in a line on the island. Overlapping peaks foil the blue water, white clouds, green trees and bright flowers. The air is refreshing. Only electric-powered vehicles are permitted on the island, so the whole place is free from the noise and pollution of combustion engines and is particularly quiet. All these render an atmosphere of a fairyland. After the Opium War in 1842, 13 countries including Great Britain, France and Japan had established consulates, churches and hospitals here, turning the island into a common concession. From the Baroque buildings to the Gothic cathedral, from the Shanghai-style alley to the Fujian-style courtyards, Gulangyu Island is filled with different architectural styles, making it a veritable "Architecture Museum", attracting architecture students from across the nation and the world to find their source of inspiration. The island is also known as the Cradle of Musicians and Island of Pianos because of the passion local people have for music. Many accomplished musicians were born here and the percentage of piano ownership ranks at the top in the whole country.

The island boasts many scenic spots, among which the most attractive are Sunlight Rock and Shuzhuang Garden.

Located in the south-central part of the island, Sunlight Rock is the island's highest point with an altitude of 92.7 meters. Though it may not rank with high mountain peaks, it appears superb and grand when seen from afar. Here huge and precipitous rocks form many caves and gullies. The name "Sunlight" comes from a sun-shaped formation in the granite. When the sun rises, the morning light illuminates the granite in Sunlight Temple and the rocks are bathed in sunlight.

At the foot of Sunlight Rock stands the Memorial Hall of Zheng Chenggong, built in honor of the hero's feats which included expelling the Dutch colonists and reoccupying Taiwan. Wandering up the steep rock path, visitors will see many profound inscriptions left by poets, the oldest of which dates back to over 400 years ago. This is the main cultural sight on the hill. Continuing on, you will see the preserved training grounds of Zheng Chenggong's troops. Near the fields is a huge rock bridging two cliffs, forming a natural entrance to a cave. This is called Old Summer Cave where you can feel a pleasant cool breeze. It's the perfect viewing spot to appreciate the scenery of Gulangyu Island. A fantastic panorama of Xiamen City, including Nanputuo Temple, Xiamen University and Hulishan Battery, is within view.

Shuzhuang Garden, situated on the seashore to the south of Sunlight Rock, was first built in 1931 as a private villa by a rich merchant named Lin Erjia, who migrated here with his family. He named the Villa Shuzhuang, which is a homonym to his mother's name. Now a bronze statue of the former owner stands in the park. Shuzhuang Garden became a garden park open to the public in 1955. It consists of two sections: the Garden of Hiding the Sea and the Garden of Making-up Hills. It was exquisitely designed in harmony with its topography. The Garden of Hiding the Sea is named so because the ocean remains hidden from view even if you walk right up to the garden gate. However, once you emerge from the bamboo forest, the seascape leaps into view. The Tower of Tide-viewing can really get you a terrific look at the sea. The former owner also made clever use of the naturally available scenery. Using the original slopes facing the sea, the reefs in the bay and the shape of the shoreline, the owner built bridges and pavilions at various levels. The panorama changes from a small bay to a vast ocean as you ascend. It is an ideal place for tasting the spray of the surging waves and getting a bird's-eye view of other charming islands. Both Sunlight Rock and Hero Hill are visible. The garden also possesses another characteristic—combining "active" with "static". Its unique arrangement joins a rockwork that includes a maze of connected caves with fine pavilions on the side of the slope. Lovely children chasing in the caves represent movement and activity, while people resting in the pavilions give a feeling of tranquility and harmonious contemplation.

A highly recommended spot in Shuzhuang Park which no tourists can afford to miss is the nation's largest Piano Museum, the only one in China with exhibits of world-famous pianos, some more than a century old and coming from Germany, France, America and Australia.

Gulangyu Island has other sights worth seeing including the Bright Moon Garden, the Seasight Watch Garden, Yu Park, Island Ring Boulevard, Bathing Beach, Underwater World Oceanarium and Xiamen Museum. The Bright Moon Garden is located in the southeast of the island with an area of over 20,000 square meters. It is a statuary garden to commemorate the national hero Zheng Chenggong with enchanting views. The appealing Seasight Watch Garden boasts villas of various styles of China and the West. It has become a noted resort for visitors. Yu Park was built in 1984 in memory of a doctor named Lin Qiaozhi.

a. Answer the following questions according to the passage.

1. What is Gulangyu Island renowned for?
_____

2. What are the factors that contribute to the atmosphere of a fairyland on Gulangyu Island?
_____

3. Why is Gulangyu Island attractive for architecture students?
_____

4. Give a brief introduction to Sunlight Rock.
_____

5. Give a brief introduction to Shuzhuang Garden.
_____

b. Translate the expressions into Chinese or English.

1. permanent residents _____   永久的幸福 _____
   a permanent job _____   永久地址 _____
   permanent assets _____   常设委员会 _____
   five permanent members _____   永久性军事基地 _____
2. delicate natural beauty _____   精密的仪器 _____
   a delicate violin passage _____   精致的瓷器 _____
   a critic's delicate perception _____   精细的手术 _____
   delicate questions _____   精致的花边 _____
3. source of inspiration _____   互相支持，互相鼓励 _____
   a fount of inspiration _____   从大自然中获得灵感 _____
   have a sudden inspiration _____   从……得到启示 _____
   give the inspiration to _____   从实验中得到启发 _____
4. the cradle of musicians _____   文明的发源地 _____
   in the cradle _____   自幼，自在襁褓时 _____
   stifle in the cradle _____   从生到死 _____
   the cradle of the deep _____   看着长大 _____

c. *Choose an appropriate word to fill in each blank to make each sentence meaningful, and change its form when necessary.*

| render | illuminate | wander | expel | boast |
| afar | ascend | permanent | fantastic | alley |

1. My daughter likes to describe her _____ dreams to me.
2. I'm not a _____ employee; I'm working here on a fixed-term contract.
3. The gift itself may be light as a goose feather, but sent from _____, it conveys deep feeling.
4. It is dangerous to walk the back _____ alone in the night.
5. His fatness _____ him unable to bend down.
6. The river _____ through some beautiful countries.
7. The headmaster decided to make an example of the pupil and _____ him from the school.
8. The airplane _____ higher and higher.
9. A sudden smile _____ her face.
10. Don't believe him; he is just _____.

d. *Translate the following sentences into English with words or phrases given in the brackets.*

1. 这座纪念碑是为了纪念为国牺牲的士兵而建立的。(in honor of)
_____
2. 大海和天空和谐地构成一幅美丽的图画。(harmony)
_____
3. 我们从直升飞机上俯瞰到城镇全景。(a bird's-eye view)
_____
4. 那些岩石从河中突兀地冒出来。(steeply)
_____
5. 从峰巅俯瞰，阿尔卑斯山壮丽的景色尽收眼底。(panorama)
_____

Vocabulary List

| accomplished | [əˈkʌmplɪʃt] | *adj.* 有造诣的；精湛的 |
| afar | [əˈfɑː] | *adv.* 从远处；在远处；遥远地 |

alley	[ˈæli]	n. 小巷
altitude	[ˈæltɪtjuːd]	n. 高度
architecture	[ˈɑːkɪtektʃə]	n. 建筑，建筑学
ascend	[əˈsend]	v. 攀登，上升
atmosphere	[ˈætməsfɪə]	n. 大气，空气，气氛
attraction	[əˈtrækʃn]	n. 吸引，吸引力；有吸引力的事物
baroque	[bəˈrɒk]	n. 巴洛克式
		adj. 巴洛克式的
boast	[bəʊst]	n. 自夸，值得夸耀的事物
		v. 自夸，以有……而自豪
breeze	[ˈbriːz]	n. 微风
		v. 吹微风
cathedral	[kəˈθiːdrəl]	n. 大教堂
colonist	[ˈkɒlənɪst]	n. 殖民地居民；殖民者
concession	[kənˈseʃn]	n. 让步
consulate	[ˈkɒnsjələt]	n. 领事，领事馆
contemplation	[ˌkɒntəmˈpleɪʃn]	n. 注视；沉思
cradle	[ˈkreɪdl]	n. 摇篮，发源地
delicate	[ˈdelɪkət]	adj. 精巧的，精致的
enchanting	[ɪnˈtʃɑːntɪŋ]	adj. 迷人的，迷惑的，妩媚的
expel	[ɪkˈspel]	v. 驱逐，排除
exquisite	[ɪkˈskwɪzɪt]	adj. 精巧的，敏锐的
exquisitely	[ˈekskwɪzɪtli]	adv. 精巧地，敏锐地
fairyland	[ˈfeərilænd]	n. 仙境，乐园，奇境
fantastic	[fænˈtæstɪk]	adj. 幻想的，奇异的
foil	[fɔɪl]	v. 烘托，衬托
Gothic	[ˈgɒθɪk]	n. 哥特式
		adj. 哥特式的
granite	[ˈgrænɪt]	n. 花岗岩
gully	[ˈgʌli]	n. 溪谷
		v. 水流冲成沟渠
harmonious	[hɑːˈməʊniəs]	adj. 和谐的，和睦的，悦耳的
homonym	[ˈhɒmənɪm]	n. 同音异义字
illuminate	[ɪˈluːmɪneɪt]	v. 照亮，照明；阐释，说明
inspiration	[ˌɪnspəˈreɪʃn]	n. 灵感

inscription	[ɪn'skrɪpʃn]	n. 题字，碑铭
laudatory	['lɔ:dət(ə)ri]	adj. 赞美的，赞赏的
opium	['əʊpiəm]	n. 鸦片
panorama	[ˌpænə'rɑ:mə]	n. 全景，全景画
pavilion	[pə'vɪliən]	n. 亭台，楼阁，大帐篷
		v. 搭帐篷
permanent	['pɜ:mənənt]	adj. 永久的，持久的
placid	['plæsɪd]	adj. 平静的
pound	[paʊnd]	v. 打击，敲击，重击
precipitous	[prɪ'sɪpɪtəs]	adj. 陡峭的，急躁的
profound	[prə'faʊnd]	adj. 深刻的，意义深远的
reef	[ri:f]	n. 暗礁
refreshing	[rɪ'freʃɪŋ]	adj. 提神的；凉爽的；使人喜欢的
relic	['relɪk]	n. 遗迹，遗物，废墟
render	['rendə]	v. 致使；给予补偿
resident	['rezɪdənt]	n. 居民
seascape	['si:skeɪp]	n. 海景，海景画
spray	[spreɪ]	n. 喷雾
		v. 喷射
statuary	['stætʃʊəri]	n. 雕像
steep	[sti:p]	adj. 陡峭的，险峻的
		n. 悬崖，峭壁
superb	[su:'pɜ:b]	adj. 庄重的，华丽的，极好的
surge	[sɜ:dʒ]	n. 汹涌，澎湃
		v. 涌浪，汹涌
topography	[tə'pɒɡrəfi]	n. 地形学
tranquility	[træŋ'kwɪlɪti]	n. 宁静
veritable	['verɪtəbl]	adj. 真正的
villa	['vɪlə]	n. 别墅

Phrases

be renowned for	因……而有声望
in harmony with	与……一致（协调）
in honor of	向……表示敬意，为祝贺……

Terms

Architecture Museum	万国建筑博览
Bathing Beach	天然海滨浴场
Garden on the Sea	海上花园
Gulangyu Island	鼓浪屿
Hen Hill	鸡母山
Hoisting Flag Hill	升旗山
Hulishan Battery	胡里山炮台
Island of Pianos	钢琴岛
Island Ring Boulevard	环岛路
Lin Erjia	林尔嘉
Lin Qiaozhi	林巧稚
Memorial Hall of Zheng Chenggong	郑成功纪念馆
Nanputuo Temple	南普陀寺
Old Summer Cave	古避暑洞
Piano Museum	钢琴博物馆
Shuzhuang Garden	菽庄花园
Sunlight Rock	日光岩
the Bright Moon Garden	皓月园
the Cradle of Musicians	音乐家的摇篮
the Dragon Head Hill	龙头山
the Garden of Hiding the Sea	藏海园
the Garden of Making-up Hills	补山园
the Ming Dynasty	明朝
the Opium War	鸦片战争
the Tower of Tide-viewing	听涛轩
Underwater World Oceanarium	海底世界
Yu Park	毓园
Yuanshazhou Island	圆沙洲

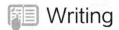 Writing

Task 1 Writing Skills

On-the-way Introduction

On-the-way introduction is an important part of guiding service. It may take hours for tourists to arrive at the destination. A tour guide should try to arouse the interest of the tourists who may feel boring because of the long journey. So on-the-way introduction is one of the best ways to keep tourists in high spirits and aspiring for the tourist site. The following four aspects should be observed while making an on-the-way introduction:

A general introduction of the destination so as to create a good image or the mental picture in the mind of tourists;

Briefly introduce the location, distance and the expected arrival time of the destination;

Describe the cities or scenic spots en route when tourists pass, but they won't visit them;

Briefly explain the travel schedule for the present day or the next day upon arrival.

Task 2 Sample Writing

(1) On-the-way tour from Guilin to Yangshuo (the first section: from Guilin to Ox Gorge)

Ladies and gentlemen, we are taking the Li River cruise from Guilin to Yangshuo. Gorgeous Karst peaks will give you surprises at each bend of the limpid river under the blue sky. Along the river, you will see water buffalo patrolling the fields, peasants reaping rice paddies, fisherman floating by on bamboo rafts. With its breathtaking scenery and taste of a life far removed from the concrete metropolis, the scenery along the Li River is worth visiting more than once.

Our trip starts from the dock south of Liberation Bridge in Guilin downtown area. The river trip is over eighty kilometers long and is estimated to take seven to eight hours. The eye-feasting landscape and country scenery will never disappoint you.

It is a Chinese tradition to divide the long trip into sections (just as the Three Gorges along the Changjiang River) and give each peak an imaginative name. Although some take much of your imagination to see what it is like, listening to my legendary stories behind them is sure to be a delightful experience when you are appreciating the landscapes.

Now let's start our impressive Li River trip from section to section. In the first section, which is from Guilin to Ox Gorge, you can enjoy the following scenery: Elephant Trunk Hill, Rooster Fighting Hill, Pagoda Hill, Daxu Ancient Town, and Ox Gorge.

Look at the hill situated majestically on the western bank of Li River! What does it look like? Yes, the hill resembles an elephant sucking water from the river with its long trunk. It is supposed to be the landmark of Guilin landscape, which you can find on travel brochures or books. The most impressive may be the water reflection of a moon-like cave when the moonlight sprinkles over the river.

A few minutes down from the Elephant Hill on the west bank is a small hill topped with a pagoda. The hexagonal pagoda is called Longevity Buddha Pagoda (Shoufo Ta) dating from the Ming Dynasty (1368~1644). It is said the second floor has stone Buddha figurines on display and the hill is compassed in Chuanshan Park. In autumn, the hill illuminated with red maples is very charming.

Perching on the northern bank of Li River, the ancient town Daxu keeps in its antique style from the Ming Dynasty (1368~1644). A flagging street, lined with old residences, shops and stalls, runs two kilometers along the river bank through the town. Some well-preserved residences hidden behind the street door may give you surprises when you occasionally explore further into a shop. These are quarters for businessmen in the past times. People in the town are very kind to tourists. Further to south, there is a single-arched bridge in the town named Longevity Bridge.

(2) On-the-way tour from Guilin to Yangshuo (The second section is omitted. The third section: from Water-Dropping Village to Yangshuo).

Ladies and gentlemen, the third section of our Li River trip goes from Water-Dropping Village to Yangshuo where you can see Snail Hill, Green Lotus Peak (Bilian Peak), and Schoolboy Hill (Shutong Hill). The scenery is equally beautiful.

One of Yangshuo's renowned pictographic hills, Snail Hill is about 1 kilometer (0.6 mile) south of Xingping Town, and is 64 kilometers (40 miles) from Guilin. The stratiform veins that twist up from the bottom to the hill make it look like a big snail. Hence the name Snail Hill.

South of Snail Hill lies Snail Cave, a name derived from the hill. Stalactites, in shapes of birds, beasts, fruits and flowers, are scattered around the cave. The most attractive and astonishing sights are the three snail stones which are hanging upside down. One is as white as snow, one is as dark as black lacquer and the other is as green as emerald. It is probable that they may capture your imagination and consider them to be the babies of the big snail.

Have you ever seen a green lotus flower? Besides the lovely pink and white lotus blooms, there is also a "green lotus flower". Green Lotus Peak (Bilian Peak) is on the west bank of Li River, southeast of Yangshuo County. A landmark of the county, the peak resembles a budding lotus bloom in contrast to the other peaks found in the area.

Shutong Hill rises up on the right bank of the Li River. It is the smallest peak along the bank of the Li River. According to legend, long ago, there was an evil dragon in the Li River. It often hovered on the Li River and endangered the local people. One day, a schoolboy received a sealed book from his teacher. The book taught him how to conquer this vicious creature. So when the dragon saw this book, it fell down to the river. For fear that the dragon might play a trick of opossum, the schoolboy, holding the book, stood by the riverside and changed into a hill (Shutong Hill) to protect the local people.

Hi, friends, we are approaching Yangshuo, which becomes a well-known small town to foreigners by Li River cruise. Located some 90 kilometers south of Guilin City, this town is the downstream end of the cruise but not the least. Guilin's scenery is often noted as the most beautiful of the world. Yangshuo's scenery is, arguably, superior to that of Guilin. The West Street in the town lined with western cafés, restaurants and hotels is the best choice for people who want to explore Chinese life.

Yangshuo is a great place for hikes and cycling excursions. Take a close-up exploration to the country villages, you will have a taste of the rural life. One thing surprised us was the one-hour bamboo raft trip along Yulonghe River. We didn't expect the scenery to be such a paradise.

Task 3 Writing Practice

Make an on-the-way introduction to a scenic spot which you are familiar with.

Vocabulary Development

World Heritage Sites in China and Other Important Attractions

	进入世界遗产名录的 中国文化自然遗产景点
Cultural Heritage	文化遗产
The Great Wall	长城
The Imperial Palace of the Ming and Qing Dynasties (The Forbidden City and Shenyang Imperial Palace)	明清皇宫 （北京故宫和沈阳故宫）
"Peking Man" Site at Zhoukoudian	周口店北京猿人遗址
Mogao Grottoes in Dunhuang	甘肃敦煌莫高窟
Mausoleum of Qin Shi Huang and Terra-cotta Warriors and Horses in Shaanxi	陕西秦始皇陵兵马俑
Chengde Mountain Summer Resort and Eight Outer Temples	河北承德避暑山庄及外八庙

Potala Palace in Lhasa, Tibet	西藏拉萨布达拉宫
The Temple, Mansion and Cemetery of Confucius in Qufu, Shandong Province	山东曲阜孔庙、孔府、孔林
Ancient Building Complex in the Wudang Mountains	武当山古建筑群
Mount Lushan	庐山
Ancient City of Pingyao	平遥古城
Suzhou Classical Gardens	江苏苏州古典园林
Ancient Town of Lijiang	云南丽江古城
The Summer Palace	北京颐和园
The Temple of Heaven	北京天坛
Dazu Rock Carvings	重庆大足石刻
Imperial Mausoleums of Ming and Qing Dynasties	明清皇家陵寝
Longmen Grottoes	龙门石窟
Mount Qingcheng and Dujiang Dam	青城山、都江堰
Ancient Villages in South Anhui：Xidi and Hongcun	安徽古村落：西递、宏村
Yungang Grottoes	云冈石窟
The Capital Cities and Tombs of the Ancient Koguryo Kingdom	高句丽王城、王陵及贵族墓葬
The Historic Center of Macao	澳门历史城区
The Yin Ruins	安阳殷墟
Natural Heritage	自然遗产
Jiuzhaigou Valley	九寨沟
Huanglong Scenic Spot	四川黄龙风景名胜区
Wulingyuan Scenic Spot	湖南武陵源风景名胜区
Three Parallel Rivers of Yunnan	云南三江并流
Sichuan Giant Panda Habitat	四川大熊猫栖息地
Natural and Cultural Heritage	自然文化双遗产
Mount Taishan	泰山
Mount Huangshan	黄山
Mount Emei and the Leshan Giant Buddha	峨眉山、乐山大佛
Mount Wuyi	武夷山

(The Other Famous Tourist Attractions in the World) 世界其他著名游览胜地

Asia 亚洲

Mount Fuji, Japan	日本富士山
Taj Mahal, India	印度泰姬陵
Angkor Wat, Cambodia	柬埔寨吴哥窟
Bali, Indonesia	印度尼西亚巴厘岛
Borobudur, Indonesia	印度尼西亚波罗浮屠
Sentosa, Singapore	新加坡圣淘沙
Crocodile Farm, Thailand	泰国北榄鳄鱼湖
Pattaya Beach, Thailand	泰国芭堤雅海滩
Babylon, Iraq	伊拉克巴比伦遗迹
Mosque of St, Sophia in Istanbul(Constantinople), Turkey	土耳其圣索菲亚教堂

Africa 非洲

Suez Canal, Egypt	苏伊士运河
Aswan High Dam, Egypt	阿斯旺水坝
Nairobi National Park, Kenya	肯尼亚内罗毕国家公园
Cape of Good Hope, South Africa	南非好望角
Sahara Desert	撒哈拉大沙漠
Pyramids, Egypt	埃及金字塔
The Nile, Egypt	埃及尼罗河

Oceania 大洋洲

Great Barrier Reef	大堡礁
Sydney Opera House, Australia	悉尼歌剧院
Ayers Rock	艾尔斯巨石
Mount Cook	库克山
Easter Island	复活节岛

Europe 欧洲

Notre Dame de Paris, France	法国巴黎圣母院
Eiffel Tower, France	法国埃菲尔铁塔
Arch of Triumph, France	法国凯旋门
Elysee Palace, France	法国爱丽舍宫

Louvre, France	法国卢浮宫
Kolner Dom, Koln, Germany	德国科隆大教堂
Leaning Tower of Pisa, Italy	意大利比萨斜塔
Colosseum in Rome, Italy	意大利罗马斗兽场
Venice, Italy	意大利威尼斯
Parthenon, Greece	希腊帕特农神庙
Red Square in Moscow, Russia	莫斯科红场
Big Ben in London, England	英国伦敦大本钟
Buckingham Palace, England	英国白金汉宫
Hyde Park, England	英国海德公园
London Tower Bridge, England	英国伦敦塔桥
Westminster Abbey, England	英国威斯敏斯特大教堂
Monte Carlo, Monaco	摩纳哥蒙特卡罗
The Mediterranean	地中海

The Americas 美洲

Niagara Falls, New York State, USA	美国尼亚加拉大瀑布
Bermuda	百慕大
Honolulu, Hawaii, USA	美国夏威夷火奴鲁鲁
Panama Canal	巴拿马大运河
Yellowstone National Park, USA	美国黄石国家公园
Statue of Liberty, New York City, USA	美国纽约自由女神像
Times Square, New York City, USA	美国纽约时代广场
The White House, Washington DC., USA	美国华盛顿白宫
Central Park, New York City, USA	美国纽约中央公园
Yosemite National Park, USA	美国约塞米蒂国家公园
Grand Canyon, Arizona, USA	美国亚利桑那州大峡谷
Hollywood, California, USA	美国加利福尼亚好莱坞
Disneyland, California, USA	加利福尼亚迪士尼乐园
Las Vegas, Nevada, USA	美国内华达拉斯维加斯
Miami, Florida, USA	美国佛罗里达迈阿密
Metropolitan Museum of Art, New York City, USA	美国纽约大都会艺术博物馆
Acapulco, Mexico	墨西哥阿卡普尔科
Cuzco, Peru	秘鲁库斯科

Shopping
旅游购物

Unit Objectives

After learning this unit, you should

- understand how to give shopping information;
- master the basic words and expressions about shopping in traveling;
- get some cultural knowledge about shopping information;
- be familiar with some domestic typical goods;
- find ways to improve your writing skills about A Letter of Complaints.

Background Knowledge

As an important part of a tour, shopping can sometimes be the main reason for traveling. You need to know the following knowledge.

Types of Stores

大型的：

department store	百货公司
shopping mall	购物中心

小型的：

dime store	一角钱商店
grocery store	杂货店
discount store	折扣商店

Types of Counters

tea and coffee counter	茶叶咖啡柜台
fruit and vegetable counter	水果蔬菜柜台
cotton fabric counter	棉布柜台
silk and satin counter	丝绸柜台
sweater counter	毛衣柜台
daily necessities counter	日用品柜台
jewellery counter	珠宝柜台
hardware and electric articles counter	五金电器柜台
stationery counter	文具柜台
toys counter	玩具柜台
musical instrument counter	乐器柜台
cigarettes and wine counter	烟酒柜台
men's wear counter	男士衣装柜台
ladies' wear counter	女士衣装柜台

Types of Payment

cash	现金
check	支票
credit card	信用卡
direct deduction from bank account	直接从银行账户扣除
money order	汇款单

 Practice Materials

Listening

Dialogue 1

a. Listen to Dialogue 1 and decide whether each of the following sentences is true (T) or false (F).

1. _____ The woman wants to buy a bag to deal with the stuff.
2. _____ The woman likes a suitcase of medium size.
3. _____ She still wants to buy a wallet in the same place.
4. _____ The assistant shows the woman a very popular wallet.
5. _____ At last, the woman doesn't buy the wallet that the assistant recommended.

b. Listen to the dialogue and answer the following questions.

1. What does the woman want to buy?
_____

2. Which style does she like, a small one or a medium one?
_____

3. Does she prefer a real leather one?
_____

4. How does she feel about the wallet at first?
_____

5. How much money does she spend in total?
_____

c. Listen to the dialogue again and supply the missing words.

1. Do you want a large size or _____?
2. Are they all _____ real leather?
3. Let me see if it can hold _____ in the two bags.
4. A single suitcase is easier _____ than two bags.
5. It can _____ in this way.

Notes

1. style	型号，式样，款式
2. medium	中间的，中等的
3. real leather	真皮
4. be made of	由……做成
5. artificial leather	人造革
6. spacious	宽敞的，宽广的，广大的

Dialogue 2

a. Listen to Dialogue 2 and decide whether each of the following sentences is true (T) or false (F).

1. _____ The woman wants to buy some presents for her family.
2. _____ There are 18K gold necklace, chain and earrings only.
3. _____ The price of the gold necklace is $66.
4. _____ The price of a key ring is $1.2.
5. _____ The woman believes these key rings are good presents for her friends.

b. Listen to the dialogue and answer the following questions.

1. What does the woman want to do?
_____

2. Is she interested in jewellery?
_____

3. How much money does she spend on buying the gold necklace?
_____

4. What is the price of the key ring?
_____

5. How many key rings does she buy?
_____

c. Listen to the dialogue again and supply the missing words.

1. All the jewellery is _____ here today.

2. We have 14K and 18K _____, chain and _____.

3. Its _____ price is $66, and you can have it with a forty percent discount.

4. Couldn't you _____ a little bit more?

5. OK, give me _____ like this.

Notes

1. jewellery	(总称)珠宝
2. necklace	项圈，项链
3. chain	链，项圈，表链，手链
4. forty percent discount	百分之四十的折扣，六折
5. key ring	钥匙环，钥匙链
6. knock off	从(价格中)减去；迅速而不费力地做成；下班；停止(工作)
7. the last price	最后的价格，最低的价格
8. a dozen	一打(12个)

 **Speaking**

Dialogue 1

Chinese Paper-cuts

(Two friends are discussing what they have bought in China.)

L: Miss Liu   J: Jeremy

L: What did you buy at the market?

J: I bought some special local products.

L: You seem to have bought the whole market!

J: Yes. I really wanted to do so. I love those handicrafts, especially the paper-cut.

L: Paper-cuts are all hand-made. Let me see the paper-cuts you bought. They are all animals.

J: Aren't animals the main content of Chinese paper-cuts?

L: All right. Animals, especially Chinese zodiac, are the most common theme in paper-cuts. But there are other themes.

J: Then I will buy some tomorrow.

L: Why do you want to buy so much?

J: Because I want to send them to my friends.

L: I see.

Notes

1. paper-cut   剪纸
2. special local product   特产
3. handicraft   手工艺品
4. hand-made   手工制造
5. main   主要的
6. content   所容纳的东西，所含之物，内容
7. zodiac   黄道带（占星家用于表示星体位置的图表，有十二个等份区，各有其名称和符号，尤用于推算行星对人生的影响）
8. theme   主题

Dialogue 2

Shopping in the Arts and Crafts Store

(Lucy, the local guide, together with her tourists, has arrived at a store which sells arts and crafts. The following dialogue is between them.)

Lucy: Ladies and gentlemen, attention please. We have arrived at an arts and crafts store. This store is the best you can find in this city.

Tourist: What does it sell?

Lucy: It mainly covers jade wares, silk products, paintings and calligraphy.

Tourist: Does the store sell the "Four Treasures of Study"? I want to buy one set for my son.

Lucy: Yes, the store does sell writing brushes, ink sticks and paper.

Tourist: How about the quality of the articles in this store?

Lucy: You can rest assured. This store is designated by the state and provides authentic articles.

Tourist: Excuse me. But could you tell me how to choose jade wares?

Lucy: You have to pay attention to its color, design and carving skills. Chrysolite is the best of Chinese jade. It has the color of white and green. Agate ranks the second in terms of value. It has the color of red or white. If you need help, please don't hesitate to ask.

Tourist: What about the price?

Lucy: The price here is moderate.

Tourist: Can we bargain here?

Lucy: Sorry to say that this is a store operated by the state, so bargaining here is not allowed.

Notes

1. art and craft —— 艺术手工艺品
2. jade ware —— 翡翠饰品，玉器
3. silk product —— 丝织品
4. calligraphy —— 书法作品
5. Four Treasures of Study —— 文房四宝
6. writing brush —— 毛笔
7. ink stick —— 墨
8. article —— 商品；文章
9. designate —— 指出，指示，命名，指派
10. authentic article —— 真货
11. carving skill —— 雕刻技术
12. chrysolite —— 贵橄榄石
13. agate —— 玛瑙
14. in terms of —— 就……而言
15. hesitate —— 犹豫，踌躇
16. moderate —— 适中的，一般的，有节制的
17. bargain —— 议价，订约；廉价货

Key Sentences

1. This store is the best you can find in this city.

这家店是这个城市中最好的。

2. It mainly covers jade wares, silk products, paintings and calligraphy.

它主要经营翡翠饰品、丝织品、画卷作品和书法作品。

3. How about the quality of the articles in this store?

这家店里商品的质量怎么样？

4. Agate ranks the second in terms of value.

玛瑙就其价值来说排第二位。

5. If you need help, please don't hesitate to ask.

如果你需要帮助，尽管直说。

6. The price here is moderate.

这里的价格是合理的。

7. Can we bargain here?

这里能砍价吗？

Dialogue 3

Buying Embroidery

Tourist: Excellent as they are, they aren't worth that much. This morning a peddler showed me a piece of Su embroidery. The pattern was great. He only asked for 300 yuan.

Assistant: Did you take it?

Tourist: Yeah, I took it for only 240 yuan. Here it is.

Assistant: They are quite different. Yours is machine-made, I mean it is mass produced. It isn't worth that much. At most it can sell at 150 yuan. You were overcharged.

Tourist: Really?

Assistant: But look at all the embroidery I'm dealing in. They are all hand-made. Both sides display exactly the same pattern. It's worth every penny I asked for.

Tourist: How about 400 yuan?

Assistant: 500 yuan is the last price I can accept. I know some foreigners never bargain, so I've never overpriced my goods. You can compare mine with other sellers'. Then you will find 500 yuan is quite reasonable for such an excellent item.

Tourist: OK, I do love it. I'll take it. Here is the money.

Assistant: Thank you. Anything else you need?

Tourist: No, thank you, bye.

Assistant: Goodbye. Have a good trip!

Notes

1. workmanship	手艺，技巧；工艺品
2. tri-colored pottery of the Tang Dynasty	唐三彩
3. embroidery	刺绣，装饰，镶边
4. brocade	织锦，锦缎
5. jade carving	玉雕
6. lacquer ware	漆器，瓷漆
7. fragile	易碎的
8. cloisonne	景泰蓝
9. delicate	细致的，精致的
10. peddler	叫卖者
11. machine-made	机器制造
12. mass produced	批量生产
13. deal in	交易

14. hand-made　　　　　　　　　　手工制作
15. reasonable　　　　　　　　　　合理的

Key Sentences

1. I want something typically Chinese and easy to carry.
我想买一些带有中国特色的且容易携带的东西。

2. I suggest you buy some embroideries.
我建议你买刺绣。

3. Feel the material. Look at the pattern.
摸摸它的质地，看一看样式。

4. They aren't worth that much.
它们不值那么多钱。

5. You were overcharged.
你买贵了。

6. It's worth every penny I asked for.
它值我要的价钱。

7. I've never overpriced my goods.
我从来都不要高价钱。

Background Information

When shopping in China, the following tips will be useful for tourists from abroad.

1. When buying antiques, you should make sure that they are permitted to be exported. According to Chinese relevant laws, antiques that dated before 1795 are not allowed to be exported. The suggestion is that you always examine things carefully before buying.

2. When buying expensive antiques, you should make sure that they bear a seal (in sealing wax). This little seal indicates that the article is authentic and can be taken out of China legally.

3. Remember not to buy such items as made from rare wild animals. Recently, the production of some animal medicines has been restricted in order to protect endangered species like antler, leopard, tiger, rhinoceros and elephant. So, medicines made from endangered animals are not allowed to be exported.

4. Receipts are needed when buying and should be kept after buying. When going through the customs at the airport, you may be asked to show these receipts before leaving China.

Reading

Shopping in China

There are many exotic and unusual things to buy in China which make wonderful souvenirs and gifts for relatives and friends back home. The following is a sample of the amazing range of goods available.

Silk

Chinese silk is famous all over the world for its magnificent quality, color and variety. Silk products from Hangzhou, Sichuan, Suzhou and Dandong are particularly good.

In ancient times, there were cloths made of silk in China, especially for the nobleman to make clothes. Despite technological development, a silkworm can only produce a certain amount of silk—1,000 meters (3,280 feet) in its lifespan of 28 days. The rarity of the raw material is the deciding factor of both the value and the mystery of silk. The development of productivity popularizes silk and it is no longer a luxury just for aristocrats.

Tea

Tea from China, along with her silk and porcelain, began to be known by the world over a thousand years ago and has since always been an important Chinese export. In summer or warm climate, tea seems to dispel the heat and bring on instant cool together with a feeling of relaxation. Tea is also rich in various vitamins; for smokers, it helps to discharge nicotine out of the system. There are varied tastes and kinds of tea in China, with each of them having different positive effects.

There are hundreds of varieties of Chinese tea. They can be classified into five categories — green tea, black tea, brick tea, scented tea, and oolong tea. The top ten types of teas in China are as follows; any of them would make a wonderful gift for your friends.

Longjing (龙井) produced near West Lake, Hangzhou, Zhejiang

Biluochun (碧螺春) from Wu County in Jiangsu

Huangshan Maofeng(黄山毛峰) from Mount Huangshan in Anhui

Junshan Silver Needle(君山银针) from Junshan Island on Dongting Lake

Qimen Black Tea(祁门红茶) from Qimen County in Anhui

Lu'an Guapian(六安瓜片) from Lu'an County in Anhui

Xinyang Maojian(信阳毛尖) from Xinyang in Henan

Duyun Maojian(都匀毛尖) from Duyun Mountain in Guizhou

Wuyi Rock Tea(武夷岩茶) from Wuyi Mountain in Fujian

Tieguanyin (铁观音) from Anxi County in Fujian

Wines and Spirits

Alcoholic drinks, in ancient China, were regarded as sacred and were used only in sacrifices. Today, however, wines and spirits are becoming popular as accompaniments to Chinese food.

The following wines and spirits have won many international awards:

Yanghe Daqu (洋河大曲) and Shuanggou Daqu (双沟大曲) from Jiangsu

Gujing Tribute Liquor (古井贡酒) from Anhui

Maotai (茅台) and Dong Liquor (董酒) from Guizhou

Wuliangye (五粮液), Jiannanchun (剑南春) and Luzhou Laojiao (泸州老窖) from Sichuan

Fen Liquor (汾酒) from Shanxi

Antiques

If you're an antique enthusiast, China is the place for you! Fascinating antique and curio shops and market stalls are to be found in most cities and towns. Care is needed, however. When buying expensive items you must make sure, for example, that the item carries the official red seal of the shop and the sale documents are in order. Chinese law forbids the export of antiques dated earlier than 1795.

Chinese Medicinal Materials

Traditional Chinese medicine is an integral part of Chinese life and culture. With its unique diagnostic methods, systematic approach, abundant historical literature and materials, traditional Chinese medicine has found many adherents in Western countries. The use of traditional herbs and potions lies at the core of Chinese medicine. Mostly made from animal and plant materials, these medicines have proved effective for treating a wide range of illnesses and disorders. Tonics based on herbs are also popular. Examples of the materials used in the preparation of medicines and tonics are ginseng, antler, rhubarb horse-tails, bezoars, angelica, Tianqi, licorice root, apricot kernel and the root of balloon flower.

In recent years, for the sake of protecting endangered animals, the preparation of medicinal materials from rare animals, such as musk, antler, leopard and tiger bone, rhinoceros horn and elephant skin, has been restricted. Such medicines cannot be exported from China; however, tourists can export Chinese herbs with a total value of less than RMB 300 yuan (per person).

Arts and Crafts

Arts and crafts products make ideal souvenirs and gifts. These include bronze ware, cloisonne, folk toys, jade, kites, lacquer wares, paper-cutting, porcelain, pottery, seal, prints and scrolls, silk, embroidery and printed and dyed fabrics. Cloisonne made in Beijing, porcelain made in Jingdezhen in Jiangxi, embroidery from Suzhou, Hunan, Guangdong and Sichuan, Tang tri-colour pottery horses and camels from Luoyang and Xi'an, and batik (蜡染) from Guizhou and Yunnan are all highly recommended.

The "four treasures of study" (文房四宝) —namely writing brush, ink stick, ink slab, paper—play an important part in Chinese culture. You may want a set for your own study or to give as a unique gift to your friends. The best writing materials are said to be Xuan paper and Hui ink stick from Anhui, Duan ink slab from Guangdong and Hu writing brush from Zhejiang.

a. Answer the following questions according to the passage.
1. What are the typical Chinese goods?
_____
2. How many categories can tea be classified into according to the passage?
_____
3. What is the famous wine of Anhui?
_____
4. Why are some of Chinese medicine not allowed to be exported from China?
_____
5. What are the "four treasures of study"?
_____

b. Translate the expressions into Chinese or English.

1. be regarded as	_____
give best regards to sb.	_____
_____	尊重某人
_____	关于
2. an integral whole	_____
_____	积分方程
_____	整体的组成部分
3. make preparations for	_____
be in preparation	_____
_____	事前准备，预先准备
4. arts and crafts	_____
_____	有技巧地，巧妙地
aerial craft	_____

c. Choose an appropriate word to fill in each blank to make each sentence meaningful, and change its form when necessary.

| particularly | exotic | range | available | magnificent |
| discharge | forbid | rare | include | recommend |

1. These _____ palaces impressed the foreigners deeply.
2. How long will the _____ of the cargo take?
3. We need about twelve excellent football players, _____ in age from 18 to 23, to reinforce our college team.
4. The house itself is not _____ to my mind, but I like its environment.
5. Lack of time _____ any further discussion at the point.
6. The film retains much of the book's _____ flavor.
7. The graphic arts _____ calligraphy and lithography.
8. Soon after the accident, the motorist was sent to hospital by the people _____ at the scene.
9. Can you _____ to me a good dictionary?
10. Parliament has passed an Act forbidding the killing of _____ animals.

d. Translate the following sentences into English with words or phrases given in the brackets.

1. 法国以它的美酒和佳肴闻名于世。(be famous for)
_____

2. 他们的市场策略是根据对顾客花钱的情况所作的研究而制定的。(be based on)
_____

3. 本省的丝绸工业有很长的历史了，刺绣产品在世界上声誉很好。(embroidery, well-established)
_____

4. 一般来说，陶瓷产品可以分为两类，即实用品和艺术品。(classify into)
_____

5. 在许多大型的购物中心里，宠物禁止入内。(forbid)
_____

Vocabulary List

accompaniment　　[ə'kʌmpənimənt]　　　n. 自然的伴随物，陪伴物

adherent	[əd'hɪərənt]	adj. 黏着的，依附的
alcoholic	[,ælkə'hɒlɪk]	adj. 酒精性的，含有乙醇的，含有酒精的
angelica	[an'dʒɛlɪkə]	n. [植] 白芷
antler	['æntlə]	n. 鹿角，多叉鹿角，茸角
approach	[ə'prəʊtʃ]	n. 接近；门径
apricot	['eɪprɪkɒt]	n. 杏
available	[ə'veɪləbl]	adj. 可用的；有效的
award	[ə'wɔ:d]	n. 奖，奖品
batik	['batɪk]	n. 巴蒂克印花法；蜡防印花（法）；蜡防法印染的花布
bezoar	['bi:zɔ:]	n. [药] 毛粪石，胃石，牛黄，马宝（均为解毒剂）
category	['kætəgəri]	n. 种类，部属；类目
cloisonne	[klwɑ:'zɒneɪ]	adj. 景泰蓝制的
curio	['kjʊərɪəʊ]	n. 古董，古玩，珍品
diagnostic	[,daɪəg'nɒstɪk]	adj. 诊断的
discharge	[dɪs'tʃɑ:dʒ]	v. 卸下，放出；解雇；放电；解除
disorder	[dɪs'ɒ:də]	n. 混乱，杂乱，无秩序
dye	[daɪ]	n. 染料
		v. 染色
enthusiast	[ɪn'θju:ziæst]	n. 热心家，热情者，热衷……者
exotic	[ɪg'zɒtɪk]	adj. 异国的，外来的
fabric	['fæbrɪk]	n. 布；（毛，丝）织物
forbid	[fə'bɪd]	v. 禁止，不准
ginseng	['dʒɪnsɛŋ]	n. 人参
herb	[hɜ:b]	n. 草；草本植物；香草，药草
include	[ɪn'klu:d]	v. 包括，包含，连……在内
integral	['ɪntɪgrəl]	adj. 构成整体所必需的；完整的
kernel	['kɜ:nl]	n. （果实的）核，仁；[计算机] 核心
lacquer	['lækə]	n. 真漆；（中国、日本等地产的）天然漆
leopard	['lepəd]	n. 豹
licorice	['lɪk(ə)rɪʃ]	n. 甘草，甘草制剂，甘草精
literature	['lɪtrətʃə]	n. 文学，文学作品
magnificent	[mæg'nɪfɪsnt]	adj. 壮丽的，宏伟的
musk	[mʌsk]	n. 麝香

particularly	[pə'tɪkjələli]	adv. 特别，尤其
porcelain	['pɔːsəlɪn]	adj. 瓷制的，精美的，脆的
pottery	['pɒtəri]	n. [集合词] 陶器类
rhinoceros	[raɪ'nɒsərəs]	n. 犀牛
range	[reɪndʒ]	n. 范围，行列
		v. 排列，归类于，延伸
rare	[reə]	adj. 稀罕的，罕见的，珍贵的
recommend	[ˌrekə'mend]	v. 建议，推荐，劝告，介绍
rhubarb	['ruːbɑːb]	n. [植]大黄；食用大黄；大黄根(药用)
sacred	['seɪkrɪd]	adj. 神圣的，庄严的
sacrifice	['sækrɪfaɪs]	n. 牺牲，牺牲品；祭品，献祭
scroll	[skrəʊl]	n. (羊皮纸)卷轴；(纸)卷；卷形物
seal	['siːl]	n. 印章；海豹
slab	[slæb]	n. 平板；厚的切片
souvenir	[ˌsuːvə'nɪə]	n. 纪念品
systematic	[ˌsɪstə'mætɪk]	adj. 有系统的；分类的；体系的
tonic	['tɒnɪk]	n. 滋补剂

Phrases

brick tea	砖茶
scented tea	花茶
oolong tea	乌龙茶
horse-tails	马尾
licorice root	甘草根
bronze ware	青铜器
along with	与……一起
based on	建立在……基础上
be famous for	因……而著名
classify into	分类
in order	按顺序，井然有序

Terms

Cloisonne	景泰蓝
Tang tri-color	唐三彩

Writing

A Letter of Complaints

Task 1　Writing Skills

当自己的正常生活受到骚扰、自己的合法权益受到侵犯、社会服务有失规范时，人们有权通过某种途径对其提出批评或指责，其途径之一就是写信。

西方人在表达不满情绪或提出批评意见时，十分重视摆事实、讲道理。在写此类书信时，他们不习惯拐弯抹角，更不会编造、歪曲事实。即使在盛怒之下，他们也仍讲求实事求是。

人们写信进行抱怨和批评的最终目的是解决问题，并非为了发泄而发泄。尽管人们有时会用词尖刻、口气生硬，但其用意仍是为了纠正错误或帮助当事人改正错误，因此，信中很少掺杂与之无关的感情色彩。当用英语写这类书信时，应首先揣摩例行的行文思路，不可按照自己的思维方式故意伤害当事者的感情，也不要为了出气而将问题搞得更加复杂。

抱怨及批评信的信体结构一般为：描述问题的经过——论述问题引起的后果——提出批评及处理意见。

Task 2　Sample Writing

Subject：Complaint about a restaurant's service

Dear Mr. Carl,

　　My wife and I had heard from friends that dining at the Seaside was an enjoyable experience. Therefore, we reserved a table for last Saturday night and invited another couple to join us. Things got off to a shaky start when no table was ready when we arrived. After a 40-minute wait we were finally seated.

　　The waiter seemed hurried and annoyed. Two of us ordered the vichyssoise and were disappointed. The salmon with crabmeat stuffing fell short of expectations.

　　Since our guests included my law firm's most important client, I avoided any complaint about the food or confrontation with the irritable waiter, but I'm disappointed nonetheless.

　　From the reputation you've built, I can only conclude that our experience was an exception. It was, however, enough to keep us from ever returning.

Yours faithfully,
(Signature)

【译文】

主题：向饭店老板反映其服务质量问题

尊敬的卡尔先生：

我和妻子从朋友处得知在你们海滨饭店进餐是一种享受，因此我们上周六在贵店预订了一张餐桌并邀请了另一对夫妇共进晚餐。事情一开始就不顺利，因为在我们到达时，居然没有一张布置好了的餐桌。在足足等了40分钟后，我们才最终就座。

服务员看起来既匆忙又生气。我们中的两位点了奶油浓汤但很失望，而鲑鱼配蟹肉这道菜也不符期待。由于邀请的客人中有我们律师事务所最重要的客户，因此我没有对食物进行抱怨或与急躁的服务员起冲突，但不管怎样我感到很失望。

从贵店已经建立的名声来看，我只能得出结论说我们的经历是一次例外。然而，这足以让我们不再光临贵店。

您诚挚的 ××

（签名）

Common Sentence Patterns about Complaints and Criticisms

(1) I had always enjoyed doing business with your firm until recently when I felt much disappointed by your...

过去我一直愿意与贵公司共事，然而，近日来贵公司却……，这使我很失望。

(2) The dismissal of ... is not just a loss of a clever and humorous tour guide, but also a loss of our faith and confidence in your agency.

你们更换×××不仅使你们失去了一位富有智慧和幽默感的导游，而且也使我们对你们旅行社失去了信心和信任。

(3) I understand and appreciate your policy change ... but what I can't understand and appreciate is your receptionist's way of handling the new policy.

我理解并赞同你们政策的改变，但我无法理解和赞同的是你们的接待员执行新政策时的那种方式和方法。

(4) My wife and I had heard from friends that dining at your restaurant was an enjoyable experience, but our recent experience proved otherwise.

我和我的妻子听朋友说，在您那儿吃饭是一种享受，而就近来我们的亲身体验而言，事实并非如此。

(5) One annoying aspect of your service is...

你们的服务项目中一个令人不满的方面是……

(6) It would seem not an unreasonable expectation to be treated with common courtesy in return.

礼尚往来，希望受到基本的礼貌接待，这不算过分吧。

(7) I have been pleased with your service for years, but now I am just plain frustrated.

多年来我一直很满意你们的服务，但是现在我简直失望透顶。

Task 3　Writing Practice

a. Fill in the following complaint letter by translating the Chinese in the brackets.

Dear Mr. Worthington,

　　_____ (一个令人相当烦恼的方面) of the otherwise satisfactory commuter train service from Lancaster to downtown Manchester is the playing of the radio over the loud speaker system.

　　This was particularly objectionable this morning on the 6:40 train where riders were subjected to the incessant blaring of KIOU for _____ (几乎全程). Evidently whoever calls the stops is unaware that the background noise of his radio accompanies his announcements. _____ (而更糟的是), he apparently forgets to press his off switch, and _____ (一千名乘客被迫聆听) this clatter.

　　Noise pollution on city buses is usually confined to an individual carrying a loud radio. Old Smoky Railroad does it on a loud radio. Old Smoky Railroad does it on a grand scale. I think it should stop.

　　　　　　　　　　　　　　　　　　　　　　　　　　　Yours truly,
　　　　　　　　　　　　　　　　　　　　　　　　　　　Tom Wallace

b. Write a letter according to the situation below. Add some more information if necessary.

假如你是海伦，和朋友一起到餐厅吃烤肉。由于服务员 Bud Andrews 的不慎，将肉汁泼到你新买的毛衣和短裙上。为此，你给餐厅老板 Mr. Dewey 写了一封 150 字左右的抱怨信，信中包括以下内容：

1. 你到餐厅就餐的日期是 10 月 24 日；
2. 你们当日是免费消费，但仍因此遭受了重大损失；
3. 希望老板考虑赔偿相应的购衣和干洗费用共计 181 美元。

Vocabulary Development

Words and Expressions

Chinese knot	中国结
clay figurine	泥人
dough figurine	面人
waxwork	蜡像
gold plate	(总称)金器
silverware	银器
tapestry	挂毯
brocade	锦缎
scarf	围巾
necktie	领带
high heels	高跟鞋
calf skin	小牛皮
imitation leather	人造皮
shoe store	鞋店
bookstore	书店
record shop	唱片行
pharmacy	药店
bakery	面包店
antique shop	古董店
souvenir shop	纪念品店
optician	眼镜商
floor	楼层
fitting room	试衣间
shape	形状
design	设计
pattern	式样
stripe	条纹
flaw	瑕疵

Common Commercial Slogans

sold out	已售完
on sale	特价中
closed	打烊
exit / way out	出口
pull	拉
push	推
out of order	故障中
no parking	禁止停车
staff only	员工专用
gentlemen	男用厕所
ladies	女用厕所

Useful Sentences

May I help you?	我可以帮你吗?
I'm just looking, thank you.	随便看看，谢谢。
I'll take this.	我要买这个。
What are the opening hours?	请问营业时间到几点?
Let me look in the mirror.	让我照下镜子。
This doesn't fit well.	这个不是很合适。
What is the material?	这是什么材料?
Can you make it less?	能便宜点吗?
Please give me a discount.	给我打个折吧。
I can give you a ten percent off.	我可以给你打九折。
I will take it if you lower the price.	如果便宜一点儿我就买。
This is the best I can do.	这已经是最低价了。
Can I have a refund on this?	这个可以退货吗?
Does the price include tax?	这个价格含税吗?
Can I get a tax refund for this?	请问这个可以退税吗?
Should it be dry-cleaned?	请问它要干洗吗?

Unit 13

Settling Complaints
解决投诉

Unit Objectives

After learning this unit, you should

- understand what is the definition and classification of complaints;
- master the basic words and expressions about settling complaints;
- get some background information about tourism complaints;
- find ways to improve your writing skills about A Claim Letter;
- be familiar with the UK Travel Industry and the process of settling complaints.

Background Knowledge

Tourism complaint is a common phenomenon in tourism activities. Tourism complaint is that tourists and overseas traveling salesmen, domestic tourism operators and others make a complaint about the damage to the legitimate standards of tourism operators and related services units in order to safeguard their own legitimate rights of the tourism, in written or oral request of handling the complaints to the tourism administration departments.

Types of complaints

1. complaints of domestic tourism   国内旅游投诉
2. outbound tourism complaints   出境旅游投诉
3. inbound tourism complaints   入境旅游投诉

The topics of complainants

1. travel agencies   旅行社
2. hotels   酒店
3. dining   餐饮
4. interesting places   景点
5. shopping   购物
6. transportation   交通
7. the others   其他

Practice Materials

Listening

Dialogue 1

a. Listen to Dialogue 1 and decide whether each of the following sentences is true (T) or false (F).

1. ___ Frank lives in Room 158.
2. ___ Frank wants to change the room at first.
3. ___ There is something wrong with the air-conditioner.
4. ___ The assistant manager will send a repairman to check that air-conditioner at once.
5. ___ At last Frank doesn't want to change his room.

b. Listen to the dialogue and answer the following questions.

1. What's the guest's name?

_____

2. What's wrong with the air-conditioner?

_____

3. Do you know the phrase "she said it was too much for her"?

_____

4. Do they have a spare room for Frank today?

_____

5. Do you know the phrase "have a sound sleep"?

_____

c. Listen to the dialogue again and supply the missing words.

1. My child was woken up several times by the _____ the bad air-conditioner made.

2. I'm _____ sorry, Sir.

3. The American & Chinese _____ Delegation will be leaving tomorrow morning.

4. I hope we'll be able to enjoy our stay in _____ tomorrow evening and have a sound sleep.

5. Be sure. I'll _____ of that.

Notes

1. assistant manager	副经理
2. air-conditioner	空调
3. prearrange	预先安排
4. wake up	醒来
5. too much for somebody	受不了
6. repairman	修理工
7. spare room	备用房间
8. delegation	代表团
9. sound	有效彻底的
10. suite	套房

Dialogue 2

a. Listen to Dialogue 2 and decide whether each of the following sentences is true (T) or false (F).

1._____ The conversation happened on the phone.

2._____ The madam will live in Room 490.

3._____ The madam isn't satisfied with five items in the room.

4._____ The room is untidy because the housemaid is too lazy to clean the room.

5._____ The last solution is to change another room for the madam.

b. Listen to the dialogue and answer the following questions.

1. When does the conversation happen?

_____

2. How did the madam feel when she entered into her room?
_____

3. Which is the worst thing in the madam's opinion?
_____

4. Who will be sent to the room and help the madam with her luggage?
_____

5. What does the madam think about the last solution?
_____

c. *Listen to the dialogue again and supply the missing words.*
1. I'm simply shocked to find the room in such an _____.
2. First the room is _____ and has _____.
3. And _____ hasn't been _____.
4. Then the _____ is always _____ in the washroom.
5. Oh, dear, we are _____ for all this mess.

Notes

1. receptionist	招待员，传达员
2. shock	打击，震惊，冲突
3. intolerable	无法忍受的，难耐的
4. pillow	枕头
5. faucet	龙头
6. inconvenience	麻烦，不方便之处
7. previous	在前的，早先的
8. occupant	占有者，居住者
9. access	通路，访问，入门
10. chambermaid	（寝室的）女仆，（旅馆里负责清理卧室的）女服务员
11. make up	整理，包装
12. peak season	旅游旺季
13. porter	行李搬运工
14. reasonable solution	合理的解决办法

Background Information

Hotel Service

Hotel service is one of the most important tasks for tour guides to concentrate. Proper maintenance and provision of hotel services have a significant effect on the attitude of a guest toward the hotel. A lobby, elevator, or room that has not been maintained properly, that looks shabby, or that contains items requiring repair creates a bad impression on the guest. And of course, inadequate air conditioning, poor heating, or improper plumbing will result in immediate complaints. The guest pays a substantial amount of money for accommodations and expects the equipment to function at least as well as it does at home. Therefore, the chief engineer and staff have an important role to fulfill in satisfying the guests' demands and thus helping to maintain the profit level for the hotel. At the same time, the engineering department's cost must be properly monitored and controlled.

Speaking

Dialogue 1

A Complaint about Noise

R: Receptionist   **B**: Mr. Barratt

R: Good evening, Sir. How can I help?

B: I'm in Room 554 and it's too noisy.

R: I'm sorry about that. What kind of noise can you hear?

B: I need to have my window open because it's too hot but the noise from the night club is too loud. They should turn the volume down.

R: I do apologize. Let me see if we can find you a room at the back of the hotel. It's quieter there.

B: Thank you. I have had a very busy day and I need peace and quiet to sleep.

R: I understand. We can put you in room 534. Is that acceptable?

B: That will be OK if it is quiet.

R: I will have someone take your bags to the room. It will be ready in 10 minutes.

B: Thank you.

R: That's OK. Sleep well.

> **Notes**
>
> 1. noisy　　　　　　　　吵闹的，喧闹的，充满噪音的
> 2. night club　　　　　　夜总会
> 3. turn down　　　　　　关小，调低
> 4. volume　　　　　　　（广播、电视或音响系统的）音量
> 5. peace　　　　　　　　安静，宁静，安宁
> 6. acceptable　　　　　　可接受的
> 7. Sleep well.　　　　　　睡个好觉。

Dialogue 2

Tourism Complaints to Dalian

A: Good morning. May I help you?

B: Could I speak to the manager?

A: Our manager has been out. What can I do for you, Sir?

B: I'm afraid I have to make a complaint. My whole family chose a tour line to Dalian in your travel agency last week. On the way to the lido in Dalian, there was something wrong with the sightseeing bus. We had to wait for half an hour for the driver to fix it. But he couldn't fix it well. Then the guide called the local travel agency for help. He said we would wait for about forty minutes for another sightseeing bus. But it was just traffic jam, so we had to wait for nearly two hours for that bus. As a result, we had no spare time to the lido. It made my family members very disappointed, especially for my son. When he heard the bad news, he cried. It made our mood too bad. You must examine the bus condition before you start a tour. How do you explain that?

A: I'm terribly sorry, but that is the situation. We have reported the case to the superior leadership of our company. I believe that it will have a good reply soon.

B: It's hard to believe that there happened such a bad thing in a well-run company.

A: Yes, Sir. I understand how you feel. Please calm yourself. We'll try our best to solve the problem, but I cannot guarantee anything now because we haven't got any reply from our superior leadership. We do try to check the case as thoroughly as possible and give you a reasonable reply. Would you tell us your demands?

B: Well, the tour guide should make an apology to us for the matter. And your agent must send back our lido fee and make compensation for us.

A: Well, we'll report your demands to the superior leadership of our company soon. Please wait for our reply with patience. Please fill in the form, and we'll call you.

B: (After filling in the form) I hope it won't be long.

A: No, we'll give you a reply as soon as possible.

> **Notes**
>
> 1. lido　　　　　　　　　　　　海滨浴场，露天游泳池
> 2. sightseeing bus　　　　　　　观光巴士
> 3. fix　　　　　　　　　　　　 修理
> 4. traffic jam　　　　　　　　　塞车，交通拥堵
> 5. disappointed　　　　　　　　失望的
> 6. especially　　　　　　　　　 特别，尤其
> 7. bus condition　　　　　　　　车况
> 8. superior leadership　　　　　 上级领导
> 9. Please calm yourself.　　　　 请你平静一下。
> 10. make an apology to ...　　　　向……道歉

Dialogue 3

Tourism Complaints to Hainan

A: Good morning. Is there anything I can help you?

B: Yes. I'm Mrs. Haden. Excuse me, I think I have a complaint about our travel to Hainan.

A: I'm sorry to hear that. What was the problem?

B: Well, we chose the travel line named 'Free Trip' to Hainan in your travel agency. At first you promised to provide the same personal tour guide to accompany us for the whole trip. And you promised that it was a fine line with wonderful interesting places. But we found the tour guide disappeared when we checked in the flight. After we got off the plane, we were sent to a hotel by another tour guide. Afterward we knew the guy was a local tour guide in Hainan. The worst thing was that they changed two tour guides for us throughout the whole tour.

A: Well, you know, madam, in general, one local tour guide is responsible for the tasks in one destination. So we usually change local tour guides according to different traveling lines.

B: But you didn't tell us in advance. What's more, the last tour guide made a bold change for the arranged line. If we refused to do so, he became angry and left us alone. At last, we had to obey him. So we didn't see that so-called wonderful interesting place. One doesn't expect this sort of thing in a well-run travel agency.

A: Thank you for telling us about it. I'm sorry, madam, there may be some misunderstanding. In general, our tour guides must obey the travel contract. I will look into it and give you a reply as soon as possible. Could you give me your number that I can reach you?

B: My mobile telephone number is 13978787656.

A: We do try to check it as thoroughly as possible. Is there anything else?

B: No, thank you.

A: You are welcome. Sorry for the inconvenience. I'll give you a reply as soon as possible.

Notes

1. Free Trip	自由行
2. tour guide	导游
3. promise	允诺，答应
4. personal	私人的，针对个人的
5. accompany	陪伴，伴奏
6. interesting place	景点
7. disappear	消失，不见
8. local tour guide	地陪
9. throughout	遍及，贯穿
10. in advance	提前
11. make bold to	擅自，胆敢；冒昧
12. travel agency	旅行社
13. misunderstanding	误解
14. travel contract	旅行合同
15. mobile telephone	手机
16. thoroughly	十分地，彻底地

Reading

Introduction to the UK Travel Industry

What is the Travel Industry?

The travel industry provides facilities and services for people traveling away from the area where they normally live and work. It is a massive international industry dedicated to

meeting the needs of millions of travelers each year including:
- transport
- accommodation
- food and drink
- things to see and do
- help to plan and book their travel and to make the most of their stay at a destination

The travel industry therefore includes a number of different sectors and types of organizations which work together.

The Structure of the Travel Industry

International travel is a complex business and many different organizations are likely to be involved in any trip. Travel service providers can be divided into three types: producers (often referred to as principals), wholesalers and retailers. These work together to form what is known as a distribution chain.

Producers provide and operate essential components such as accommodation or transport.

In the travel industry, producers include:
- Accommodation operators: hotels, holiday centres, guesthouses, bed and breakfast accommodation, self-catering operators, camping and caravan parks and motels.
- Transport operators or carriers: airlines, ferries, cruise operators, railways, bus and coach operators.

Backing up these producers are a range of support services including excursion operators, catering services, guiding services, car hire, travel insurance companies and transfer agents, etc.

Wholesalers are tour operators or brokers. Tour operators buy products such as hotel rooms or aircraft seats in bulk and package them together to create a package or inclusive tour. Brokers also buy items in bulk and sell these on, often to smaller tour operators with limited buying power.

Travel agents are retailers who sell inclusive tours developed by tour operators, as well as separate travel components from producers (such as flights or cruises) and ancillary services such as travel insurance and airport car parking. These products are bought by members of the public.

In the UK, the travel industry provides services for:
- Outbound tourists: who are traveling from the UK to an overseas country, for example, a family from Birmingham traveling to Spain for a summer holiday.
- Domestic tourists: traveling from their home to a destination elsewhere in the UK,

for example, a couple traveling from Edinburgh for a short break in the Lake District.
- Incoming tourists: visiting the UK from an overseas country.

Travel Industry Products

Accommodation is a key requirement for people traveling away from home, and a key element of inclusive tours developed by tour operators. Some travel agents book accommodation direct for clients.

Most countries, including the UK, operate systems of classifying and grading accommodation establishments to assist consumers in selecting accommodation to meet their needs. In England, there are classification and grading schemes for hotels, guesthouses, etc., for example, 4-star hotels and 3-diamond guesthouses. There are also separate schemes operating in Scotland and Wales. Other countries have different systems and some tour operators have developed their own systems for grading hotels.

The following types of rooms are usually available in hotels:
- Single rooms: containing a single bed and suitable for occupation by one person.
- Twin rooms: containing two beds and suitable for occupation by two people.
- Double rooms: containing one double, queen-size or king-size bed and suitable for occupation by two people.
- Family rooms: suitable for use by a family.
- Suites: sets of connecting rooms with one or more bedrooms and bathrooms, plus a sitting room. A junior suite is a large room with a separate sitting area(rooms with en-suite facilities have private bathrooms).

There is often a supplement payable for a balcony, terrace or sea view in resort hotels.

Hotels normally operate one or more bars and restaurants and may offer guests a range of other services such as laundry facilities, a gym, swimming pool, games rooms, hairdressers and shops. In larger hotels in beach resorts, there is often a programme of daytime sporting and other activities and evening entertainment.

Many packages in hotels and holiday centre include meals. Different arrangements apply including:
- Full board (FB): breakfast, lunch and dinner each day. Full board arrangements can also be described as American Plan (AP).
- Half board (HB): breakfast and lunch or dinner each day.
- Bed and Breakfast (BB): Bermuda Plan (BP) includes English breakfast. Continental breakfasts include tea or coffee, bread, toast or rolls, butter and preserves, and often fruit juice, cold meat and cheese. English breakfasts include cooked meals such as

bacon and eggs.
- All inclusive (AI): all meals and drinks.

Transport

Transport is another key element of packages developed by tour operators and agreements for the sale of transport products can also be made between travel agents and principals.

Transport products include:
- scheduled or charter flights with the UK or overseas airlines.
- ferry, jetfoil or hovercraft crossings. Sailings can be booked for passengers only or for passengers plus their cars, motor cycles or caravans.
- coach travel in the UK or to European destinations.
- rail travel in the UK or internationally.

Inclusive Tours

There are a wide range of mainstream and specialist tours developed by tour operators and sold by travel agents. Some have a broad appeal and attract a range of different types of customers and others, more specialist tours attract only those with a particular interest or within a specific age group.

Handling Complaints

Travel agents and tour operators make great efforts to ensure that their customers are satisfied with the service they receive and that they enjoy the holidays they have booked. However, things do occasionally go wrong and in such cases dissatisfied clients may demand compensation.

Some dissatisfied clients will not say anything at all. However, they may well not be prepared to use the same company again.

Others will complain:
- to their travel agent
- to the transport operator
- in the resort to the resort representative or accommodation provider
- to the tour operator's office in the UK

Dealing with complaints can be difficult. However, it is important for any employee handling a complaint face-to-face or on the telephone to:
- follow their employer's complaints procedure
- listen carefully to the complaint and make appropriate notes in order to establish the facts
- remain calm, even if the client is angry and aggressive

- empathize with the client but do not admit liability, i.e. do not admit that anyone was at fault
- suggest appropriate action and attempt to agree this with the client

It is very important for agents and operators to deal with all complaints in a professional manner and for ABTA members to meet the requirements of the ABTA Code of Conduct.

In most cases, it will be possible to reach a mutually acceptable agreement. However, in a small number of cases it may not be possible to resolve the dispute amicably.

a. Answer the following questions according to the passage.

1. Could you name a type of transport about the travel industry?
_____

2. Decide if the following are outbound, domestic or incoming tourists on the side of the author.

(1) A family from Cardiff (英国港市) traveling to Greece.

(2) A couple from London holidaying in Wales.

(3) An Australian resident touring Scotland.
_____

3. Could you name different types of rooms usually available in hotels?
_____

4. Please list the range of facilities and services available to guests in a large resort hotel.
_____

5. To whom will some dissatisfied clients complain in the UK?
_____

b. Translate the expressions into Chinese or English.

1. international travel   _____
   wholesalers and retailers _____
   _____   分配链
   guesthouses   _____
2. outbound tourists   _____
   _____   境内游客
   incoming tourist   _____
3. twin room   _____
   double room   _____
   suite   _____

4. _____	全膳
half board	_____
bed and breakfast	_____
travel agent	_____
transport operator	_____
_____	达成协议

c. Choose an appropriate word or phrase to fill in each blank to make each sentence meaningful, and change its form when necessary.

facility	provide	massive	millions of
book	handle	make the most of	accommodation
reach a mutually acceptable agreement			dedicated…to

1. We must make _____ efforts to improve things.
2. Are there washing _____ in the school?
3. It is _____ in the contract that the work should be accomplished within a year.
4. She _____ a difficult argument skillfully.
5. The two countries finally _____ on their borders.
6. We must _____ natural materials.
7. The traveling students found _____ at moderate prices.
8. He _____ his life _____ the service of his country.
9. The secretary _____ the manager in at the Hilton Hotel.
10. There are _____ bicycles on the road.

d. Translate the following sentences into English with words or phrases given in the brackets.

1. 如果你当时不支持我，是没有人相信我的。(back up)

    _____

2. 外出旅游时，我们整个部门分成了三个小组。(divide into)

    _____

3. 因为严重的交通堵塞，他有可能会晚到一会儿。(be likely to)

    _____

4. 消除贫困是社会主义本质要求。(essential)

5. 我要是你就不去介入他们的问题。(involve in)

Vocabulary List

acceptable	[əkˈseptəbl]	*adj.* 可接受的；合意的
accommodation	[əˌkɒməˈdeɪʃn]	*n.* 住处，膳宿
aggressive	[əˈgresɪv]	*adj.* 有闯劲的；侵略性的
airline	[ˈeəlaɪn]	*n.* 航线
amicably	[ˈæmɪkəblɪ]	*adv.* 友善地
ancillary	[ænˈsɪləri]	*adj.* 辅助的；副的
appropriate	[əˈprəʊpriət]	*adj.* 适当的
appeal	[əˈpiːl]	*n./v.* 请求，要求；吸引力
assist	[əˈsɪst]	*v.* 援助，帮助
attempt	[əˈtempt]	*v.* 努力，尝试，企图
bacon	[ˈbeɪkən]	*n.* 培根，咸肉，熏肉
balcony	[ˈbælkəni]	*n.* 阳台；包厢，(戏院)楼厅
book	[bʊk]	*v.* 登记，预订；控告
broker	[ˈbrəʊkə]	*n.* 中间人，经纪人
bulk	[bʌlk]	*n.* 体积；大批
caravan	[ˈkærəvæn]	*n.* 旅行队，大篷车
catering	[ˈkeɪtərɪŋ]	*n.* 公共饮食业；给养
charter	[ˈtʃɑːtə]	*v.* 租，包(船、车等)
cheese	[ˈtʃiːz]	*n.* 干酪；<俚>头等的人或事物
classify	[ˈklæsɪfaɪ]	*v.* 分类，分等
classification	[ˌklæsɪfɪˈkeɪʃn]	*n.* 分类，分级
coach	[kəʊtʃ]	*n.* 四轮大马车，长途汽车；教练
compensation	[ˌkɒmpenˈseɪʃn]	*n.* 补偿，赔偿
complex	[ˈkɒmpleks]	*adj.* 复杂的，合成的，综合的
component	[kəmˈpəʊnənt]	*n./adj.* 成分；组成的，构成的
cruise	[kruːz]	*vi./n.* 巡游，巡航
dedicated	[ˈdedɪkeɪtɪd]	*adj.* 专注的，献身的
destination	[ˌdestɪˈneɪʃn]	*n.* 目的地
element	[ˈelɪmənt]	*n.* 要素，元素

empathize	['empəθaɪz]	v. 移情；神会
employee	[ɪm'plɔiː]	n. 职工，雇员，店员
ensure	[ɪn'ʃʊə]	v. 保证，担保
essential	[ɪ'senʃl]	n./adj. 要素，要点；基本的，精华的
establish	[ɪ'stæblɪʃ]	v. 建立，设立
establishment	[ɪ'stæblɪʃmənt]	n. 确立，设施
excursion	[ɪk'skɜːʃn]	n. 远足，游览，短程旅行
facility	[fə'sɪləti]	n. 设备，工具
ferry	['feri]	v./n. 摆渡；渡船，渡口
hire	['haɪə]	n./v. 租金；租用，雇用
hovercraft	['hɒvəkrɑːft]	n. 气垫船
jetfoil	['dʒetfɔɪl]	n. <主英>喷流水翼船
liability	[ˌlaɪə'bɪləti]	n. 责任；倾向；债务
mainstream	['meɪnstriːm]	n. 主流
massive	['mæsɪv]	adj. 厚重的；大块的
motel	[məʊ'tel]	n. 汽车旅馆
mutually	['mjuːtʃuəli]	adv. 互相地，共同地
occasionally	[ə'keɪʒnəli]	adv. 有时候，偶尔
occupation	[ˌɒkju'peɪʃn]	n. 职业；占有
particular	[pə'tɪkjələ]	adj. 特殊的；详细的
preserve	[prɪ'zɜːv]	v./n. 保护，保藏；蜜饯，果酱
principal	['prɪnsəpl]	n./adj. 首长，校长；主要的，首要的
procedure	[prə'siːdʒə]	n. 程序，手续
professional	[prə'feʃnl]	n./adj. 自由职业者，专业人员；专业的，职业的
representative	[ˌreprɪ'zentətɪv]	n./adj. 代表；典型的，有代表性的
requirement	[rɪ'kwaɪəmənt]	n. 需求，要求，必要条件
resolve	[rɪ'zɒlv]	v. 决心，决定解决
resort	[rɪ'zɔːt]	n./vi. 凭借，手段；胜地；求助，诉诸
retailer	['riːteɪlə]	n. 零售商人
schedule	['ʃedjuːl]	n. 时间表，进度表
scheme	['skiːm]	n. 计划，方案
self-catering	[ˌself'keɪtərɪŋ]	adj. 自给的，自供伙食的
specialist	['speʃəlɪst]	n. 专门医师，专家
specific	[spə'sɪfɪk]	n./adj. 特效药，细节；特殊的，特效的

suitable	['suːtəbl]	adj. 适当的，相配的
supplement	['sʌplɪmənt]	n. 补充；附录；增刊
terrace	['terəs]	n. 露台，阳台
toast	[təʊst]	n./v. 烤面包（片），敬酒；烤（面包等）
wholesaler	['həʊlseɪlə(r)]	n. 批发商

Phrases

a range of	一套
a short break	短暂休息
attract...with	吸引
back up	支持，倒退
be divided into	被分成
be known as	被认为是
be likely to	可能
be satisfied with	对……感到满意
be prepared to	准备
deal with	处理
dedicate...to	献身
involve in	使陷入
meet the needs of	满足……需要
make the most of	充分利用
meet the requirements of	满足……需求
provide for	做准备，供养
reach a mutual agreement	达成双边协议
in bulk	散装，大批

Terms

All inclusive (AI)	包全餐和饮料
Bed and Breakfast (BB)	住宿加（次日）早餐
Code of Conduct	行为准则，管理法典
Cold meat	（西餐）冷盘肉
Double room	双人房（带一张大床的双人房）
Family room	家庭房（适合一家人住宿的房间）
Full board (FB)	全膳（包早、中、晚三餐）
Half board (HB)	半膳（包早、中或晚两餐）
Inclusive tour	包办旅行

Single room	单人房
Suite	套房
Twin room	双人房（带两张单人床的双人房）

Notes

Bermuda	百慕大群岛
Birmingham	伯明翰
Edinburgh	爱丁堡
Scotland	苏格兰
Wales	威尔士
Lake District	湖泊地区

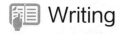

Writing

A Claim Letter

Task 1　Writing Skills

在欧美国家，当人们付了款而得不到应有的服务时，大多数人不是忍气吞声或无动于衷，而是通过各种方式要求有关部门给予退款或赔偿。

一般来说，写这类书信的人虽然气愤，但大多数情况下仍能把握行文的分寸，这主要是因为他们懂得写信的目的是解决问题，而不是发泄怒气或怄气。当然，这并不能排除人们会用带有命令、威胁字眼的可能性。正如本单元索赔信范例所示，口气生硬、态度坚决的书信不在少数。在很多情况下，这样的书信反倒加速问题的最终解决。但需要中国读者注意的是，写这类书信的欧美人一般懂得自己的权利范围，他们写信的用词和口气是以这种权限为基础的。换言之，他们十分清楚得到退款或赔偿的可能性，因为他们熟悉有关法律或规定。我们在写这类书信时，切勿不分青红皂白地照搬本单元信例中的口气或用词，否则会引起额外的麻烦。

在书写索赔信时，一般应首先向有关部门或负责人陈述事情的经过，具体要求或提出的条件放在信尾。有些写信人在信的开头先向收信人提出表扬或赞扬，然后再提出问题，这不失为一种礼貌的写作手法。

书写索赔信时，需要读者根据具体情况酌情安排，信例结构一般如下：描述事件的开始及背景——详述事情的经过——提出要求（退款或赔款金额）及根据——提出具体的解决办法——感谢对方的合作或向对方提出带有威胁口吻的督促。

Task 2 Sample Writing

1) Claim for the lost baggage

Dear Mr. Stewart,

On May 2, I arrived on your Flight 603 from Baltimore to St. Louis. However, the suitcase I checked at your counter prior to the flight never arrived in St. Louis and hasn't been found in the six weeks since. Nor have I been reimbursed for the value of the suitcase and its contents.

When it became apparent that my luggage was missing I reported it to your Miss Rachel at the baggage claim area in St. Louis. Before leaving the airport I filled out a report. I am enclosing a copy of that report with this registered letter. Also enclosed is a copy of the claim check I was issued in Baltimore, along with an itemized list of the contents of the suitcase and the approximate value.

I realize that your liability covers only the depreciated value of the missing items and not the cost of replacing them. Since the total amount of the claim is well under the 75% of passenger liability limit for baggage-loss claims on domestic flights, I see no point in further delay in processing the claim.

Yours truly,
Henry Lee

【译文】

主题：因空运行李丢失而要求赔偿

尊敬的斯图尔特先生：

我于5月2日乘坐贵公司603航班从巴尔的摩飞往圣路易斯。然而，航班起飞前我在贵公司柜台办理托运的手提箱却根本没有抵达圣路易斯，此后六周也毫无音信，而且也无人就手提箱及其中物品的价值对我进行任何补偿。

很显然我的行李已丢失，于是我向圣路易斯行李领取区的雷切尔小姐报告了此事。在离开机场前，我还填写了报告单。现将此报告单的复印件连同此信一起挂号寄给您，随信还附上我在巴尔的摩被发到的行李认领牌的复印件以及一份提箱内物品的详细清单及大概价格。

我知道贵方只负责承担丢失物品的折旧价格而不是全额的赔偿。由于我索赔的总金额在规定的国内航班对每位乘客行李丢失索赔限额的75%以下，因此我看不出在处理本索赔中有进一步耽搁的理由。

您真诚的
亨利·李

2) Claim for the interference

Dear Mr. Paul,

On the weekend of June 3-5, three friends and I attended the Political Women's Seminar held in your hotel. We had a room reserved for the two nights, but on one of those nights we were able to get very little sleep.

On the night of the third there was a high school prom in the hotel. From midnight till 3:00 A.M., the teens were roaming the halls, shouting, banging on doors and being as rowdy as they could. Our calls to the desk brought promises, but no action.

The next morning we went to the registration desk and asked for a refund for that night and were told that was impossible. Since we had paid for the two nights in advance, we were stuck.

We understand these were unusual circumstances, Mr. Paul, but if you wish to continue to draw seminar groups to your hotel, some changes in policy must be made. If we do not receive a refund for that night we will make sure the Political Women no longer have their annual seminar in your hotel.

Yours truly,
Jane Smith

【译文】

主题：因住宿受打扰而要求旅馆赔偿

尊敬的保罗先生：

在6月3日至5日的周末，我和三位朋友参加了在贵旅馆举行的妇女政治研讨会。我们定了一个房间住了两夜，但其中一个夜晚我们几乎无法入睡。

其原因是在3日晚旅馆里举行了一场高中生的舞会。从午夜到凌晨3点，青年学生们在大厅里到处闲逛、喊叫、猛敲房门，竭尽所能地吵闹。我们打电话给服务台，他们承诺解决问题，却不见动静。

第二天早晨我们到登记处要求退还当晚房费，但被告知没有可能。由于我们已提前支付两晚费用，因而无法脱身。

保罗先生，虽然我们理解这些并不是通常的情形，但如果你希望继续吸引研讨会团体来贵旅馆，就必须做出一些政策改变。如果我们没有收到当晚的退款，将肯定不再在贵旅馆举办妇女政治研讨班年会。

您真诚的
简·史密斯

Common Sentence Patterns about Claim

(1) I'm willing to concede that luggage is occasionally lost, even on a well-run airline like... but...

我承认，丢失行李的事偶尔会发生，即使是在像……那样管理很好的航空公司也是如此，然而……

(2) I have just returned from a week's vacation which your ads bill as, "Island living at its best." In reality, it was a disaster.

我刚刚结束一周的度假回来，你们的广告说这是"海岛最佳时节之旅"，可事实上却是一场灾难。

(3) This letter is to confirm my phone call this afternoon in which I requested that my reservation for the tour to Hawaii be cancelled.

谨以此信证实今天下午我的电话内容：我请求取消预定，不去夏威夷了。

(4) According to our contract, you should... but you obviously can't... so I'm writing to...

根据我们的合同，你们应该……，但是你们明显不能……，因此我写信要求……

(5) I'm writing to request a refund since...

既然……，我现写信要求退款。

(6) We understand these were unusual circumstances, Mr. Keyes, but if you wish to continue to draw seminar groups to your hotel, some changes in policy must be made.

凯斯先生，我们能理解这种情况非比寻常，但是，假如你希望继续吸引会务组去你的饭店的话，你就应该改变政策。

(7) I regret the inconvenience this unavoidable cancellation has caused you.

对于此次不得不取消预定而给你带来的不便，我深感抱歉。

(8) Rather than just chalk it up to experience, I have decided to extract some measure of compensation in return for the miserable week caused by your misrepresentations and negligence.

你们的不称职和玩忽职守造成了一周的不愉快，为此，我决定向你们要求一定的赔偿，而不仅仅将此事归咎于你们缺少经验了事。

Task 3   Writing Practice

a. Fill in the following claim letter by translating the Chinese in the brackets.

Dear Mr. Hobing,

In early April I sent a check for a $50 deposit for my son, Brad, to attend the summer camp. Brad _____ (多年来一直盼着参加夏令营).

Two days ago he _____ (骑自行车出了事故).

He broke his right wrist and sprained his left ankle and, needless to say, is in no shape to attend the camp next week.

I am enclosing a note from Dr. Ted outlining the extent of Brad's injuries. I realize you've had a space reserved for him, but in view of his accident and my prompt notification, _____ (请退还 50 元押金，我们不胜感激).

Cordially yours,

Jack Han

b. Write a letter according to the situation below. Add some more information if necessary.

假如你是李红，和家人一起入住某酒店，但你预定的客房没有及时准备好。为此，你写信给该酒店的经理 Mr. Pane。信长约 150 字，信中包括以下内容：

1. 你到达酒店的时间是 7 月 14 日下午 5 点；
2. 直到晚上 9 点半客房还没准备好，影响了孩子们的休息；
3. 要求酒店为此退还当晚房费 162 美元。

Vocabulary Development

complain	抱怨，悲叹，控诉
complain about	抱怨
complain of	抱怨，抗议
complainant	发牢骚的人，原告
complaining	诉苦的，抱怨的
complainingly	诉苦地，抱怨地
complaint department	顾客意见接纳处
lodge a complaint	提出不满意见，对……提出控告
make a complaint	提出不满意见，对……提出控告
make a complaint against	提出不满意见，对……提出控告
complaint and claims	抗议与索赔
complaint desk	障碍报告 (服务) 台
complaint investigation	陈诉调查
complaint note	催询通知，意见书
complaint notice	催询通知
find fault	挑剔

grumble	怨言，满腹牢骚
justified complaint	合理的投诉
mutter	咕哝，嘀咕
pour out	倾诉
squawk	诉苦，抗议
unjustified complaint	不合理的投诉
for attention	关注
inconvenience	麻烦，不方便之处
failure	失败；故障；疏忽

Dealing with Special Problems
应对难题

Unit Objectives

After learning this unit, you should

- understand how to deal with problems & emergencies;
- master the basic words and expressions about illnesses and disasters;
- get some knowledge about travelers' check;
- find ways to improve your writing skills about A Letter on a Reply to a Guest's Complaint;
- be familiar with first aid techniques.

Background Knowledge

During the journey, a variety of special problems and emergencies may occur sometimes. Therefore, it's necessary for a travel agency to have plans to deal with such crises.

Types of Problems & Emergencies

1. food poisoning	食物中毒
2. typhoon & hurricane	台风和飓风
3. tsunami	海啸
4. elevator incident	电梯故障
5. physical assault	人身伤害
6. terrorist attack	恐怖袭击
7. equipment breakdown	设备故障

8. earthquake	地震
9. fire	火灾
10. lose the way	迷路
11. street fights	街头打斗
12. explosion	爆炸
13. get sick	生病
14. lose properties	遗失财物
15. traffic accident	交通事故
16. flood	洪水
17. gas leakage	气体泄漏
18. power failure	停电
19. kidnap	绑架
20. hijack	劫持

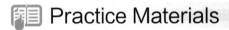 Practice Materials

Listening

Dialogue 1

Explosion

a. Listen to Dialogue 1 and decide whether each of the following sentences is true (T) or false (F).

1. _____ The tourist is an American.
2. _____ The tourist wants to enter a train station.
3. _____ The station is closed because of an explosion.
4. _____ All the stations are closed except Euston Station.
5. _____ The tourist wants to take a plane to China.

b. Listen to the dialogue and answer the following questions.

1. How long has the tourist been lining up for?

2. Why are the stations closed?

3. When will the plane to China take off?

4. Where did the explosion happen?
_____

5. How does the tourist go to the airport?
_____

c. Listen to the dialogue again and supply the missing words.

1. A tourist is _____ to enter the station, but something unusual happened.
2. Attention, please! Something _____ has happened.
3. _____ should be evacuated at once.
4. I think you can go to the Russell Square to _____.
5. Would you give me _____?

Notes	
1. stand in a line	排队
2. explosion	爆炸
3. evacuate	撤离
4. Huston Station	休斯敦地铁站
5. the Russell Square	罗素广场
6. a double-decker bus	双层巴士

Dialogue 2

Losing one's handbag

a. Listen to Dialogue 2 and answer the following questions.

1. Why does the tourist go to the police station?
_____

2. Can he remember where he lost it?
_____

3. What is the color of his handbag?
_____

4. What were the tourist and his friend doing when they sat at the table?
_____

5. What's inside the handbag?
_____

b. Listen to the dialogue again and supply the missing words.

1. But _____, I was in the shopping mall with my friend.
2. But the most unlucky thing is, _____ is in the bag.
3. Now please fill in this _____.
4. Write down your name, _____.
5. We'll try to look for it _____.

Notes

1. shopping mall   购物广场
2. zipper   拉链
3. makeup   化妆品
4. passport   护照
5. lost form   失物登记表
6. embassy   大使馆

Background Information

Qualities of a Tour Guide

Pleasantness breeds pleasantness, and one of the first essential qualities for a tour guide is a naturally pleasant manner. This will be a great skill in dealing with people, for the attitude of the guide is so often reflected quickly in the person with whom he/she is dealing. A real liking for people which springs from a genuine desire to help them is another necessary quality. This is based on unselfishness and the ability to put the needs and wishes of tourists before his/her own.

Speaking

Dialogue 1

Settling a Complaint about Services

P: Mr. Pink   **M**: Manager

P: I want to complain about the terrible service in this hotel.

M: I'm sorry you are not happy, Sir. What has happened?

P: This morning I wanted a wake-up call at 7 A.M., but I didn't get one so I was late for my meeting.

M: I do apologize, sir.

P: Also, your staff are very slow. I waited an hour for the service in your restaurant and when the waiter came he was very rude and he upset my wife.

M: I'm sorry, he's French.

P: I would like to know what you are going to do about this awful service.

M: I will talk to my staff and make sure it doesn't happen again.

P: Good. If the service doesn't get better I will never stay here again.

M: It will get better. Can I give you a discount to make you happy?

P: That's very nice of you.

Notes

1. wake-up call　　　　　（旅馆等提供的）叫醒电话，叫醒服务
2. staff　　　　　　　　　员工，全体职员
3. upset　　　　　　　　　使生气，使心烦意乱
4. awful　　　　　　　　　让人讨厌的，糟糕的，使人不快的
5. discount　　　　　　　折扣，打折

Dialogue 2

A Careless Guest

(A careless guest, Mr. Bell, has locked himself out of the hotel room. Now he is asking a clerk for help.)

A: I've locked myself out of the room. May I borrow a duplicate key?

B: Don't worry, Mr. Bell. I'll open the door for you.

(She opens the door with a duplicate key.)

A: Thank you very much. Sometimes I'm quite absent-minded.

B: It doesn't matter, Mr. Bell. What else can I do for you?

A: Ah, I'm afraid there's something wrong with the TV. The picture is wobbly.

B: I'm sorry. May I have a look at it?

A: Here it is.

B: (Try to fix it, but in vain) I'll send for an electrician from the maintenance department. We can have it repaired. Please wait for just a few minutes, Mr. Bell.

(She leaves the room. Ten minutes later, there is a knock at the door.)

E (**Electrician**): May I come in?

A: (Open the door) How do you do?

E: How do you do? The TV set is not working well. Is that right, Mr. Bell?

A: No, it isn't.

E: Let me have a look. (Finishes the repairing and checks other electric facilities in the room) Mr. Bell, everything is OK now.

A: What efficiency! Thanks a lot.

(Taking out some fee) This is for you.

E: Oh, no. We won't accept tips, but thank you anyway. We wish you a nice stay with us, Mr. Bell.

Notes

1. duplicate key　　　　　备用钥匙
2. absent-minded　　　　心不在焉的
3. wobbly　　　　　　　摇摆不定的
4. electrician　　　　　　电工，电学家
5. maintenance　　　　　维修、保养
6. facility　　　　　　　设备工具（常用复数）
7. efficiency　　　　　　效率

Oral Practice

Make a dialogue according to the information that a hotel guest calls from his room for a repairman to come to attend to the toilet, which is out of order.

Dialogue 3

Claiming for Damage and Loss

Scene: *A careless guest (G) has thrown a cigarette end on the bedcover and burnt a hole in the bedcover and the blanket. The housekeeper (H) is talking to the guest.*

H: Good morning, Mr. Smith.

G: Good morning.

H: I am the housekeeper. May I know what happened here?

G: Sure. I met some friends in the room last evening. We smoked and talked a lot. When I was going to bed, I suddenly found there was a cigarette end in the bed. The bedcover and the blanket were burnt.

H: I'm sorry to hear it. But let me take a look first.

G: OK, here they are.

H: Oh, I am sorry to say they are badly damaged. These are all quite new and have been used no more than a week.

G: I do apologize for what I have done.

H: Well, I am afraid we have to charge them to your account.

G: May I know how much they are?

H: About 350 yuan.

G: That's about two nights' room price.

H: If a fire started, you couldn't imagine the outcome.

G: That's true. I'll never forget the lesson. By the way, what are you going to do with the bedcover and blanket?

H: Don't worry, Sir. I'll ask the chambermaid to give you a new bedcover and a blanket for this evening.

G: And the damaged ones?

H: Now, they are all your belongings. You may take them with you.

G: Oh, I don't think my wife will like to see them. She always advises me to give up smoking.

Notes

1. cigarette   香烟
2. bedcover   床罩
3. hole   洞，破洞
4. damage   损坏，毁坏
5. chambermaid   清理房间的女服务员

Role–play

A guest throws cigarette ends on the carpet in his room and burns it. Practice the dialogue he might have with the housekeeper.

Reading

Passage 1

Traveler's Cheques

When traveling abroad, it's always wise to carry your money in travelers' cheques because cheques are protected against loss or theft. If your cheques are lost or stolen, the issuing authority will refund your money.

Not only are they safe, they are also convenient. They are available in different denominations and different currencies and they can be cashed at most banks throughout the world. Most shops, hotels and restaurants also accept them.

To obtain travelers' cheques, you usually go to your bank. They can be paid for in cash or debited to your account. Large amounts, however, must be ordered in advance.

For the safety and convenience of travelers' cheques, you are charged two commissions. An insurance commission when you buy them, and an encashment commission when you cash them.

They are very easy to use. When you collect them you sign each cheque once. The cashier enters the amount in your passport. When you cash you sign each cheque again. The cashier will usually ask to see your passport again too.

It is advisable to make a note of the serial numbers and denominations of your cheques in case they are lost or stolen. Keep this separate from the cheques.

a. Decide whether each of the following statements is true (T) or false (F).
1. _____ Travelers' cheques cannot be lost or stolen.
2. _____ You must always order travelers' cheques.
3. _____ You pay twice for travelers' cheques.
4. _____ You must sign each cheque twice.
5. _____ You must keep a record of your cheques.

b. Translate the expressions into Chinese or English.
1. _____ 旅行支票
   commercial traveler
   _____ 旅费
   travel-soiled
2. protect against loss
   _____ 防止袭击
   protect from the cold
   _____ 防御危险
3. _____ 保险佣金
   _____ 兑现佣金
   on commission
   out of commission

4. _____   做好记录

sound a note of warning   _____

strike the right note   _____

_____   记下，记录

c. Choose an appropriate word to fill in each blank to make each sentence meaningful, and change its form when necessary.

| steal | order | charge | refund | denomination |
| issue | available | advisable | abroad | cheque |

1. He told me that I could pay by _____ instead of in cash.
2. How much do you _____ for mending a pair of shoes?
3. In view of the delay, the customers obtained a _____ of a deposit.
4. The US coin of the lowest _____ is the cent.
5. He loves collecting stamps and he always buys new stamps on the day of_____.
6. The judge _____ that the prisoner should be remanded.
7. Do you think it _____ to have kept waiting for him here?
8. The tour guide received a group of visitors who have come from _____ warmly.
9. The old lady found that her purse was _____ as soon as she arrived at the airport.
10. You'd better note that these tickets are _____ for one month only.

d. Translate the following sentences into English with words or phrases given in the brackets.

1. 你能将这张支票兑换成现金给我吗？(cash)

_____

2. 如果空中交通被严格控制的话，飞行就会相对安全一些。(in case)

_____

3. 在一间房住一个晚上他们想要我付八十英镑！(charge)

_____

4. 我们选择这个酒店是取其方便：它离商店很近，而且交通也很便利。(convenience)

_____

5. 她把有毛病的收音机退还给商店并要求退款。(refund)

_____

Vocabulary List

account	[ə'kaʊnt]	n. 计算，账目，说明
advisable	[əd'vaɪzəbl]	adj. 可取的，明智的
authority	[ɔː'θɒrəti]	n. 权威，威信，权威人士；权力
cash	[kæʃ]	v./ n. 兑现，现金
cashier	[kæ'ʃɪə]	n. (商店等的) 出纳员
charge	[tʃɑːdʒ]	v. 装满，控诉，收费
commission	[kə'mɪʃn]	n. 委托，佣金
convenient	[kən'viːniənt]	adj. 便利的，方便的
currency	['kʌrənsi]	n. 流通，货币
debit	['debɪt]	v. 记入借方
denomination	[dɪˌnɒmɪ'neɪʃn]	n. 命名，(货币等之) 单位或类别，面额
encashment	[ɪn'kæʃmənt]	n. <英> 付现，兑现
insurance	[ɪn'ʃʊərəns]	n. 保险，保单，保险费
issue	['ɪʃuː]	v. 发行 (钞票等)；流出，出版 (书等)
refund	['riːfʌnd]	v. 退还，偿还
serial	['sɪəriəl]	adj. 连续的
theft	[θeft]	n. 偷，行窃，偷窃行为

Phrases

travelers' cheques	旅行支票
make a note of	记下，记录
pay for	付款，支付
protect against	防御，保护
separate from	分开，分离
in advance	预先，提前
in case	以免，万一
in cash	用现金
throughout the world	全世界

Passage 2

An Accident

Jack is the manager of a 120-seat restaurant in a resort area in Hong Kong. As the dinner crowd starts to thin out one night, he hears a sound outside the door of his restaurant.

When he opens the door, he sees that the wife of one of his customers is sitting on the steps holding her ankle. The light beside this door isn't very bright, but he thinks he sees her husband rushing to the car. Jack asks if there's anything he can do to help and the woman tells him that her husband is taking her right to the emergency room to get her ankle checked out. She tells Jack that he'll be sure to get the hospital bill and more. Her husband pulls up alongside her, gets his wife in the car, and tells Jack, "You'll hear from me!"

As promised, the next day her husband drops off the hospital bill to Jack and threatens a lawsuit. Jack tells him that he doesn't understand, after all he did ask if he could help, and he explained that the door they used was not the proper exit for guests. It was an employee entrance and exit. At this point, the man tells Jack, "You'll hear from my lawyer."

a. Answer the following questions according to the passage.

1. Who is Jack?

_____

2. What does he see when he opens the door one night?

_____

3. What does the husband do the next day?

_____

4. What isn't safe about the employees' door?

_____

5. What should Jack have done to make sure customers do not use the employees' door?

_____

b. Translate the expressions into Chinese or English.

1. resort area　　　　　　　　　　_____
   health resort　　　　　　　　　_____
   _____　　　避暑胜地
   _____　　　凭借，求助

2. the side door
   _____　　　_____
   　　　　　　　　　　　　　　　并肩地，互相支持地
   put on side　　　　　　　　　　_____
   on/from all sides

3. emergency room
   _____　　　_____
   　　　　　　　　　　　　　　　紧急出口
   an emergency fund
   _____　　　_____
   　　　　　　　　　　　　　　　在紧急情况时

4. _____   停下车
   pull sb. up
   _____   追上
   pull-up

c. Choose an appropriate word or phrase to fill in each blank to make each sentence meaningful, and change its form when necessary.

| drop off | accident | crowd | check | hear from |
| after all | thin out | step | entrance | lawsuit |

1. His mother was killed in a road _____ when he was still a young boy.
2. The policeman told the old man that the bus would _____ at the station.
3. The accountant _____ all these figures before she leaves the company every day.
4. The young soldier failed _____, in spite of all that had been done.
5. There were large _____ of people in the streets on Christmas Eve.
6. After a long _____ of 5 years, the murderer was sentenced to death in the end.
7. His parents were very glad to hear that he had passed the university _____ examination.
8. I wonder how often you _____ your elder sister.
9. Mind the _____ when you go down into the cellar.
10. The farmer _____ the seedlings, pulled up some of them to allow the others to grow better.

d. Translate the following sentences into English with words or phrases given in the brackets.

1. 如果其他手段都失败的话，我们将诉诸武力。(resort to)

_____

2. 在过去的十年里，战争和疾病已使这个国家的人口减少了。(thin out)

_____

3. 他那出乎意料的批评使我停下来认真思考。(pull up)

_____

4. 恐怖分子威胁要把飞机炸毁，如果他们的要求得不到满足。(threaten)

_____

5. 结完账后他匆匆忙忙地驾车赶往机场，把他的手机落在了旅馆。(check out)

_____

Vocabulary List

alongside	[ə,lɒŋ'saɪd]	*adv.* 在旁
ankle	['æŋkl]	*n.* 脚踝
exit	['eksɪt]	*n.* 出口
lawsuit	['lɔːsuːt]	*n.* 诉讼（尤指非刑事案件）
lawyer	['lɔːjə]	*n.* 律师
resort	[rɪ'zɔːt]	*v./ n.* 求助，诉诸，凭借；胜地
threaten	['θretn]	*v.* 恐吓，威胁

Phrases

hospital bill	医疗费用清单
check out	结账，检查
drop off	将某物送到某地
emergency room	急诊室
hear from	收到某人的信件、消息等
pull up	停止，拉起，拔起
thin out	减少

Writing

A Letter on a Reply to a Guest's Complaint

Task 1　Writing Skills

妥善处理客人的投诉是修复或重建企业信誉、重新赢得客户信任的重要手段。回复投诉有两种形式：口头和书面，书面形式显得更为正式。无论投诉是否合理，回复客户的投诉信都要及时，信件的重点要放在问题的解决方案上，且要注意语言的委婉和礼貌，内容要符合国家相应法规和企业相关规定。

回复投诉信大致包括以下内容：

一、感谢对方来信。

二、诚恳地表示歉意，简单解释出错的原因。

三、告知补救方案，如有可能给客户提供适当的补偿以示诚意。承诺下次不再发生这样的情况，并诚挚地邀请对方再次光临。

Task 2 Sample Writing

Reply to a Guest's Complaint

Dear Mrs. Mary,

We are sorry to see your letter dated May 15 that you have not received good service on the journey from Wuhan to Yunnan.

We have learned that the relevant tour guide has just graduated from Traveling College. She has made such a mistake because she lacks enough practical experience. We believe that she will know "A fall into the pit, a gain in your wit." At the same time, we will call for all staff to strengthen their study of professional knowledge. We guarantee that this won't happen again.

We are extremely sorry for the incident. As a measure of compensation, we would like to give a further 5% discount on your following tour in our traveling agency. We hope this arrangement will give you satisfaction.

Yours faithfully,
Zhao Liang

General Manager

回复投诉常用句型

(1) I'm awfully sorry, Sir.

非常抱歉，先生。

(2) I do apologize (for what had happened).

我向您道歉。

(3) I'm sorry, Sir, there must be some misunderstanding.

对不起，先生。我想这里面可能有点误会。

(4) Sorry, Sir. I'll solve the problem for you as soon as possible.

先生，很抱歉，我将尽快解决这个问题。

Task 3 Writing Practice

a. Fill the following replying letter to a justified complaint by translating the Chinese in the brackets.

Dear Sir/Madam,

_____ (您关于服务的投诉已转交给我并引起关注). I am very sorry that you have been inconvenienced by our failure to provide the level of services to which you are entitled.

I have made enquiries and found that the problem was caused by carelessness. _____

（我向您保证我们已经采取了措施，确保这样的情况不会再发生。）

Please accept our apology and appreciation of your highly valued custom. Please contact me personally if you experience any problems with our services in the future.

Yours sincerely,
Jones

b. Fill the following blanks：*Mr. Weimar, the manager of Complaint Department in St. Paul Hotel, will reply a letter to an unjustified complaint letter from Miss Lily on June 21st.*

Dear Miss Lily,

Thank you for your letter of June 12th, concerning service of complaint. _____ _____（我已经彻底调查了这次投诉）and have interviewed all the staff involved. However, _____（我没有发现证据支持您的索赔）. Indeed, I am satisfied that our staff acted properly and with due courtesy and efficiency. _____ ____（如果您觉得我们在处理中有玩忽职守的行为，请接受我的歉意）. If, however, _____（您能提供任何证据支持您的索赔）, I shall be pleased to review the situation. If you would like to discuss the matter in person, please contact me directly.

Yours sincerely,
Weimar
Complaint Department Manager
St. Paul Hotel

Vocabulary Development

Words about Symptoms

headache	头疼
stomachache	胃疼
running nose	流鼻涕
dizzy	头晕
sore throat	嗓子疼
toothache	牙疼
ulcer	溃疡
appendicitis	阑尾炎

fracture/break	骨折
heat stroke	中暑
vomit	呕吐
heart attack	心脏病
sunburnt	晒伤
nose bleeding	流鼻血
breathing difficulty	呼吸困难
cold	感冒
flu	流感
high fever	高烧
allergic/sensitive to	过敏
pneumonia	肺炎
hepatitis	肝炎
arthritis	关节炎
diarrhoea	痢疾，腹泻
cut finger	割破手指
abdominal pain	腹痛

Useful Sentences

1. 抗击疫情，人人有责！Everyone is responsible for fighting the epidemic!

2. 勤开窗、勤洗手、常消毒，预防新型冠状病毒肺炎。Open Windows frequently, wash hands frequently and disinfect frequently to prevent COVID-19.

3. 早发现、早报告、早隔离、早诊断、早治疗！Early detection, early report, early isolation, early diagnosis, early treatment!

4. 做好自我防护就是关爱他人，遵守文明行为就是奉献社会。To do a good job in self-protection is to care for others, and to abide by civilized behaviors is to contribute to the society.

5. 祝愿大家都平安，齐心协力渡难关。May everyone be safe and work together to overcome the difficulties.

Unit 15

Checkout Services
退房服务

Unit Objectives

After learning this unit, you should
- learn how to ask and offer information about checkout at a hotel;
- be familiar with the procedures of settling the bills;
- master the basic words and expressions used during checkout;
- get some knowledge about checkout;
- find ways to improve your writing skills about Resume.

Background Knowledge

Introduction to Checkout at a Hotel

Checkout is one of the primary jobs of front desk personnel. Guests can check out at the cashier of the front desk. Checkout time varies from one hotel to another. In most cases, checkout time at the latest is 12:00 noon or 1:00 P.M. If the guest leaves after the time, he or she will have to pay half or full of the rate. It is important to set a proper checkout time when the guest is to check out. As many tourists in hotels set off at about 8:00 A.M. or 9:00 A.M., they may have to queue for checkout. Therefore, if the guest would like to settle the bill during the time, he or she must allow enough time to do it. However, if the guest notifies the front desk the departure time beforehand, the clerk may get the bill ready. Thus it will save the guest much time when he or she checks out.

When checking out, the guest can either pay in cash or by credit card or with a travelers' check. If the guest checks out by credit card or with traveler's check, he or she will be informed to sign the name.

If the guest needs help to take the baggage to the lobby, he or she may call the bellboy counter. The bellboy will come to the room to take the baggage, but the guest should not forget to tip him. If the guest wants the hotel to deposit the valuables or the baggage, he or she can ask the front desk for help. Most hotels provide this free service.

Before paying the bill, the guest must check each item carefully in case there are some mistakes. If the guest disagrees with the bill, he or she can ask the cashier to explain it or revise it.

Practice Materials

Listening

Dialogue 1

a. Listen to Dialogue 1 and decide whether each of the following sentences is true (T) or false (F).

1. _____ Nobody had breakfast at the dining room this morning.
2. _____ The total amount at the hotel is US$ 3,640.
3. _____ The Travel Agency pays everything for the tourists, including the charge in such places as lobby bar.
4. _____ The check out time is from ten to eleven.
5. _____ One of our tourists will fly to Hong Kong first instead of Wuhan.

b. Listen to the dialogue and answer the following questions.

1. What's Karen Zhou?

_____

2. Which rooms are they staying in?

_____

3. Did Karen find something wrong with the bill?

_____

4. What will Peter pay for separately?

_____

5. How much will be paid by the tourist if he still wants to stay in the room after 12:00?

_____

c. *Listen to the dialogue again and supply the missing words.*

1. Three nights at _____ each, and here are the meals and others you had at the hotel. It totals US$ 3,460.

2. But the amount of money paid by our _____ does not include this kind of charge.

3. Certainly. But if he leaves after 12:00, he'll have to be charged 50% of the price since it's _____ now.

4. _____ is a good idea.

5. Have _____ home.

Notes

1. calculate	计算
2. item	项目，一条，一项
3. sign for	签收
4. brandy	白兰地酒
5. lobby	前厅，厅堂；议会休息室
6. check out time	结账时间
7. Hong Kong	香港
8. charge	收费，要价
9. peak season	高峰期，旺季
10. deposit	订金，押金，保证金
11. refund	归还，退还
12. invoice	发票

Dialogue 2

a. *Listen to Dialogue 2 and decide whether each of the following sentences is true (T) or false (F).*

1. _____ Mr. Green stayed in Room 608.

2. _____ Mr. Green checked out in the evening of 9th.

3. _____ The clerk agreed that Mr. Green hadn't used the mini-bar and refunded him the money.

4. _____ Mr. Green had three bottles of beer from the mini-bar in the evening of 7th.

5. _____ Mr. Green paid the bill with credit card.

b. Listen to the dialogue and answer the following questions.

1. How much is the total amount?
_____

2. How many mistakes are there in the bill?
_____

3. How many days did Mr. Green stay in the hotel?
_____

4. Did Mr. Green use the mini-bar?
_____

5. How much does each bottle of beer cost in the mini-bar?
_____

c. Listen to the dialogue again and supply the missing words.

1. I'm sorry there might be _____ with the bill.
2. But it shows that I have to pay for _____.
3. Excuse me for a moment, Sir, while I _____.
4. Thanks, Mr. Green. Here is your bill, _____.
5. I'll try to be _____ another time.

Notes

1. mini-bar	酒店内的小吧柜
2. detail	细目，细节，详情
3. receipt	收据，发票

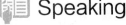
Speaking

Dialogue 1

I'd Like to Settle My Bill

A：clerk   B：Mr. Black, a guest

A：Good morning, Sir. May I help you?

B：Yes, I'd like to settle my bill.

A：Certainly, Sir. May I have your room key, please?

B：Sure. Here you are.

A：Just a moment, please. I'll draw up your bill for you... Thank you for waiting, sir.

Your bill totals two thousand six hundred and fifty-eight yuan, including the phone and laundry.

B：That much! Would you mind letting me have a look at it?

A：Not at all, Sir. Here you are.

B：Thanks. Well, it seems to be right. How much is that in dollars, please?

A：Just a moment, Sir. I'll calculate that for you. It comes to 305 dollars and 52 cents at today's exchange rate.

B：I see. OK.

A：How would you like to make the payment?

B：In cash, please. Here you are.

A：Thank you, Sir... Here is your change. Could you check it, please? Thank you for choosing our hotel. I hope you enjoyed your stay.

B：By the way, please forward my mail to this address.

A：Certainly, Sir. We hope you have a good trip.

Notes

1. settle		结算（账单），结（账）
2. draw up		起草，拟定
3. total		总计达，共计
4. laundry		刚洗好的衣服
5. calculate		计算
6. come to		共计
7. exchange rate		兑换率，汇率
8. forward		（按新地址）转寄，转交

Dialogue 2

Checking out

A：clerk　B：Nancy Baker, a guest　C：bellboy　D：another clerk

A：Good morning! May I help you?

B：Yes. I'm leaving right now. Could you send a bellboy to take the baggage for me?

A：Of course. Which room are you in?

B：Room 425.

A：All right. The bellboy will be up right away.

B：Thank you.

(*After a while*)

C: Bellboy.

B: Come in, please.

C: Good morning, Madam. What can I do for you?

B: Could you please take this baggage for me? I have three pieces of baggage.

C: OK. I'll take them down to the lobby.

B: Thank you.

(Soon they come to the lobby.)

C: Madam, shall I leave the baggage here?

B: Yes, thank you very much. (She gives tip to the bellboy.)

C: Thanks.

(Then Mrs. Baker comes to the front desk to check out.)

B: Hello! I'd like to check out now. I'm in Room 425. Can I have my bill now?

D: Of course. Your name, please?

B: Nancy Baker.

D: One moment, please. (The clerk checks it in the computer.) So you stayed here for two nights. This is your bill 960 yuan. Please check it.

B: Does it include service and tax?

D: Yes, that's everything.

(Mrs. Baker checks it carefully.)

B: OK. Exactly. Do you accept traveler's check?

D: Certainly.

B: Here you are.

D: (The clerk takes an imprint of it.) Mrs. Baker, please sign your name here.

B: Oh, yes.

D: Thanks. Here is your card, bill and receipt. Please take care of them. Hope you have a nice trip and hope to see you soon.

B: Thanks. Bye.

D: My pleasure. Bye.

Notes

1. bellboy 服务生，男侍者
2. baggage 包裹，行李
3. tip 小费
4. traveler's check 旅行支票
5. imprint 印，印记；特征；痕迹

Dialogue 3

Explaining the bill

C: clerk **G**: guest

C: Good morning, Sir. What can I do for you?

G: I'd like to check out. My name is Jack Brown.

C: Excuse me, Mr. Brown. Could you tell me your room number?

G: Room 3308. May I see the bill?

C: Of course, Sir. One moment while I print out your bill... Here you are. The total is RMB 2,508 yuan. Please have a check.

G: (Check the bill) ... I'm sorry. What's this charge of RMB 245 yuan? Could you explain it to me?

C: Sure. That's a 10 percent service charge.

G: Oh, OK. And what's this for?

C: That's for the taxi you called to the World Exposition.

G: Oh, I see. Can I pay in US dollars?

C: No, Sir. I'm sorry. But you can get your money changed at the Foreign Exchange Counter in our hotel.

G: Then would credit card be all right?

C: What kind of card are you holding, Sir? We only accept Visa, MasterCard, American Express, Diners Club.

G: American Express.

C: That's fine... Here is your bill and receipt, Sir. We hope you enjoyed your stay with us here and hope you'll have a nice trip home.

G: Thank you.

Notes

1. total   总计，总数
2. World Exposition   世界博览会
3. Foreign Exchange Counter   外币兑换台
4. Visa, MasterCard, American Express, Diners Club   信用卡名（维萨，万事达，美国运通，大来卡）

 Reading

How Hotels Help Themselves to Your Money

If you think your hotel is done with you when you check out, think again. It might just be getting started.

Charges can be quietly added to your hotel bill after you've left. And increasingly, they are.

When Andrew Fox was a weekly guest at a W Hotels & Resorts property, the items he found on his credit card bill after checkout were often bogus — a candy bar he hadn't eaten or a bottle of water he hadn't drunk. Although he successfully fought to have the charges reversed, "It got to the point that before I checked in, I would ask them to remove the goodie-box from my room," he says.

Just a year ago, about one in 200 bills at full-service hotels was revised after checkout, according to Bjorn Hanson, an associate professor at New York University. Today, as hotels struggle with slipping occupancy levels and flat-lining growth, properties are wasting no opportunity to add late charges. As a result, the number of rebillings has doubled.

The late charges are usually correct, say experts. And if they aren't, most hotels are quick to correct the error. But not always. Some properties either resist crediting their customers or refuse. That's what happened to Charles Garnar when he stayed at the Renaissance Fort Lauderdale Hotel recently. "When we checked out, we were told there were no charges so we had a zero balance," he remembers. But when he returned home after a cruise vacation, he found an unwelcome surprise on his credit card statement: a $57 charge. "It took two days to get through to the accounts payable department," he says, "They said we used the mini-bar."

The hotel only removed the charges after he proved it couldn't have been his. How? Garnar had turned down the mini-bar key when he checked in.

This shouldn't be happening, of course. The latest hotel accounting systems let you see your room charges in real time, often from your TV screen. There's no reason the bill that is slipped under the door on the morning of your checkout shouldn't include all of your charges, with the possible exception of your breakfast check. "It should be your final bill," says Robert Mandelbaum, a hotel expert with PKF Consulting.

In depth

I contacted several hotel chains to find out about their policy on late charges, including Marriott (which owns the Renaissance) and W Hotels. Only one of the major hotels,

InterContinental, bothered to respond. My favorite non-answer came from W, where a spokeswoman told me that, "Because of transitions in the company, we don't have an appropriate spokesperson to speak on this topic right now."

Oh, too bad.

Here's what InterContinental, which owns the Crowne Plaza, Holiday Inn and Hotel Indigo Suites brands, had to say about late billing. It's rare, and usually only happens when guests choose the express checkout option—that's where the bill is slipped under your door on the day of checkout. If someone bills something to your room after 3 A.M., chances are that you'll get a late charge.

Normally, guests aren't notified about the charges, because they've agreed to them as part of the terms of their express checkout. But when there's a significant additional fee, a hotel typically notifies travelers before billing them. What if they disagree with the bill? Contact the hotel and tell a representative you have a problem with the charge, recommends InterContinental spokesman Brad Minor.

"Our hotels value our guests and we want to make sure our guests are satisfied with all aspects of their stay," he says.

I'm pretty confident that the other hotels would have said more or less the same thing. But guests don't necessarily agree with that. After I posted Fox's story on my blog, I received a firestorm of comments accusing the hotels of deliberately charging guests after their stay.

It doesn't really matter. What matters is that you, the guest, don't get socked with a surprise charge on your credit card days or weeks after your vacation. Here are three excuses hotels use for separating you from your money after you're long gone. You might hear some of these reasons articulated by a hotel employee—other excuses are probably reserved for the privacy of the break room or the hotel's executive offices.

Are you sure you didn't take something from the mini-bar?

A vast majority of late checkout charges—about 75 percent, according to Hanson—are from those little refrigerators stocked with vastly overpriced snacks. Hotel mini-bars have become figurative traps that guests get stuck in. Often, they don't even know about it until it's too late. The newest mini-bars have sensors that charge your room the moment an item is moved. Here's a first-person account of guest falling into one of these traps at a Los Angeles hotel.

The solution? Don't accept the key to your mini-bar. If there's no key, ask to have the mini-bar (or goody-basket) removed. It's the only way to be sure.

But you checked out before we could charge you!

Unless you're talking about breakfast on the day you check out, this is an empty excuse. Remember, most hotel accounting systems are lightning-fast. The moment you sign your check for an activity or meal, your account is charged. But if a major charge shows up on your credit card, it's worth calling the hotel.

The solution? Review your bill before checking out to make sure nothing is missing. And check out your credit card bill after your stay to make sure nothing is added.

We didn't think you would notice.

I have no proof—no memos or transcripts, scheming hotel employees saying this. Scores of guest experiences suggest this attitude is pervasive behind the front desk. For example, Eugene Santhin, who was a frequent business traveler from Mt. Laurel, New Jersey, before retiring, says he was often billed for water and mini-bar items that weren't consumed. "Many properties charged for breakfast when it was included in the room rate," he adds. To their credit, the hotels quickly removed the items when he protested. But it was the speed with which they did so that made him suspicious. Were they adding these extras to his bill, hoping he wouldn't notice? It's difficult to say for certain.

The solution? Pay attention! Your hotel may be trying to pull a fast one, despite its denials. Keep all of your receipts.

Not all late billings hurt hotel guests. Reader Kate Trabue remembers a recent stay at the InterContinental Sydney where she was hit with unexpected room charges after she checked out. "A call to the billing department got the charges reversed without a problem," she remembers. "The interesting part of this transaction was that because of the exchange rate, I was credited more dollars than the original charge."

a. Answer the following questions according to the passage.

1. Why does the author think the hotel isn't done with him when he check out and it might just be getting started?

_____

2. What makes the number of rebillings doubled?

_____

3. Why did the hotel remove Garnar's $57 charge?

_____

4. What are the three excuses hotels use for separating you from your money after you have long gone?

_____

5. Do all late billings hurt hotel guests?
_____

b. *Translate the expressions into Chinese or English.*

1. be representative of the people　　　_____
   a representative body　　　　　　　　_____
   _____　　　　　　派代表参加会议
   the House of Representatives　　　　　_____
2. make comments on something　　　　_____
   offer comments　　　　　　　　　　　_____
   no comment　　　　　　　　　　　　_____
   _____　　　　　　征求意见
3. value somebody's advice　　　　　　_____
   _____　　　　　　平均值
   good value　　　　　　　　　　　　　_____
   value securities　　　　　　　　　　　_____
4. _____　　　　　　采取……态度
   attitude towards this question　　　　_____
   maintain a firm attitude　　　　　　　_____
   strike an attitude　　　　　　　　　　_____
5. _____　　　　　　把桌上的桌布拿走
   remove one's shoes　　　　　　　　　_____
   remove all doubts　　　　　　　　　　_____
   be removed from school　　　　　　　_____

c. *Choose an appropriate word to fill in each blank to make each sentence meaningful, and change its form when necessary.*

consume	recommend	typically	attitude	handle
aspect	significant	original	reserve	normally

1. They studied every _____ of the subject.
2. Mr. Yu, we'll have a week vacation. Where do you _____?
3. The liver is functioning _____.
4. The _____ plan was better than the plan we followed.

5. The weather in Siberia is _____ continental.

6. The front seats _____ for the leaders and the foreign guests. Would you please move?

7. Can you _____ the situation?

8. Last night Professor made a _____ speech in our college.

9. Thermal engines (热能机), whether they are large or small, have to _____ fuel.

10. What is your _____ towards this question?

d. Translate the following sentences into English with words or phrases given in the brackets.

1. 投诉必须向适当的主管当局提出。(appropriate)
_____

2. 这个顾客的批评有些是没有什么道理的，但他的大部分都是公正的评语。(majority; comment)
_____

3. 这是一种很困难的局势，但他应付得很好。(handle)
_____

4. 她申明自己对被偷的货物一无所知。(protest)
_____

5. 这种厕所是专门留给残疾人用的。(be reserved for)
_____

Vocabulary List

accounting	[əˈkaʊntɪŋ]	n. 会计；记账；清算账目
accuse	[əˈkjuːz]	vt. 控告，谴责，非难
appropriate	[əˈprəʊpriət]	adj. 适当的，恰当的
articulate	[ɑːˈtɪkjuleɪt]	vt. 用关节连接，接合；清晰明白地说
aspect	[ˈæspekt]	n. (问题等的) 方面；外表，方位
associate	[əˈsəʊsieɪt]	adj. 副的，伙同的
attitude	[ˈætɪtjuːd]	n. 态度，看法，意见；姿势
bill	[bɪl]	n. 账单；钞票；票据，清单；法案 vt. 给……开账单；用海报宣传
bogus	[ˈbəʊgəs]	adj. <美> 假的，伪造的
chain	[tʃeɪn]	n. 链(条)，镣铐，一连串，一系列
comment	[ˈkɒment]	n. 评论，意见，批评

confident	[ˈkɒnfɪdənt]	*adj.* 确信的，肯定的；有信心的，自信的
consulting	[kənˈsʌltɪŋ]	*adj.* 商议的，顾问资格的，咨询的
consume	[kənˈsjuːm]	*vt.* 消耗，消费，耗尽
credit	[ˈkredɪt]	*n.* 信任，信用；声望，荣誉
		vt. 相信，信任；把……记入贷方，存入（账户）
cruise	[kruːz]	*n.* 乘船游览，巡游
deliberately	[dɪˈlɪbərətli]	*adv.* 故意地
denial	[dɪˈnaɪəl]	*n.* 否认；拒绝，拒绝给予
executive	[ɪgˈzekjətɪv]	*adj.* 执行的，行政的；实行的；有行政能力的
figurative	[ˈfɪgərətɪv]	*adj.* (用词上) 形象的，比喻的
firestorm	[ˈfaɪəstɔːm]	*n.* 大爆发
handle	[ˈhændl]	*vt.* 处理，操作，控制，应付，对待
increasingly	[ɪnˈkriːsɪŋli]	*adv.* 日益，愈加，越来越多地
majority	[məˈdʒɒrəti]	*n.* 多数，大多数；票数差距，超过的票数
memo	[ˈmeməʊ]	*n.* 备忘录
normally	[ˈnɔːməli]	*adv.* 通常地；正常地
notify	[ˈnəʊtɪfaɪ]	*vt.* 通知，告知，报告
occupancy	[ˈɒkjəpənsi]	*n.* 占有，使用，居住
option	[ˈɒpʃn]	*n.* 选择 (的自由)；选项；可选择的办法
original	[əˈrɪdʒənl]	*adj.* 原先的，最初的，最早的；新创的
overprice	[ˌəʊvəˈpraɪs]	*v.* 将……标价过高，索价过高
payable	[ˈpeɪəbl]	*adj.* 应付的，可付的
pervasive	[pəˈveɪsɪv]	*adj.* 无处不在的；遍布的；充斥各处的
policy	[ˈpɒləsi]	*n.* 政策，方针；策略
property	[ˈprɒpəti]	*n.* 财产；资产；所有物
protest	[ˈprəʊtest]	*vt./vi.* 声明；抗议；拒付
rare	[reə]	*adj.* 稀少的，罕见的
recommend	[ˌrekəˈmend]	*vt.* 劝告，建议；推荐，介绍
refrigerator	[rɪˈfrɪdʒəreɪtə(r)]	*n.* 冰箱，冷藏库
remove	[rɪˈmuːv]	*vt.* 移走；排除；开除
representative	[ˌreprɪˈzentətɪv]	*n.* 代表，代理人
respond	[rɪˈspɒnd]	*vt./vi.* 回答；回报；响应；作出反应
reverse	[rɪˈvɜːs]	*vt./vi.* 取消；撤销；推翻；(使) 翻转废除

revise	[rɪ'vaɪz]	vt. 修订，修改，修正
scheming	['skiːmɪŋ]	adj. 惯搞阴谋的；诡计多端的；狡诈的
sensor	['sensə]	n. 传感器，灵敏元件
significant	[sɪg'nɪfɪkənt]	adj. 重要的，有意义的；意味深长的
slip	[slɪp]	vi./vt. 滑，滑倒；偷偷地塞给，塞入
snack	[snæk]	n. 小吃；点心；快餐
spokeswoman	['spəʊks,wʊmən]	n. 女发言人，女代言人
statement	['steɪtmənt]	n. 声明，陈述，综述
suspicious	[sə'spɪʃəs]	adj. 猜疑的；可疑的；表示怀疑的
transaction	[træn'zækʃn]	n. 处理，办理；(一笔)交易；(一项)事务
transition	[træn'zɪʃn]	n. 过渡；转变；变迁
transcript	['trænskrɪpt]	n. 抄本；誊本；打字本；副本
trap	[træp]	n. 陷阱；圈套；(对付人的)计谋，陷阱
typically	['tɪpɪkli]	adv. 代表性地，典型地，作为特色地
value	['væljuː]	vt. 估价，重视，尊重
vast	[vɑːst]	adj. 极大的，大量的，巨额的

Phrases

a candy bar	一块糖
additional fee	额外费用
a vast majority of	绝大多数
express checkout	快速结账
first-person account	第一人称叙述
goodie-box	糖果盒
late checkout	延迟退房
zero balance	零余额；偿清款项
accuse sb. of	指责、谴责某人……
be stuck in	陷住，卡住，动弹不得
be reserved for	留作，(专)供……之用
get to the point	抓住重点，进入正题
pull a fast one	欺骗
waste no opportunity	利用一切机会
at full-service	提供全方位服务

Notes

Marriott：万豪国际酒店，总部位于美国。

the Renaissance Fort Lauderdale Hotel：万丽酒店。

W Hotels & Resorts：W 酒店。喜达屋酒店 (Starwood Hotels & Resorts Worldwide) 的附属公司。

InterContinental：洲际集团成立于 1777 年，是目前全球最大及网络分布最广的专业酒店管理集团，拥有洲际酒店 (InterContinental)、皇冠假日酒店 (the Crowne Plaza)、假日酒店 (Holiday Inn) 及英迪格酒店 (Hotel Indigo) 等多个国际知名酒店品牌和超过 60 年的国际酒店管理经验。

PKF Consulting：一家国际知名集团公司，提供会计师业务及管理咨询业务，在酒店咨询业久负盛名。

Writing

Resume

Task 1　Writing Skills

下面介绍英文简历的几种常见形式。

英文简历并无固定形式，应聘者完全可以根据个人的具体情况来灵活设计。一般来说，根据个人经历的不同侧重点，可以选用以下三种形式。

(1) 以学历为主的简历 (basic resume)

这种形式适用于应届毕业生或毕业后仍在待业的求职人员。因为没有工作经历，所以将重点放在学业上，从最高学历往下写。

在 basic resume 中，一般包括下列元素。

1) personal data（个人资料）：name（姓名）、address（通讯地址）、postal code（邮政编码）、phone number（电话号码）、birth date（出生日期）、birthplace（出生地点）、sex（性别）、height（身高）、weight（体重）、health（健康状况）、date of availability（可到职日期）、number of identification card（身份证号码）。因为求职者是应届毕业生或毕业不久，一般没有结婚，因而可省略 marital status（婚姻状况）和 children（儿女情况）两项。当然，如果是研究生毕业已婚，则应写明。

2) job/career objective（应聘职位）。

3) education（学历）：就读学校及系科的名称、学位、起止时间，以及应聘职位相关的课程与成绩、社会实践、课外活动、奖励等。

4) special skills（特别技能）。

5) hobbies/interests（业余爱好）。如果在学历项目的课外活动中已经注明，此项则不必重复。

(2) 以经历为主的简历 (chronological resume)

以这种形式出现的英文简历，往往侧重于工作经历，把同应聘职位有关的经历和业绩按时间顺序写出来，把工作经历放在学历之前。经历和学历的时间顺序均是由近至远。

毫无疑问，这种形式的英文简历适用于有工作经验的求职人员。

在 chronological resume 中，通常包括以下元素。

1) personal data（个人资料）。具体内容同以学历为主的简历相同。不过，因为你参加工作多年，已进入结婚年龄，所以不管是否结婚，都应注明婚姻状况和儿女情况。

2) job/career objective（应聘职位）。

3) work experience（工作经历）。务必写明自己在每个工作单位的职位、职责、业绩和工作起止时间。

4) education（学历）。因为你已工作多年，雇主重点考虑你的工作经验是否能胜任你所应聘的职位，所以学历只是一个参考因素，因而不必像以学历为主的简历那样写得详细，只需注明你就读的校系名称、起止时间和学位即可。

5) technical qualifications and special skills（技术资格和特别技能）。

6) scientific research achievements（科研成果）。

(3) 以职能为主的简历 (functional resume)

这种形式的英文简历，也是突出工作经历，因而所含元素和以经历为主的简历相同。二者的根本差别在于：以经历为主的简历是按时间顺序来排列工作经历；而以职能为主的简历则按工作职能或性质来概括工作经历，并无时间上的连贯性，旨在强调某些特定的工作能力和适应程度。例如，你曾在两个不同的工作单位担任相同的职务或负责相同的业务，便可归纳在一个项目之中。例如：

functional summary of work experience *(Sample 1)*

purchasing manager:

July 2013 to May 2015 Guangzhou Friendship Store

December 2017 to September 2019 Nanfeng Department Store

sales manager:

June 2015 to November 2017 Dongshan Department Store

October 2019 to February 2022 Guangzhou Department Store

Increased turnover by 25% in 2021 and by 30% in 2022

工作经历的职能概述（例1）

采购部经理：

2013年7月—2015年5月 广州友谊商店

2017 年 12 月—2019 年 9 月 南丰商场

销售部经理：

2015 年 6 月—2017 年 11 月 东山百货大楼

2019 年 10 月—2022 年 2 月 广州百货大楼

2021 年提高了 25% 的营业额，2022 年提高了 30% 的营业额

work experience: *(Sample 2)*

8/2012-10/2019 Shandong Light Industrial Products Import and Export Corp.

11/2019-4/2022 Guangdong Light Industrial Products Import and Export Corp.

work covered: international marketing

Importing sport shoes from Italy. Decreased purchasing cost by 10-15% between 2013 and 2019.

Exporting rain boots to Europe. Increased profit by 15-20% between 2020 and 2021.

工作经历：（例 2）

2012 年 8 月—2019 年 10 月 山东轻工业品进出口集团公司

2019 年 11 月—2022 年 4 月 广东轻工业品进出口集团公司

工作范围：国际营销

从意大利进口运动鞋。2013 年至 2019 年之间降低购买成本 10%-15%。

往欧洲出口雨鞋。2020 年至 2021 年之间增加利润 15%-20%。

英文简历写作七大技巧

现在许多单位都希望应聘者有比较扎实的英文基础，特别是外企和涉外交往比较多的单位，一份漂亮的英文简历会帮助你给用人单位留下好印象。

那么，如何将英文简历写得更充实呢？在此介绍一些简单技巧。

(1) 教育背景中写相关课程。不要为了拼凑篇幅，把所有的课程一股脑儿地都写上，如体育等。这样会使阅读者产生疲劳感和厌烦感。

(2) 奖学金一项一行。

(3) 语言精练，表达准确。

(4) 加大字号。可将 10 号、小五号改成 12 号或小四号，方便阅读。

(5) 社会工作细节放在工作经历中，这样会弥补工作经验少的缺陷。例如，你在担任团支书、学生会主席等职务时组织过什么活动等。

(6) 暑期工作。作为大学生，雇主通常并不指望你在暑期工作期间会有什么特别突出的成绩，当然如果有就更好了。

(7) 中学情况。一般都写，但不要写太多。小学就不用提了。

Background Information

Tips on How to Write a Resume

To be competitive in the job market you must have the right Selling Tool. The resume is your powerful business and professional resources. A well-planned presentation and the ability to project confidence can lead you to greater revenues, help you to attain instant recognition and place you in a career of choice.

1. A resume should be:
   - Original
   - Informative at a glance
   - Geared toward the industry / company targeted
   - One page in length (preference) or two pages (acceptable)
   - Free from error, visibly crisp and clean
   - Brief and clear in content

2. A resume should not:
   - Use the word "I"
   - Abuse the word "all"
   - Present meaningless information
   - Use the phrase "same as above"
   - Show frequent changes in employment
   - Inject meaningless hot words
   - Expect a cover letter to replace a resume

3. Key elements:
   - An objective
   - Qualifying skills
   - Education, training or related experience
   - List of certifications, licenses or languages spoken
   - Brief company description
   - Employment highlights
   - Pattern of growth or increased responsibilities
   - List of accomplishments, awards, nominations or honors

Task 2 Sample Writing

应聘宾馆客房部主管 (Room Service Supervisor)

Resume	
Name：Xiaofeng Liu　　　　　　　　　　Nationality：the Dong	
Birth date：26/7/2000　　Gender：Male　　Health：Excellent	
Career Objective：Hotel Room Service Supervisor	
Address	Graduating Class, Hotel Management Speciality, College of Management, Fudan University, Shanghai 200433
Date	Education
2018-2022	B.S. in Hotel Management at Fudan University Courses completed: Management Principles, Introduction to Hotel Management, Hotel Personnel Management, Tourist Psychology, Tourism Marketing, Tourism Economics, Room Service Management, Public Relations Science, etc.
2015-2018	Guiyang No.16 Middle School
Summer Jobs	Assistant Room Supervisor at Shanghai International Hotel, 2021 Public Relations Boy at Pudong Hotel, 2020 Assistant Food Supervisor at Shanghai Guest Hotel, 2019
Special Skills	College English Test—Band Six Computer Operation：IBM-PC

英文简历中的其他有用词汇

(1) 应聘职位

objective	目标
career objective	职业目标
position wanted	希望职位
job objective	工作目标
position applied for	申请职位
position sought	谋求职位

(2) 离职原因

for prospects of promotion	为晋升的前途
for higher responsibility	为更高层次的工作责任
for wider experience	为扩大工作经验
due to close-down of company	由于公司倒闭
offered a more challenging opportunity	获得了更有挑战性的工作机会

sought a better job	找到了更好的工作
to look for a more challenging opportunity	找一个更有挑战性的工作机会
to seek a better job	找一份更好的工作

(3) 科研成果

scientific achievements	科研成果
publications	发表作品
daily	日报
evening news	晚报
periodical	期刊
magazine	杂志
monthly	月刊
weekly	周刊
bimonthly	双月刊
semimonthly	半月刊
journal	学刊，学报
issue	(报刊)期号
be published	出版
be carried	登载
publishing house	出版社
invention	发明
innovation	革新
patent	专利

(4) 业余爱好

hobby	业余爱好
go boating	划船
listening to pop music	听流行音乐
listening to classical music	听古典音乐
listening to symphony	听交响乐
reading	阅读
singing	唱歌
skating	滑冰
writing fiction	写小说
skiing	滑雪
do boxing	拳击
traveling	旅游

take pictures	拍照
play cards	打扑克
play chess	下棋
play bridge	打桥牌
Peking Opera	京剧
play basketball	打篮球
play volleyball	打排球
play football	踢足球
play table tennis	打乒乓球
play badminton	打羽毛球
jogging	慢跑
long distance running	长跑
collecting stamps	集邮
collecting coins	收藏硬币
hiking	长途徒步旅行
camping	露营
play the guitar	弹吉他
play the flute	吹笛子
play the accordion	拉手风琴

(5) 课外活动

课外活动 (extracurricular activities) 主要包括以下几种活动。

1) 体育活动 (physical activities)

captain of the university basketball team 大学篮球队队长

player of the college volleyball team 学院排球队队员

won the first place in men's one-thousand-meter race at the University Student Sports of Jiangsu Province in 2022

在 2022 年江苏省大学生体育运动会中获男子 1000 米跑第一名

won championship in women's five-hundred-meter swimming race at the college sports meet in 2021

在 2021 年的校体育运动会中获女子 500 米游泳赛冠军

2) 文娱活动 (recreational activities)

violin (piano, etc.) player of the university orchestra 校管弦乐团小提琴（钢琴等）演奏员

member of the college choir 校合唱团成员

member of bridge club 桥牌俱乐部成员

won the first place in the university chess contest in 2021

2021 年获全校象棋比赛第一名

won the runner-up in the college dancing contest in 2020

在 2020 年全校舞蹈比赛中获亚军

3) 学术活动 (academic activities)

editor of *Campus Life*, a weekly

《校园生活》周报编辑

won the second place in the eloquence competition in the university in 2022

2022 年在本校举行的口才比赛中获第二名

won the calligraphic contest in the college in 2022

2022 年在本校书法比赛中获优胜奖

won the second class prize in the university drawing contest in 2021

2021 年在本校绘画比赛中获二等奖

4) 社会活动 (social activities)

senior year：president of College Student Council

四年级：校学生会主席

senior year：Party secretary of the department student branch

四年级：系学生党支部书记

junior year：League secretary of the class

三年级：本班团支部书记

sophomore year：commissary in charge of organization of the League branch of the class

二年级：本班团支部组织委员

sophomore year：commissary in charge of sports in the Student Council

二年级：学生会体育委员

freshman year：commissary in charge of studies in the class

一年级：本班学习委员

freshman year：monitor of class

一年级：本班班长

(6) 奖励

在校期间曾经获得的奖学金、论文奖、三好学生、优秀团员、优秀干部等荣誉奖均可列举出来。例如：

scholarship from the university in 2022　2022 年获校级奖学金

won the title of excellent League member in 2022　2022 年荣获优秀团员称号

elected a "three goods" student in 2021 2021年被评为"三好学生"。

won the title of excellent leader of the university student council in 2020 2020年荣获校学生会优秀干部称号

(7) 技术资格与特别技能

1) 技术资格 (technical qualifications)

通过考试和评审所获得的各种任职资格都可算作技术资格。例如：

got an accountant qualification certificate in 2021

2021年获会计资格证书

passed the examination for tour guide qualification and got a certificate in 2019

2019年通过导游资格考试并获证书

took out a driving licence in 2018

2018年领取驾驶执照

2) 特别技能 (special skills)

typing proficiency：50 wpm 打字熟练程度：每分钟50个单词

languages：Mandarin, Cantonese, English 语言：汉语普通话，广东话，英语

English：College English Test—Band Six 英语：大学英语六级

competent for speaking and writing in Japanese 能说写日语

fluent in English reading, writing and speaking 英语读、写、说流利

French：working knowledge (conversational) 法语：应用知识 (会话方面)

English word-processing：110 wpm 英语文字处理：每分钟110个单词

shorthand：95 wpm 速记：每分钟95个字

computer language：cobol, basic, pascal 计算机语言：cobol, basic, pascal

microcomputers：experienced in IBM-PC (0520), Intel (8086/8088), Compact

微型计算机：熟悉 IBM-PC (0520), Intel (8086/8088), Compact

Task 3 Writing Practice

a. Translate the following sentences into English with words or phrases given in the brackets.

1. 你还应填入你的目标。(include, objective)

_____

2. 你能否帮我看一下我还需做任何改动吗？(go over, change)

_____

3. 他曾就读于广州市第八中学。(attend)

_____

4. 你也已经有了一些工作经历。(experience, as well)

_____

5. 她有可能得到她所喜欢的秘书工作。(be likely to, job)
_____

b. *The following is a resume form. Fill in the blanks so that it fits your case.*

Resume

Personal Data

Name: _____ Age: _____ Gender: _____

Address: _____

Tel: _____

E-mail: _____

Career Objective _____

Education

_____-_____: _____ (college/graduate school)

_____-_____: _____ (high school)

Work Experience

_____ - present: _____

_____ - _____: _____

_____ - _____: _____

Achievements _____

Special Skills _____

Hobbies _____

Other Factors _____

References _____

Vocabulary Development

advanced deposit	预付押金
B & B (Bed and Breakfast)	提供床位和早餐
bell captain	服务生领班
bell desk	服务台(服务生领班和服务生待命的柜台)
bookkeeper	记账员
chambermaid	清理房间的女服务员
change money	换钱
charge...to	记账
coin	硬币

Customer Affairs Manager	客服经理
discount	折扣
guest folios	客户账单
heating fee	供暖费
hotel directory	旅馆指南
hotel rates	酒店价格
hotel register	旅馆登记簿
identification card	身份证
information desk	问讯处
invoice	发票
in the name of	在(某人)的名下，以(某人)的名义
key card	钥匙卡
left-luggage office	行李暂存处
luggage depository	行李存放处
night porter on duty	夜间有行李搬运服务生
note	纸币
overdue	过期的
overpay	多付(钱款)
payment in full	全额付款
peak rate	高峰时间价
porter	门童，门房，行李员
prepayment	预付款
procedure fee	手续费
refund	退款
room card	房卡
room charge sheet	房价表
room service	客房服务
self checkout	自助结账
settle the account	结账
tariff	价目表
the means of settlement	结算方式
trunk	大衣箱
voucher	凭证，凭单

Unit 16

Traditional Chinese Festivals

中国传统节日

 Unit Objectives

After learning this unit, you should

- understand what and how to introduce traditional Chinese festivals;
- master the basic words and expressions about traditional Chinese festivals;
- get some cultural knowledge about traditional Chinese festivals;
- find ways to improve your writing skills about Introduction to Traditional Chinese Festivals;
- be familiar with some traditional Chinese festivals.

 Background Knowledge

Brief Introduction

Characterized by diverse styles and themes, traditional Chinese festivals are an important part of Chinese history and culture, both ancient and modern. A close relationship exists between many of the traditional festivals and chronology, mathematics, the Chinese Calendar and the twenty-four solar terms. Many of the customs connected with the traditional festivals have links with religious devotions, superstitions and myths. The form which most of the festivals take today was established around the time of the Han Dynasty (202 B.C.—220 A.D.) and for many years, various eminent poets have written countless masterpieces describing the festivals and these masterpieces are still recited regularly today.

Almost every festival has its own unique origins and customs which reflect the traditional practices and morality of the whole Chinese nation and its people. The grandest and most popular festivals are the Spring Festival, the Lantern Festival, the Qingming Festival, the Dragon Boat Festival, and the Mid-Autumn Festival, etc.

Table of Eight Chinese Traditional Festivals

Festival	Date	Customs
Spring Festival	the 1st ~ 15th of the first lunar month	pasting the character "Fu", paper-cuts and couplets, setting off firecrackers and fireworks, paying New Year's visits, and eating *jiaozi*
Lantern Festival	the 15th day of the first lunar month	watching lanterns and fireworks, guessing lantern riddles, performing folk dances, and eating *yuanxiao*
Qingming Festival	April 4th, 5th or 6th of the solar calendar	tomb sweeping, spring outings, and flying kites
Dragon Boat Festival	the 5th day of the 5th lunar month	dragon boat racing, eating *zongzi*, wearing a perfume pouch, tying five-color silk thread, hanging mugwort leaves and calamus
Double Seventh Festival	the 7th day of the 7th lunar month	praying for skillful hands, appreciating the stars
Mid-Autumn Festival	the 15th day of the 8th lunar month	appreciating and offering sacrifice to the moon and eating mooncakes
Double Ninth Festival	the 9th day of the 9th lunar month	eating Chongyang cake, drinking chrysanthemum wine, climbing mountains and appreciating beautiful chrysanthemums
Laba Festival	the 8th day of the 12th lunar month	eating laba rice porridge.

Practice Materials

Listening

Passage 1

a. Listen to Passage 1 and decide whether each of the following sentences is true (T) or false (F).

1. _____ The Spring Festival is a popular holiday just for the Han people.
2. _____ Many customs and practices about the Spring Festival have been established for centuries.
3. _____ A month before the festival, people follow the custom of cleaning the house inside out and preparing a variety of delicious food.
4. _____ *Jiaozi* is the only course for most families on New Year's Eve.
5. _____ Very often children are given some money as a New Year gift.

b. Listen to the passage and answer the following questions.

1. When is the Spring Festival?
   _____

2. Why do rural people paste pictures of "good images" on either side of their gates?
   _____

3. What do family members usually do on New Year's Eve?
   _____

4. Why do people set off firecrackers and fireworks?
   _____

5. What do family members usually do on New Year's Day?
   _____

c. Listen to the passage again and supply the missing words.

1. The Spring Festival is a popular holiday for the Han people and other _____ groups in China.

2. This grand and traditional festival falls in the period between the first and fifteenth days of the first month of the _____ calendar.

3. Over the centuries, many customs and _____ about the Spring Festival have been established.

4. Rural people make it a rule to paste pictures of "good images" on either side of their ____.

5. Children ____ to their elders to show their respect.

Notes

1. ethnic	人种的；种族的
2. a variety of	多种多样的
3. delicious	美味的
4. paste	糨糊，面团；贴，张贴
5. exorcise	驱邪，除怪
6. evil	邪恶的；邪恶，魔鬼
7. continuance	继续，持续
8. enormous	巨大的，庞大的
9. speculate	推测，思索
10. assortment	分类
11. savory	美味的，风味极佳的；佳肴
12. climax	高潮，顶点
13. firecracker	爆竹，鞭炮
14. firework	烟火，烟花
15. usher	引导，展示；引座员，招待员
16. bestow	给予，安放
17. blessing	祝福
18. kowtow	叩头

Passage 2

a. Listen to Passage 2 and decide whether each of the following sentences is true (T) or false (F).

1. _____ Paying a New Year call is very interesting in Spring Festival celebrations.

2. _____ According to the legend, "year" was an ugly, ferocious animal.

3. _____ The animal would scurry downhill for food every night.

4. _____ Early the next morning when they opened the gates, they would work together to drive the animal away.

5. _____ Although the legend has now largely died out, the practice of paying a New Year call has continued.

b. Listen to the passage and answer the following questions.

1. What else do people do in Spring Festival?
_____

2. What did "year" do on New Year's Eve?
_____

3. What did people do to protect themselves from the animal's attack?
_____

4. What did people do early the next morning?
_____

5. What tradition do modern people still keep up?
_____

c. Listen to the passage again and supply the missing words.

1. Paying a New Year call is a lively and interesting ____ in Spring Festival celebrations.

2. It is also an occasion for people to ____ New Year's greetings.

3. In the remote past, according to the legend, there was an ugly, ferocious ____ called "year".

4. Early the next morning when they opened the gates, they would exchange greetings with their neighbors and congratulate each other on having ____ through a nightmare.

5. This legend has now largely ____ out, but the practice of paying a New Year call has continued.

Notes

1. event	事件，活动
2. celebration	庆典，庆祝
3. remote	遥远的，偏僻的
4. ferocious	凶恶的，凶残的
5. scurry	急赶，急跑
6. survive	幸免于
7. nightmare	噩梦，梦魇
8. die out	灭绝，逐渐消失

Background Information

The Spring Festival

The Spring Festival is the most important festival for the Chinese people when all family members get together, just like Christmas in the West. All people living away from home go back, and airports, railway stations and long-distance bus stations are crowded with home returnees.

The Spring Festival originated in the Shang Dynasty (1600 B.C.~1100 B.C.) from the people's sacrifice to gods and ancestors at the end of an old year and the beginning of a new one.

Many customs accompany the Spring Festival. Some are still followed today, but others have weakened. On the 8th day of the 12th lunar month, many families make laba porridge, a delicious kind of porridge made with glutinous rice, millet, jujube berries, lotus seeds, and beans etc. The 23rd day of the 12th lunar month is called Preliminary Eve. At this time, people offer sacrifice to the kitchen god. Now however, most families make delicious food to enjoy themselves. After the Preliminary Eve, people begin preparing for the coming New Year. This is called "seeing the New Year in". Then people begin decorating their clean rooms featuring an atmosphere of rejoicing and festivity, pasting Spring Festival couplets as well as pictures of the god of doors and wealth. The Chinese character "Fu" (meaning blessing or happiness) is a must. The character put on paper can be pasted normally or upside down, for in Chinese the "reversed Fu" is homophonic with "Fu comes", both being pronounced as "fudaole". A series of activities such as lion dancing, dragon lantern dancing, lantern festivals and temple fairs will be held for days in the streets and lanes. The Spring Festival then comes to an end when the Lantern Festival is finished.

China has 56 ethnic groups. Minorities celebrate their Spring Festival almost the same day as the Han people, and they have different customs.

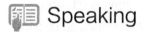 Speaking

Dialogue 1

Traditional Chinese Festivals

Li Jie: Tomorrow is a traditional Chinese festival, the Dragon Boat Festival. Would you like to go to my home to eat some zongzi (the glutinous rice dumplings)?

Linda: Great, thank you! Do you have a holiday on the Dragon Boat Festival?

Li Jie: Yes, we have holidays on some traditional Chinese festivals since 2008, such festivals as the Qingming Festival, the Dragon Boat Festival and the Mid-Autumn Festival. Also we have holidays on the Spring Festival, International Labor Day and National Day.

Linda: Are the holidays long? How many days?

Li Jie: Seven days for the Spring Festival. My family travelled to South China during this year's Spring Festival.

Linda: Spring Festival is the biggest festival in China, isn't it?

Li Jie: Yes, it is. It's as important as Christmas Day in your country.

Linda: What other traditional festivals does China have?

Li Jie: There are Lantern Festival, the Double Ninth Festival and so on.

Linda: What special food do you have at the festivals?

Li Jie: We have, for example, dumplings, sweet dumplings and mooncake.

Notes

1. dumpling 饺子
2. sweet dumpling 汤圆
3. mooncake 月饼

Make a dialogue of introducing traditional Chinese festivals to foreigners.

Words and expressions for reference:

过年 celebrate the Spring Festival　　　春联 Spring Festival couplets
剪纸 paper-cuts　　　年画 new year paintings
买年货 do shopping for the Spring Festival; do Spring Festival shopping
敬酒 propose a toast　　灯笼 lantern　　烟花 fireworks
爆竹 firecrackers (People scare off evil spirits and ghosts with the loud pop.)
红包 red packets　舞龙 dragon dance (to expect good weather and good harvests)
舞狮 lion dance (The lion is believed to be able to dispel evil and bring good luck.)
传统戏曲 traditional opera　杂耍 variety show　灯谜 riddles written on lanterns
灯会 exhibit of lanterns　　守岁 staying-up　　禁忌 taboo
拜年 pay new year's call; give new year's greetings; pay new year's visit
去晦气 get rid of the ill-fortune　　祭祖宗 offer sacrifices to one's ancestors
压岁钱 gift money; money given to children as a lunar new year gift
辞旧岁 bid farewell to the old year　扫房 spring cleaning; general house-cleaning
年糕 nian gao; rice cake; New Year cake　　团圆饭 family reunion dinner
年夜饭 the dinner on New Year's Eve　　饺子 jiaozi; Chinese meat ravioli; dumplings

Dialogue 2

Double Ninth Festival

(The tour guide is introducing the Double Ninth Festival to a group of foreign tourists.)

A: Good morning, everybody! We'll climb Mt. Huashan today. It's really a good opportunity for you to climb the mountain on this special day.

B: Why?

A: Today is the ninth day of the ninth month of the Chinese lunar calendar, a very important Chinese festival, known as the Double Ninth Festival, also called Chongyang Festival.

B: What is special on this festival?

A: In China, many people will go mountain hiking today.

B: Marvelous! We are all happy to celebrate the Double Ninth Festival with our Chinese friends! It's really a holiday tour.

A: We'll arrive at our destination at 9:30. It's a long journey. I'd like to take this chance to introduce the customs of Double Ninth Festival.

B: OK, we are glad to hear that. China has a long history of more than 5,000 years. We want to know more about China.

A: All right. The Chinese celebrate the festival in the golden season of autumn at harvest-time. The bright clear weather and the joy of bringing in the harvest make for a festive happy atmosphere. On this day, many people will go hiking and climbing in the country for the celebration.

B: How do they celebrate the festival?

A: People carry a spray of dogwood when they hike.

(To be continued)

Notes

1. Double Ninth Festival — 重阳节
2. Mt. Huashan — 华山
3. destination — 目的地
4. atmosphere — 大气，气氛
5. spray — 喷雾；飞射
6. dogwood — 山茱萸

Dialogue 3

Double Ninth Festival

(The guide is heading for Mt. Huashan with the tourists on the coach. They continue to talk about the customs of the Double Ninth Festival.)

B: Why do people carry a spray of dogwood with them when they hike in the mountain?

A: According to the legend, once a young man named Huan Jing climbed the mountain with a Taoist on the ninth day of the ninth month. The Taoist suddenly told him to put a spray of dogwood in a red bag, leave home quickly and climb to the top of a mountain. He was also advised to drink some chrysanthemum wine.

B: What happened?

A: Huan Jing rushed home and asked his family to do exactly as the Taoist said. The whole family climbed a mountain nearby and did not return until the evening. They survived from the earthquake and had a narrow escape. Since then, climbing a mountain, carrying a spray of dogwood and drinking chrysanthemum wine became the traditional activities of the Double Ninth Festival.

B: But what about those people who live in flat regions far from any mountains?

A: They go for a picnic and eat cakes instead. The Chinese word for cake is Gao, a homonym of the Chinese word for "high". Mountains are high, so eating cake can take the place of going for a climb.

B: You Chinese are romantic, too.

A: Yes. And we are also filial to our parents. Since nine is the highest odd digit, people take double nine to signify longevity. Therefore, the ninth day of the ninth month has become a special day for people to pay their respect to the elderly and for the elderly to enjoy themselves. It has also been declared as China's day for the elderly—Old Men Festival.

B: Today is really a special day. It's worth climbing Mt. Huashan on such a significant occasion.

Notes

1. legend   传说
2. Taoist   道士，道教信徒；道教的
3. chrysanthemum   菊花
4. survive   幸免于难，幸存
5. have a narrow escape 九死一生，幸免于难

6. homonym 同音异义字
7. filial 孝顺的
8. longevity 长寿，长命

 Reading

Dragon Boat Festival

The fifth day of the fifth lunar month is a traditional Chinese festival dedicated to the great patriotic poet Qu Yuan for his devotion to his native state.

Qu Yuan was a minister of the state of Chu situated in present-day Hunan and Hubei provinces, during the Warring States period (475 B.C.~221 B.C.). He was upright, loyal and highly esteemed for his wise counsel that brought peace and prosperity to the state. Chu was in danger of being invaded by the state of Qin, the strongest among the seven states then existing in central China. As one of the officers, Qu Yuan advocated that Chu should join forces with the neighbouring state of Qi to fight against Qin's troops. However, his patriotism and dedication were betrayed by those who slandered him. The king of Chu believed them. Qu Yuan was disgraced and dismissed from office, and was sent into exile. He wrote many immortal masterpieces exposing the corrupt and incompetent feudal regime. In his autobiographic works he expressed his political position and his ambition of rejuvenating his state. When Qu Yuan heard that Qin troops had occupied the Chu's capital, he threw himself into the Miluo River in despair on the fifth day of the fifth lunar month.

Local people honor the memory of Qu Yuan on this day by holding dragon-boat races. It is said that the boat races were regarded as a symbol of the people's attempt to rescue Qu Yuan. For a long time now it has been a popular sport. China has a long history of making big wooden boats sport. A typical dragon boat ranges from 50 to 100 feet in length. A wooden dragon head is attached at the bow, and a dragon tail at the stern. A banner hoisted on a pole is also fastened at the stern and the hull is decorated with red, green and blue scales edged in gold. In the center of the boat is a canopied shrine behind which the drummers, gong beaters and cymbal players are seated to set the pace for the paddlers. There are also men positioned at the bow to set off firecrackers, toss rice into the water and pretend to be looking for Qu. All of the noise and pageantry creates an atmosphere of gaiety and excitement for the participants and spectators alike. The races are held among different clans, villages and organizations. Boat races are held in rivers going either up or downstream or from bank to bank, following the strict rules and regulations set by the State Physical Culture and Sports Commission. Winners are awarded trophies, such as medals, banners, jugs of wine and festive meals. Every year the "Qu Yuan Cup" is held in China. The boat race is also very popular in Japan, Korea and Southeast Asia.

It is a tradition to eat *zongzi*, pyramid-shaped dumplings made of glutinous rice wrapped in bamboo or reed leaves. Ingredients such as beans, lotus seeds, chestnuts, pork fat and the golden yolk of a salted duck egg are often added to the glutinous rice. According to one popular story, such dumplings were thrown into the river as food for the fish and shrimp to keep them from eating Qu Yuan's body. These dumplings now are boiled and eaten on the holiday.

On this day it is also customary to take a drink of wine containing realgar, rub the wine on children's forehead, and sprinkle it on beds and mosquito nets to keep away insects.

a. Answer the following questions according to the passage.

1. Why is Dragon Boat Festival a traditional Chinese festival?
   _____

2. What happened to Chu in Qu Yuan's time?
   _____

3. What was Qu Yuan's suggestion to save Chu?
   _____

4. Why did Qu Yuan throw himself into the Miluo River?
   _____

5. What was the origin of holding dragon-boat races?
   _____

b. Translate the expressions into Chinese or English.

_____	1. a festival dedicated to the patriotic poet
_____	将一生献给教育事业
_____	dedicate one's time to going for
_____	毕生致力于科学
_____	dedicate to a goal
_____	将（所著的书）题献给某人
_____	2. devotion to one's native state
_____	对教育事业的热爱
_____	devotion to music
_____	q 忠于职守

_____ devotion of one's time to scientific research
_____ 无条件地投入去做某事
_____ 3. betray one's country to the enemy
_____ 被诱入陷阱
_____ betray one's trust
_____ 露出本来面目；原形毕露
_____ betray the cloven hoof
_____ 泄露秘密
_____ 4. in despair
_____ 陷入绝望
_____ out of despair
_____ (be) the despair of
_____ drive sb. to despair
_____ 悲观失望

c. Choose an appropriate word to fill in each blank to make each sentence meaningful, and change its form when necessary.

| advocate | patriotism | dedication | betray | corrupt |
| ambition | in despair | customary | rub | invade |

1. We resolutely wipe out any enemy that dares to _____ our territory.
2. Our family policies _____ late marriage and family planning.
3. The _____ late Qing government was not able to recover lost territories.
4. These books and films on _____ are very educational.
5. We will never be soft-hearted to people that _____ their own country.
6. The study of Chinese medicine is a serious subject and requires a lot of _____.
7. His _____ carried him to the top.
8. She was deserted by her lover, and _____ she took her own life.
9. Every time when celebrating the New Year, the village still maintains its _____ celebrations.
10. I wetted a piece of paper and tried to _____ the mark away.

d. Translate the following sentences into English with words given in the brackets.

1. 春节即将到来，街上到处飘扬着各种各样的小彩旗。(banner)
   _____

2. 在这些场合习惯上是穿礼服的。(customary)
   _____

3. 他们把拿破仑长期放逐到圣赫勒拿岛。(exile)
   _____

4. 在夏季，度假者大批涌入海滨城市。(invade)
   _____

5. 这个牧师在布道时引用了大量的圣经语录。(sprinkle)
   _____

Vocabulary List

advocate	[ˈædvəkeɪt]	vt. 提倡；倡导
ambition	[æmˈbɪʃn]	n. 抱负；信心
banner	[ˈbænə]	n. 旗帜，锦旗
betray	[bɪˈtreɪ]	vt. 背叛
chestnut	[ˈtʃesnʌt]	n. 栗子
corrupt	[kəˈrʌpt]	adj. 腐败的
customary	[ˈkʌstəməri]	adj. 习俗的
cymbal	[ˈsɪmb(ə)l]	n. 铙钹
dedication	[ˌdedɪˈkeɪʃn]	n. 献身；奉献
devotion	[dɪˈvəʊʃn]	n. 热爱；忠心
exile	[ˈeksaɪl]	n./vt. 流亡；使流放
feudal	[ˈfjuːdl]	adj. 封建的
gaiety	[ˈgeɪəti]	n. 欢乐的气氛
glutinous	[ˈgluːtənəs]	adj. 黏的，胶质的
gong	[gɒŋ]	n. 铜锣
hoist	[hɔɪst]	v. 升起
incompetent	[ɪnˈkɒmpɪtənt]	adj. 无能的
immortal	[ɪˈmɔːtl]	adj. 不朽的
invade	[ɪnˈveɪd]	vt. 侵略
jug	[dʒʌg]	n. 壶
mosquito	[məˈskiːtəʊ]	n. 蚊子
pageantry	[ˈpædʒ(ə)ntri]	n. 壮观，华丽

patriotism	['pætriətɪzəm]	n. 爱国主义；爱国精神；爱国心
prow	[praʊ]	n. 船头
realgar	[rɪ'algə]	n. 雄黄
reed	[riːd]	n. 芦苇
regime	[reɪ'ʒiːm]	n. 政权；政体
rejuvenate	[rɪ'dʒuːvəneɪt]	vt. 使恢复活力；更新
rub	[rʌb]	vt. 擦；揉
shrimp	[ʃrɪmp]	n. 虾
slander	['slɑːndə]	vt. 诽谤；诋毁
sprinkle	['sprɪŋkl]	vt. 洒
stern	[stɜːn]	n. 船尾
trophy	['trəʊfi]	n. 奖品；奖杯
upright	['ʌpraɪt]	adj. 正直的

Phrases

be in danger of	处于危险境地
dedicate to	题献给
fight against	攻打，斗争
set the pace	定调子，定速度，树榜样
in despair	绝望

Terms

lotus seed	莲子
the Miluo River	汨罗河
the State Physical Culture and Sports Commission	国家文体委员会
the Warring States period	战国时期

Writing

Introduction to Traditional Chinese Festivals

Task 1   Get more background information about the following traditional Chinese festivals.

1. Spring Festival；Chinese New Year's Day 春节（农历正月初一）
2. Lantern Festival 元宵节（农历正月十五）
3. Qingming Festival; Tomb-sweeping Festival 清明节 (4月5日前后）
4. Dragon Boat Festival 端午节（农历五月初五）
5. Double Seventh Festival 七夕节（农历七月初七）
6. Mid-Autumn (Moon) Festival 中秋节（农历八月十五）
7. Double Ninth Festival 重阳节（农历九月初九）
8. Winter Solstice Festival 冬至 (12月21日、22日或23日）
9. New Year's Eve 除夕（农历腊月三十）

Task 2   Sample Writing

Chinese Valentine's Day

The Double Seventh Festival, on the 7th day of the 7th lunar month, is a traditional festival full of romance. It often goes into August in the Gregorian calendar.

This festival is in mid-summer when the weather is warm and the grass and trees reveal their luxurious greens. At night when the sky is dotted with stars, people can see the Milky Way spanning from the north to the south. On each bank of it is a bright star, which sees each other from afar. They are the Cowhand and Weaver Maid, and about them there is a beautiful love story passed down from generation to generation.

Long, long ago, there was an honest and kind-hearted fellow named Niu Lang (Cowhand). His parents died when he was a child. Later he was driven out of his home by his sister-in-law. So he lived by himself, herded cattle and farmed. One day, a fairy from heaven—Zhi Nv (Weaver Maid) fell in love with him and came down secretly to earth and married him. The Cowhand farmed in the field and the Weaver Maid wove at home. They lived a happy life and gave birth to a boy and a girl. Unfortunately, the God of Heaven soon found out the fact and ordered the Queen Mother of the Western Heavens to bring the Weaver Maid back.

With the help of celestial cattle, the Cowhand flew to heaven with his son and daughter.

At the time when he was about to catch up with his wife, the Queen Mother took off one of her gold hairpins and made a stroke. One billowy river appeared in front of the Cowhand. The Cowhand and Weaver Maid were separated on the two banks forever and could only feel their tears. Their loyalty to love touched magpies, so tens of thousands of magpies came to build a bridge for the Cowhand and Weaver Maid to meet each other. The Queen Mother was eventually moved and allowed them to meet each year on the 7th of the 7th lunar month. Hence their meeting date has been called "Qi Xi" (Double Seventh).

Scholars have shown the Double Seventh Festival originated from the Han Dynasty (202 B.C.—220 A.D.). Today some traditional customs are still observed in rural areas of China, but have been weakened or diluted in urban cities. However, the legend of the Cowhand and Weaver Maid has taken root in the hearts of the people. In recent years, in particular, urban youths have celebrated it as Valentine's Day in China. As a result, owners of flower shops, bars and stores are full of joy as they sell more commodities for love.

Task 3 Writing Practice

Introduce one of your favorite traditional Chinese festivals.

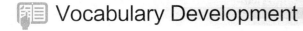

Vocabulary Development

Main Festivals in the World 世界主要节日、纪念日

1. 情人节（2月14日）—— Valentine's Day
2. 狂欢节（巴西，2月中、下旬）—— Carnival
3. 国际妇女节（3月8日）—— International Women's Day
4. 枫糖节（加拿大，3~4月）—— Maple Sugar Festival
5. 愚人节（4月1日）—— April Fool's Day
6. 复活节（春分月圆后第一个星期日）—— Easter
7. 国际劳动节（5月1日）—— International Labor Day
8. 母亲节（5月的第二个星期日）—— Mother's Day
9. 国际儿童节（6月1日）—— International Children's Day
10. 父亲节（6月的第三个星期日）—— Father's Day
11. 鬼节（万圣节前夕，10月31日夜）—— Halloween
12. 感恩节（美国，11月最后一个星期四）—— Thanksgiving Day
13. 圣诞平安夜（12月24日）—— Christmas Eve
14. 圣诞节（12月25日）—— Christmas Day

Other Festivals and Special Days 其他活动节日

1. 世界消费者权益日（3月15日）—— World Consumer Right Day
2. 世界水日（3月22日）—— World Water Day
3. 世界卫生日（4月7日）—— World Health Day
4. 世界地球日（4月22日）—— World Earth Day
5. 世界住房日（10月第一个星期一）—— World Housing Day
6. 国际红十字日（5月8日）—— International Red-Cross Day
7. 国际护士节（5月12日）—— International Nurses Day
8. 世界电信日（5月17日）—— World Telecommunication Day
9. 世界无烟日（5月31日）—— World No-Smoking Day
10. 世界环境日（6月5日）—— World Environment Day
11. 世界人口日（7月11日）—— World Population Day
12. 世界旅游日（9月27日）—— World Tourism Day
13. 世界邮政日（10月9日）—— World Post Day
14. 世界粮食日（10月16日）—— World Food Day
15. 世界艾滋病日（12月1日）—— World AIDS Day
16. 国际残疾人日（12月3日）—— International Day of Disabled Persons

Unit 17

Traveling Advertisement
旅游广告

Unit Objectives

After learning this unit, you should

- understand what and how to give traveling advertisement;
- master the basic words and expressions about traveling advertisement;
- get some cultural knowledge about traveling advertisement;
- find ways to improve your writing skills about Advertisement for A Tour Itinerary.

Background Knowledge

A tour ad generally includes: ① a headline that presents a benefit, invokes curiosity or appeals to personal interest; ② a text that resorts to figurative language for rhetoric effects; ③ pictures that are eye-catching. Traveling advertisement can be generally divided into (according to its function) the following types.

Types of Traveling Advertisement

1. Advertisement for a travel agency and its services to prospective tourists; language features: expressive, persuasive.

2. Advertisement for itineraries and travel tips to prospective tourists; language features: concise, appealing; phrases are preferred than clauses; an attractive title is indispensable.

3. Advertisement for tours; language features: expressive, persuasive, usually advertised under a title or brand name that is relevant to the trip. It is expected to be short

and appealing, presenting the most outstanding features of the tour and easy for prospective tourists to remember.

e.g. China & Yangtze River

— travel to the very heart of the Orient and experience a vastly different world of exotic culture and colorful history.

4. Advertisement for destination country/city or a tourist attraction; language features: concise, appealing; adjectives are abundantly used.

Figures of Speech Generally Contained in an Advertisement

1. 明喻 (simile)

Johnson baby soap, as gentle as her mother's hand. (强生婴儿香皂)

Smooth as silk to Samui. (泰国国际航空公司)

2. 暗喻 (metaphor)

For vigorous growth, plant your money with us. (英国法通保险公司)

Treat your sweetheart to Hilton's Romance Package—the perfect getaway. (希尔顿浪漫套餐)

3. 拟人 (personification)

The world smiles with Reader's Digest. (美国《读者文摘》)

Apple thinks different. (苹果电脑)

4. 夸张 (hyperbole)

Making a big world smaller. (德国汉莎航空公司)

Turn your legs into the ultimate accessory. (吉列女用剃毛刀)

Data at F1 speed. (美国电话电报公司)

5. 对比 (contrast)

To me, the past is black and white, but the future is always color. (轩尼诗酒)

IKEA: Spend less. Live more. (宜家家居超市)

6. 双关 (pun)

From Sharp minds, come Sharp products. (夏普产品)

Money doesn't grow on trees. But it blossoms at our branches. (莱斯银行)

7. 仿拟 (parody)

Where there is a way, there is a Toyota. (丰田汽车)

Not all cars are created equal. (三菱汽车在美国拓展市场的广告语,套用了《独立宣言》中人们耳熟能详的一句话: All men are created equal.)

8. 押韵 (rhyming)

Hi-fi, Hi-fun, Hi-fashion only from Sony. (索尼音响)

Travel your way, stress free. (美国运通广告)

9. 反复 (repetition)

Great pictures, great prints, great offer. (佳能为纪念支持美国癌症协会10周年而推出的粉色套餐 pink bundle 广告)

10. 排比 (parallelism)

Look into our land and discover us. We are strong. We are free. We are Alberta. (加拿大西南部的一个省区 Alberta 的旅游广告)

11. 设问 / 修辞问句 (rhetorical question)

You are insured, but are you protected? (美国好事达保险公司)

Can Great skin be created? (倩碧化妆品)

Where no other SUV has ever been before? (大众途锐)

Practice Materials

Listening

Passage 1

a. Listen to Passage 1 and decide whether each of the following sentences is true (T) or false (F).

1. _____ Eco Tour No. 2 is called Avana Eco Tour.
2. _____ Only three persons are allowed for each tour package.
3. _____ The three tour packages are available.
4. _____ The fare for "Round Raro Eco Tour" is $50.
5. _____ There are discounts for three tour packages.

b. Listen to the passage and answer the following questions.

1. What does the price of "Round Raro Eco Tour" include?

2. What activity can you enjoy during the second tour?

3. How many persons are allowed for each hovercraft?

4. Are there discounts for kids?

5. What's the telephone number for booking?

c. Listen to the passage again and supply the missing words.

1. We are _____ Tour Company.

2. It is called "Round Raro Eco Tour" which _____.

3. On Fridays, you will have _____ feast and fun.

4. There will be a visit to _____ and plantations in the Valley.

5. The exciting tour is made by our _____ eco-friendly hovercraft.

Notes

1. transfer		转车票
2. beach		海滩
3. kayak		爱斯基摩人用的皮船，皮船
4. lagoon		潟湖，濒海湖
5. plantation		农场

Passage 2

a. Listen to Passage 2 and decide whether each of the following sentences is true (T) or false (F).

1. _____ Hong Kong is the gateway to China's south.

2. _____ They will stay in Hong Kong for three days.

3. _____ They will leave for Guilin by air.

4. _____ They will begin their journey in Guangxi Province with cruise on Lijiang River.

5. _____ The experience in Guilin will be very different from that in Hong Kong.

b. Listen to the passage and answer the following questions.

1. Where will they meet their group and tour leader?
_____

2. Is Hong Kong a city with many amazing varieties?
_____

3. What will they do on the third day in Hong Kong?
_____

4. What will they first visit during their journey in Guangxi?
_____

5. How will they go to the countryside out of Yangshuo?
_____

c. Listen to the passage again and supply the missing words.

1. On arrival you will _____ to your hotel where you will meet your group and tour leader.

2. On Day 2 we ride the famous Star Ferry and _____ the panoramic views of China mainland from Victoria Peak.

3. We experience a delicious dim sum lunch before _____ through Kowloon's great local markets.

4. In Guilin, we experience another side of China with some of the country's most _____ that have inspired artists and writers over the centuries.

5. We take time to relax in the _____ of the town before we head into the countryside by bicycle.

Notes

1. bustling	熙熙攘攘的，忙乱的
2. commercial district	商业区
3. ferry	渡船，摆渡，渡口
4. panoramic view	全景
5. sampan	舢板，小船
6. escalator	电动扶梯，自动扶梯
7. dim sum	点心
8. Kowloon	九龙
9. stunning	极好的
10. terrace	梯田
11. legendary	传说中的
12. quaint	离奇有趣的
13. rice paddies	稻田，水田
14. lotus	莲（花），荷（花）

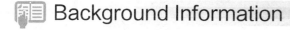

Background Information

Brief Introduction to Travel Agency

A travel agency sells either individual parts or complete of holiday packages to the customer. The main function of the travel agency is to sell the temporary use of transport (air, rail, coach, car), accommodation (hotel, motel, lodge), tours (packages) and other associated services (insurance, foreign exchange). This means that they are involved in the planning, booking, organization and documentation of travel arrangements for their clients. Often, this also involves advising, reassuring, explaining and encouraging customers. However, they generally do not operate vehicles or accompany tourists themselves.

Travel consultants (the people in a travel agency who deal with the public) are expected to gather information on travel destinations and be capable of giving advice on travel products. Travel consultants require good inter-personal and organizational skills and the ability to deal with unexpected situations.

 Speaking

Dialogue 1

Agency Giving Suggestion (1)

Staff: Where are you going for your summer vacation?

Linda: I'm thinking of traveling all over Beijing, but I haven't set up my mind yet.

Staff: How long is your vacation?

Linda: One month.

Staff: That's enough. But I still suggest you choose one or two famous scenic spots. We're setting up a sightseeing plan for you. Is there anything you'd like to see particularly?

Linda: I'll leave it to you to choose. Anything would be welcome.

Staff: How about visiting the Great Wall first? It is of high historical value.

Linda: That's a good idea.

Staff: Then we suggest you go to the Summer Palace and the Palace Museum. We're sure you will be interested in these famous spots.

Linda: Thank you for telling me that. Then I'll go to Wanshou Hill and the 17-Arch Bridge to take some photos.

Staff: That's right! Wish you have a good time!

Linda: Thanks. I hope so.

Notes

1. vacation	假期，休假
2. sightseeing	观光
3. Summer Palace	颐和园
4. Palace Museum	故宫博物院
5. Wanshou Hill	万寿山

Dialogue 2

Agency Giving Suggestion (2)

Brown: I'd like to take a sightseeing tour.

Staff: Where do you want to go then?

Brown: Well, I haven't decided. Could you tell me which tour is the best for this season?

Staff: A short-term tour or a long-distance tour?

Brown: I prefer a short-term one. I only have two days.

Staff: OK. According to your situation and the hot summer, I recommend you go to Tai Bai Mountain for sightseeing.

Brown: Could you tell me why?

Staff: Most of all, the weather is cool there at this time. You can avoid the hot temperature and enjoy a convenient tour there. For the second part, it is just three hours' ride from here, so you can go and come back during two days. For the last but not least, the environment and view there are very good for sightseeing.

Brown: Sounds good. Thank you very much.

Notes

1. three hours' ride	三小时的车程
2. Tai Bai Mountain	太白山
3. convenient	方便的，便利的
4. the last but not least	最后但并非最不重要的

Dialogue 3

Recommending a Tour Guide Service

(Tom is recommending a tour guide service called 'A friend in New York' to Jerry, who hasn't been there before.)

Jerry: I'm going to New York for the first time, but I don't have a tour guide. Can you give me any suggestions?

Tom: There's a service called "A friend in New York". It's a personal tour guide service.

Jerry: That's interesting. What does it do?

Tom: You give them your information by answering a questionnaire and they will create a perfect trip for you according to your budget.

Jerry: Good. Where can I get the questionnaire?

Tom: You can easily download it from their website.

Notes

1. A friend in New York   "纽约朋友"
2. personal   个人的，私人的
3. tour guide service   旅游向导服务
4. questionnaire   调查问卷，调查表
5. create   创造，设计
6. budget   预算
7. download   下载
8. website   网站

Dialogue 4

Traveling at the May Day Holiday

(Tom is giving Jerry advices about traveling at the May Day Holiday.)

Tom: The May Day holiday is coming up soon. Are you planning on going on vacation?

Jerry: I am. I just went to the travel agent's and picked up these brochures.

Tom: Where are you planning on going?

Jerry: I fancy going to Tibet for a few days. Have you ever been there?

Tom: I went a long time ago. At that moment, there weren't any trains going there. And now you can go by train and that's really convenient.

Jerry: Would you recommend going there for a few days?

Tom: Personally, I think it'd be better to go when you have more time. A few days aren't really enough to get acclimatize yourself and to go on a few excursions outside of the capital.

Jerry: You're probably right. What do you think about Yangshuo?

Tom: It's a beautiful city, but I think it's becoming too touristy. How about going to a cosmopolitan city like Shanghai or Hong Kong?

Jerry: I'd like to get away from the big city life.

Tom: Maybe you should consider going to a hot springs resort outside of Beijing. I heard they are very relaxing.

Jerry: I guess if I only have a few days, I should probably think about going somewhere that isn't so far away.

Tom: Since the May Day holiday is the high season, you should probably call ahead to reserve a room. Here's the phone number.

Jerry: Thanks, I'll give them a call later.

Notes

1. come up	即将到来，即将发生
2. pick up	拿起；发现；找到
3. brochure	小册子，手册
4. fancy	想要，想做
5. personally	在个人看来，就个人而言
6. acclimatize	（使）适应；（使）习惯于（新地方或新气候）
7. excursion	短途旅游，远足
8. touristy	挤满游客的；被旅游商品充斥的
9. cosmopolitan	世界性的，国际化的
10. get away from	远离
11. hot spring	温泉
12. resort	度假胜地
13. relaxing	令人轻松的，放松的
14. think about	考虑
15. high season	旺季
16. ahead	提前，预先（准备或计划）

Reading

Passage 1

Advertisements for Scenic Spots

A Brief Introduction to the Dragon Spring Cave

The Dragon Spring Cave is located in the cliff of the north bank of the Xialao Stream. It is near the exit of Xiling Gorge and 10 kilometers from Yichang City. It is the most splendid and famous limestone cave in the Three Gorges area.

After being reopened up by first-class limestone expert, the main scenery of the cave, which consists of the Palace Pagoda Forest, the Palace of Goddess, the Palace of Waterfall, the Palace of Longevity, and the Palace of Crystal, is now more beautiful and brilliant than before. In the Palace of Pagoda Forest, the jade bamboo shoots stand like spears. You are sure to be deeply impressed at the very sight of it. In the Palace of Goddess, the pearl curtain looks elegant and the spring water is glittering, making the Palace really a charming spot. In the Palace of Longevity, row upon row of strange rocks are towering. You would be surprised at the wonderful sight. In the Palace of Crystal, crystal houses and pearls are everywhere. Thousands of treasures are gathered there. The Palace is so attractive that you may even forget to return. In the Palace of Waterfall, a waterfall is running down the cliff. The scene is very magnificent and you can find satisfaction in it. The scenery in the Dragon Spring Cave is marvelous and the surroundings of it are truly unique. When you go upstairs from the cave gate, you can get a good bird's eye view of Sanyou Ancient Cave, the Gezhou Dam and the picturesque Xialao Stream. There are so many beautiful scenes in the Dragon Spring Cave that you simply can't take them all in one time. Welcome to visit the Dragon Spring Cave.

The World Largest Miniature Scenic Spots—Splendid China

Splendid China, situated by the picturesque Shenzhen Bay, is a tourist area in the Overseas Chinese Town of Shenzhen Special Economic Zone. Spreading over 450 mu of land, it is divided into Scenic Spot Area and Comprehensive Service Area. Splendid China excels its counterparts in China and the world, in area as well as in the amount of scenery reproduced.

In the Scenic Spot Area, about a hundred scenic wonders arranged in accordance with the real locations of China's scenic spots, are the epitomes of China's long-standing history, brilliant culture as well as her beautiful scenery and rich historical sites. Here you will see the Great Wall, life-size Terra-cotta Figures of Soldiers and Horses of Qinling Mausoleum, which are among the world's eight wonders. And there are many other things that rank first in the world: the world's most ancient stone arch bridge, astronomic observatory and wooden pagoda (Zhaozhou Bridge, Ancient observatory and Yingxian Wooden Pagoda), one of the world's biggest palace and Buddha statue (the Imperial Palace and Leshan grand Buddha Statue), the world's longest fresco (Dunhuang Mogao Grottoes), the world's most splendid building located at the highest point above sea level (Potala Palace), the world's most wonderful karst landscape (the Stone Forest), the world's most steep peaks (Huangshan Mountain), one of the world's biggest waterfalls (Huangguoshu Falls). Other well-known sights found here are the solemn and dignified Huangdi Tomb, the Mausoleum of Genghis Khan, and the Ming Tombs, Dr. Sun Yat-sen's Mausoleum, the resplendent and magnificent Confucius Temple, the Temple of Heaven, the imposing, majestic Taishan Mountain, the precipitous and graceful Three Gorges of the Yangtze River, the picturesque and marvelous view of the Lijiang River, the West Lake of Hangzhou, Wangshi Garden of Suzhou and other beautiful scenery of southern China, the famous pagodas, temples, towers and grottoes with an infinite variety of beauty and charm and local houses with rich and colorful customs of nationalities. Besides, one can also see the scenes of emperors praying for good harvests, the wedding of Emperor Guang Xu, holding a memorial ceremony at Confucius's Temple and local conditions and customs of weddings and funerals, etc. In a word, you will get a good idea of the ancient civilized country with a history of five thousand years by traveling numerous famous rivers and mountains all over China only in one day.

With the artistic style of Suzhou architecture and gardens, the Comprehensive Service Area has retained a traditional shopping street in Southern China. Here you can have a taste of famous dishes of Beijing, Sichuan, Suzhou and Guangzhou as well as traditional flavor of delicacies and snacks from various places of the country. You can enjoy the performance of national songs and dances, on-the-spot demonstrations of making traditional articles of handicraft art, a cinesphere with giant-screen films showing the splendid, graceful land of China. What is more, the endless array of beautiful handicrafts, antiques, herbs and tonics, famous local specialties as well as tourist souvenirs with unique characteristics of Splendid China are provided for you to choose. When night falls and when the evening lights are brilliantly lit up, to travel through Splendid China is a kind of interesting and charming enjoyment. Splendid China is, so to speak, a world of flowers and greenery and window for a glimpse of China's history and culture and her tourism resources.

Blessed with excellent transportation facilities, it takes only ten minutes by car to get to the place from Luomazhou Port. Splendid China is easy of access by CTS direct tourist coach between Hong Kong and Shenzhen and bus or light bus through Shennan Highway.

a. Choose an appropriate word to fill in each blank to make each sentence meaningful, and change its form when necessary.

picturesque	impress	glitter	excel	glimpse
rank	spread	counterpart	epitome	souvenir

1. The foreign minister is the _____ of the secretary of state.

2. He _____ others in courage as an actor.

3. Experience a region world-renowned for its rugged landscape, spectacular views and _____ village.

4. My father _____ on me the value of hard work.

5. When Uncle Bill went abroad to live, he left me his watch as a _____.

6. He is seen as the _____ of the hawkish, right-of-center intellectual.

7. All is not gold that _____.

8. The rumor quickly _____ through the village.

9. The old man caught a _____ of burglar climbing out of the window.

10. Would you _____ him among the world's great statesmen?

b. Translate the following sentences into English with words or phrases given in the brackets.

1. 联合王国由大不列颠和北爱尔兰组成。(consist of)
_____

2. 星期六要去郊游野餐，我们非常希望那天是个风和日丽的晴天。(pray for)
_____

3. 这部影片的首映式由于王室和许多著名影星出席而成为灿烂夺目的场面。(glitter)
_____

4. 山谷的壮丽景色给我们留下了深刻的印象。(imposing)
_____

5. 我们可以鸟瞰整个村庄。(bird's eye view)
_____

Vocabulary List

bamboo shoot	[ˌbæmˈbuː-ʃuːt]	*n.* 笋，竹笋
buddha	[ˈbʊdə]	*n.* 佛
cinesphere	[ˈsɪnəsfɪə(r)]	*n.* 球幕影院
cliff	[klɪf]	*n.* 悬崖，绝壁
Confucius	[kənˈfjuːʃəs]	*n.* 孔子
counterpart	[ˈkaʊntəpɑːt]	*n.* 副本，极相似的人或物；配对物
crystal	[ˈkrɪstl]	*adj./n.* 结晶状的；水晶，水晶饰品；结晶，晶体
delicacy	[ˈdelɪkəsi]	*n.* 微妙；美味，佳肴 (pl.)

dignified	[ˈdɪgnɪfaɪd]	*adj.* 有威严的；有品格的
epitome	[ɪˈpɪtəmi]	*n.* 摘要，缩影
excel	[ɪkˈsel]	*v.* 优秀，胜过他人
fresco	[ˈfreskəʊ]	*n./vt.* 在灰泥墙壁上作的水彩画，壁画；作壁画于
glimpse	[glɪmps]	*n./v.* 一瞥，一看；瞥见
glitter	[ˈglɪtə]	*vi./n.* 闪闪发光，闪烁，闪光；闪光
imposing	[ɪmˈpəʊzɪŋ]	*adj.* 使人难忘的；壮丽的
karst	[kɑːst]	*n.* 喀斯特地貌（石灰岩地区常见的地形）
limestone	[ˈlaɪmstəʊn]	*n.* 石灰石
longevity	[lɒnˈdʒevəti]	*n.* 长命，寿命；供职期限；资历
long-standing	[ˌlɒŋˈstændɪŋ]	*adj.* 长期存在的
majestic	[məˈdʒestɪk]	*adj.* 宏伟的，庄严的
mausoleum	[ˌmɔːsəˈliːəm]	*n.* 陵墓
miniature	[ˈmɪnətʃə]	*n./adj.* 缩小的模型，缩图，缩影；微型的，缩小的
pagoda	[pəˈgəʊdə]	*n.* 宝塔
picturesque	[ˌpɪktʃəˈresk]	*adj.* 生动的，美丽的
precipitous	[prɪˈsɪpɪtəs]	*adj.* 陡峭的；急躁的
resplendent	[rɪˈsplend(ə)nt]	*adj.* 辉煌的，灿烂的，光辉的，华丽的
spear	[spɪə]	*n.* 矛，枪
terra-cotta	[ˌterəˈkɒtə]	*n.* 陶瓦，赤陶；棕橙色
tonic	[ˈtɒnɪk]	*adj./n.* 激励的，滋补的；滋补剂，滋补品
tower	[ˈtaʊə]	*vi.* 高耸 (above)；超过；翱翔

Phrases

a bird's eye view	鸟瞰，俯视
an array of	一排，一大批
be sure to	肯定，必定
consist of	由……组成
pray for	为……而祈祷，祈求
run down	顺着……流下
in accordance with	与……一致，依照
in a word	一句话，总之，总而言之
so to speak	可以说，可谓

Terms

Confucius Temple	孔庙
Dragon Spring Cave	龙泉洞
Dr. Sun Yat-sen's Mausoleum	中山陵
Dunhuang Mogao Grottoes	敦煌莫高窟
Gezhou Dam	葛洲坝
Huangdi Tomb	黄帝陵
Huangguoshu Falls	黄果树瀑布
Huangshan Mountain	黄山
Leshan Grand Buddha Statue	乐山大佛
Lijiang River	漓江
Ming Tombs	明十三陵
Overseas Chinese Town	华侨城
Palace of Crystal	水晶宫
Palace of Goddess	瑶池宫
Palace of Longevity	万寿宫
Palace of Pagoda Forest	塔林宫
Palace of Waterfall	瀑布宫
Potala Palace	布达拉宫
Taishan Mountain	泰山
Terra-cotta Figures of Soldiers and Horses of Qinling Mausoleum	秦陵兵马俑
the Temple of Heaven	天坛
the Imperial Palace	故宫
the Mausoleum of Genghis Khan	成吉思汗陵
the Stone Forest	石林
the West Lake of Hangzhou	杭州西湖
Three Gorges area	三峡地区
Three Gorges of the Yangtze River	长江三峡
Wangshi Garden of Suzhou	苏州网师园
Xialao Stream	下牢溪
Yingxian Wooden Pagoda	应县木塔
Zhaozhou Bridge	赵州桥

Passage 2

Where to Stay on Cape Cod

THE CRANBERRY INN Gorgeous, ocean-front rooms with spectacular views. TV, VCR, private porches. Breakfast and gourmet dinner served daily. $219 per night, room only. Call 1-800-232-9021.

CAPTAIN AHAB'S HOUSE Unique, beautiful, and romantic small hotel close to beaches, shops and restaurants. 90-minute drive from Boston. No pets or smoking. For more information and reservations call 1-800-449-7999.

WESTPORT BED AND BREAKFAST Weekend packages available from $189 to $269. Two bedrooms available in wonderful old house on the beach. Views from every window. Tennis and golf available at nearby club. Call 1-800-636-2979.

THE CAPE COD HOTEL Luxurious hotel with 1 and 2 bedroom suites. Friendly staff, indoor swimming pool, spa, sauna, and dining room serving breakfast, lunch, and dinner daily. Call for details 1-800-720-0856.

THE OCEAN INN Cape Cod's finest place to stay. Casual but elegant, all rooms have ocean view and air-conditioning. Health club, healthy breakfast served daily. Package tours available. Call 1-800-627-8369 for more information.

ATLANTIC AVENUE BED AND BREAKFAST Cozy, family-owned B&B built in 1905. Friendly atmosphere and perfect location. Free parking. Glorious views. Great prices. Call 1-800-369-5892.

a. Answer the following questions according to the passage.

1. When was the Atlantic Avenue Bed and Breakfast built?

2. Where will you stay if you want to play golf?

3. What number will you call to find out the prices of the Ocean Inn?

4. Where can you have a romantic and unique hotel?

5. Which hotel has an indoor swimming pool?

b. Translate the expressions into English.

1. 海滨房间　　　　_____
2. 豪华酒店　　　　_____
3. 全体职员　　　　_____
4. 温泉　　　　　　_____
5. 餐厅　　　　　　_____
6. 健身俱乐部　　　_____
7. 免费停车　　　　_____
8. 美味晚餐　　　　_____
9. 套房　　　　　　_____
10. 室内游泳池　　　_____
11. 桑拿　　　　　　_____
12. 空调　　　　　　_____

Vocabulary List

casual	[ˈkæʒjuəl]	adj. 随便的，非正式的
cozy	[ˈkəuzi]	adj. 舒适的，安逸的，惬意的
glorious	[ˈglɔːriəs]	adj. 光荣的，显赫的
gorgeous	[ˈgɔːdʒəs]	adj. 华丽的，灿烂的
gourmet	[ˈguəmei]	n. 能精选品评美食、美酒的人
inn	[in]	n.（尤指乡村或公路边的）旅馆，客栈
luxurious	[lʌgˈʒuəriəs]	adj. 奢侈的，豪华的
porch	[pɔːtʃ]	n. 门廊，走廊
restaurant	[ˈrestərɔnt]	n. 餐馆，饭店
sauna	[ˈsaunə, ˈsɔːnə]	n. 桑拿浴，蒸汽浴
spa	[spɑː]	n. 矿泉，游乐胜地，矿泉疗养地
spectacular	[spekˈtækjulə]	adj. 引人入胜的，壮观的

Writing

Advertisement for A Tour Itinerary

Task 1　Writing Skills

旅游线路是旅行社提供给游客的一个旅游计划，在内容上一般包括旅游路线、景点信息、食宿安排、交通配备、娱乐项目等；在书写格式上则从出发时间开始逐日介绍行程安排。当然一个富有吸引力的标题也是必不可少的。旅游线路的语言风格应既简洁明了又具有吸引力，既具有信息性又符合游客的口味。因此，一份英语旅游线路广告多大量使用短语，且句子结构简单。

Task 2　Sample Writing

Best of China

Tour Code：SILVER-0801
9 Days Beijing — Xi'an — Shanghai
Starting from $829 per person

Making a Difference

The choice is yours, but decisions are often hard to make. Our itinerary feature page as Making a Difference will let you know the detailed arrangements of highlight attractions, accommodations, meals, special local flavors we arrange in the itinerary you will choose. Only you truly know where each of your coin will be spent, you could make your own choice! It is worth comparing the quality and value of a tour before you make your reservation.

Day by Day Itinerary

Day 1：Arrival in Beijing

Our guide will pick you up at Beijing airport and transfer you to the hotel. Relax during the remainder of the afternoon and evening to recover from the jet lag.

Accommodation：Forbidden Hotel ★★★

Day 2：Beijing

Before the tour starts, you will meet the other members of your group this morning during the pre-tour briefing in the hotel. Your first stop is the impressive Tiananmen Square. From there you will enter the "Imperial Palace" known as the Forbidden City to explore its many fascinating halls and pavilions. You will then go to the Temple of Heaven, the place where the Emperors worshipped the heaven for good harvests. To round off a memorable start to your tour, we will arrange a delicious meal at a delicate restaurant followed by a lively Acrobatic Show. (B+L+D)

Accommodation：Forbidden Hotel ★★★

Day 3：Beijing

This morning you will be taken to Badaling where you will experience at first hand the wonder of the Great Wall. To avoid having lunch at the shopping site restaurant, we specially arrange your lunch served at a local popular Sichuan restaurant. Later the journey will take you to the Sacred Way and the Ming Tombs in the peaceful shadow of Longevity Hill. This evening, you will be feasted by Beijing Duck Dinner valued at RMB 122 yuan net per person at a famous restaurant. (B+L+D)

  Accommodation: Forbidden Hotel ★★

Day 4: Beijing—Xi'an

You will take an afternoon flight to Xi'an after visiting the Summer Palace and the lovely giant pandas in Beijing Zoo. Upon arrival, you will be transferred to check in at the hotel. An a la carte dinner valued at RMB 60 yuan net per person will be arranged at a well-known restaurant. (B+L+D)

  Accommodation: Grand New World Hotel ★★★★

Day 5: Xi'an

The visit to the majestic Terra-cotta Warriors and Horses Museum will start your today's tour. In the afternoon, you will visit the City Wall and the Big Wild Goose Pagoda. A splendid evening is in store when you will be entertained at the Tang Dynasty Music and Dance Show when partaking of the famous Dumpling Banquet Dinner. (B+L+D)

  Accommodation: Grand New World Hotel ★★★★

Day 6: Xi'an

Today you will visit the Provincial History Museum, which houses a large collection of historic and cultural artifacts unearthed in Shaanxi Province. After lunch, you will be taken to visit a local family, which helps you know well about the local people's life. Then go to see the Great Mosque and have some free time to explore for some souvenirs or antiques in the bazaar near the Mosque. (B+L+D)

  Accommodation: Grand New World Hotel ★★★★

Day 7: Xi'an—Shanghai

This morning you will visit the Hanyangling Museum, the mausoleum of Western Han Emperor Liu Qi. Then you will board a flight to Shanghai, and check in at the hotel upon arrival. Dinner is served at your hotel. (B+L+D)

  Accommodation: Days Hotel Shanghai ★★★★ - Deluxe Room

Day 8: Shanghai

Visit the Shanghai Museum and the beautiful Yuyuan Garden. Then you will have some free time to stroll along the Bund to experience the thrills of old Shanghai. After dinner, you will be transferred back to your hotel. Upon returning to the hotel, our tour guide will see you into the lobby to say bon voyage. (B+L+D)

Accommodation: Days Hotel Shanghai ★★★ - Deluxe Room

Day 9: Departure from Shanghai

After breakfast, you will travel to the airport for your homeward flight by yourselves. However, should you wish to stay on rather than return home right away, we would suggest you choose our City Packages as an extension to your China adventure! (B)

B— Breakfast L— Lunch D— Dinner

Departure Dates and Prices (based on per person and shown in US dollars)

Guaranteed Departures with Even 1 Person!

Common Sentence Patterns in Tourist Advertisements

(1) On arrival in Beijing you will be met by our representative and driven to your hotel for a two-night stay.

抵达北京，导游接机，驱车前往下榻酒店，停留两晚。

(2) After dinner you will enjoy an included evening at the Beijing Opera. B, L, D.

晚餐后在北京剧院观看表演。含早、中、晚餐。

(3) After a morning visit to Shanghai Museum you'll take an afternoon flight to Wuhan, capital of Hubei Province, for an overnight stay.

上午参观上海博物馆，下午乘机飞往湖北省省会武汉，入住一晚。

(4) Full day excursion to the Great Wall.

全天在长城游玩。

(5) Fly to Xi'an in the morning and sightsee in Xi'an in the afternoon.

早晨飞往西安，下午在西安市内观光。

Task 3 Writing Practice

a. Fill the following tour itinerary by translating the Chinese in the brackets.

The Best of China Tour

14 DAYS/13 NIGHTS—Beijing/Xi'an/Shanghai/Suzhou/Hangzhou/Guilin/Guangzhou

Day 1 Arrive in Beijing

Welcome to Beijing, capital city of China. On arrival, ＿＿＿＿＿＿＿＿＿＿＿＿＿＿＿＿＿＿（我们的导游将在机场接机然后转往入住酒店）.

Day 2 Beijing

＿＿＿＿＿＿＿＿＿＿＿＿＿＿＿＿＿＿＿＿＿＿＿＿（早晨去天安门广场游览）, located in the heart of the capital, and the Forbidden City—one of the greatest feasts of ancient Chinese architecture. Afternoon sightseeing includes Summer Palace—a former summer resort area of the royal family, or a visit to the Temple of Heaven where the emperors prayed for good harvests.＿＿＿＿＿＿＿＿＿＿＿＿＿＿＿＿＿＿＿（晚餐享用著名的北京烤鸭）.

Day 3 Beijing

＿＿＿＿＿＿＿＿＿＿＿＿＿＿＿＿＿＿＿＿＿＿＿＿（全天游览长城——中国的象征）. It is one of the most amazing feasts of man-made construction on earth visible from outer space. After lunch, a drive to the Ming Tombs along the Sacred Way with giant marble figures and animals guarding the tomb area for deceased emperors of the Ming Dynasty. ＿＿＿＿＿＿＿＿＿＿＿＿＿＿＿＿＿＿＿＿＿＿＿＿（晚上观看京剧和杂技表演）

…… ……

Day 14 ＿＿＿＿＿＿＿＿＿＿＿＿＿＿＿＿＿＿＿＿＿＿＿＿＿＿＿＿＿＿＿＿（早晨旅行结束，搭乘特快列车返回香港）.

b. *Write an itinerary according to the following information.*

Date Arrangement

Day 1	Hong Kong—Hangzhou
Day 2	Hangzhou
Day 3	Hangzhou—Shaoxing
Day 4	Shaoxing—Ningbo
Day 5	Ningbo
Day 6	Ningbo—Putuo
Day 7	Putuo
Day 8	Putuo—Ningbo
Day 9	Ningbo—Hong Kong

Hotels

Hangzhou：Yellow Dragon Hotel, Xin Qiao Hotel

Shaoxing：Shaoxing Hotel

Ningbo：Asian Garden Hotel, Golden Dragon Hotel

Putuo：Island Hotel

Scenes

Hangzhou: Lingyin Temple, Yue Temple, West Lake
Shaoxing: Lanting Pavilion, Lu Xun Memorial Museum
Ningbo: Tianyi Pavilion, Seven-Pagoda Temple, Yuewang Temple, Tiantong Temple
Putuo: Puji Temple, Fayu Temple, Huiji Temple, Xitian Scenery, Guanyin Hall

References

[1] 教育部旅游英语教材编写组. 旅游英语 [M]. 北京：高等教育出版社，2002.

[2] 教育部英语教材编写组. 英语 [M]. 北京：高等教育出版社，2000.

[3] 陈丹. 巧嘴英语做导游 [M]. 北京：北京邮电大学出版社，2006.

[4] 陈克成. 旅游交际英语 [M]. 上海：华东师范大学出版社，1992.

[5] 陈克成. 旅游交际英语通 [M]. 上海：华东师范大学出版社，1992.

[6] 陈克成. 旅游交际英语通 [M]. 上海：华东师范大学出版社，2003.

[7] 崔进. 新编旅游英语 [M]. 武汉：武汉大学出版社，2003.

[8] 付昂. 旅游服务实用英语 [M]. 北京：外文出版社，2007.

[9] 范红育. 旅游英语 [M]. 北京：电子工业出版社，2008.

[10] 郭兆康. 饭店情景英语 [M]. 北京：高等教育出版社，1997.

[11] 郭兆康. 饭店情景英语 [M]. 上海：复旦大学出版社，1991.

[12] 郭兆康. 饭店情景英语 [M]. 上海：复旦大学出版社，2004.

[13] 浩瀚. 观光英语情景会话模板 [M]. 北京：国防工业出版社，2007.

[14] 浩瀚. 旅游度假英语口语即学即用 [M]. 北京：机械工业出版社，2008.

[15] 浩瀚. 旅游度假英语口语即学即用 [M]. 北京：机械工业出版社，2008.

[16] 胡朝慧. 酒店英语 [M]. 北京：北京大学出版社，2011.

[17] 靳顺则. 旅游手册 [M]. 北京：中国书籍出版社，2007.

[18] 靳顺则. 旅游手册 [M]. 北京：中国书籍出版社，2007.

[19] 李燕，徐静. 旅游英语 [M]. 北京：清华大学出版社，2009.

[20] 李燕，徐静. 旅游英语（第2版）[M]. 北京：清华大学出版社，2014.

[21] 李燕，徐静. 旅游英语 [M]. 北京：人民邮电出版社，2017.

[22] 李红. 敢说礼仪英语 [M]. 北京：机械工业出版社，2005.

[23] 林为慧. 旅游英语 Easy Fly[M]. 济南：山东科学技术出版社，2007.

[24] 刘爱仪. 老年出国英语会话 [M]. 大连：大连理工大学出版社，2006.

[25] 刘峰. 旅游接待英语 [M]. 北京：旅游教育出版社，2012.

[26] 刘倩. 旅游英语 [M]. 北京：北京理工大学出版社，2007.

[27] 陆建平. 现代旅游英语教程 [M]. 北京：商务印书馆，2008.

[28] 钱清. 礼仪与风俗 [M]. 北京：外文出版社，2006.

[29] 钱晓梅. 旅游英语 [M]. 天津：天津科技翻译出版公司，2002.

[30] 石民辉. 旅游英语 [M]. 北京：中国物资出版社，2005.

[31] 宿荣江. 酒店实用英语 [M]. 北京：中国人民大学出版社，2008.

[32] 汪福祥. 英语书信写作语言与技巧 [M]. 北京：外文出版社，2003.

[33] 王燕希. 实用商务英语写作大全一本通 [M]. 北京：对外经济贸易大学出版社，2003.

[34] 魏敬安. 北京欢迎您旅游服务英语 [M]. 北京：中国广播电视出版社，1993.

[35] 杨华. 实用旅游英语 [M]. 北京：中国人民大学出版社，2012.

[36] 吴光华. 现代英汉综合大辞典 [M]. 上海：上海科学技术文献出版社，1993.

[37] 吴云. 旅游实践英语 [M]. 北京：旅游教育出版社，2007.

[38] 谢先泽. 中国旅游英语读本 [M]. 成都：西南财经大学出版社，2006.

[39] 许酉萍. 旅游服务英语 [M]. 成都：西南财经大学出版社，2015.

[40] 徐晓贞. 新世纪高职高专英语综合教程 [M]. 上海：上海外语教育出版社，2005.

[41] 杨淑惠. 旅游英语 [M]. 天津：天津科技翻译出版公司，2007.

[42] 张迪. 职场英语加油站 [M]. 北京：国防工业出版社，2006.

[43] 赵伐. 旅游英语 [M]. 杭州：浙江大学出版社，2006.

[44] 张道真. 现代英语用法词典 [M]. 上海：上海译文出版社，1985.

[45] 章小瑾. 旅游英语 [M]. 北京：北京理工大学出版社，2012.

[46] 郑树棠. 新视野英语教程 [M]. 北京：外语教学与研究出版社，2004.

[47] 郑仰霖. 旅游英语自由行 [M]. 北京：世界图书出版社，2008.

[48] 周评. 出国旅游应急英语 [M]. 北京：北京工业大学出版社，2002.

[49] 周玮. 旅行社英语 [M]. 广州：广东旅游出版社，1999.

[50] 朱华. 四川英语导游教程 [M]. 北京：中国旅游出版社，2007.

[51] 卓美玲. 新餐馆英语会话 [M]. 北京：外文出版社，2001.

[52] 邹晓燕. 旅游专业英语实用教程 [M]. 北京：清华大学出版社，2005.

[53] Carol Rueckert. 餐厅英语情景口语50主题 [M]. 北京：外文出版社，2014.

[54] Marsden. 英语口语生存手册 [M]. 海口：南方出版社，2007.

[55] http://www.cnta.gov.cn/

[56] http://baike.baidu.com/

[57] http://wenku.baidu.com

扫码下载本书配套资源